Toronto

Fourth Edition

*Toronto is one of the great cosmopolitan cities and in my opinion,
it's the city that really justifies the country. It's interesting
to me that Toronto is now becoming a literary city
in the way that London has been for years.*

Margaret Atwood, author, contributor to "Incredible Ontario,"
Ontario: The Inside Story (1990)

Travel better, enjoy more

ULYSSES
Travel Guides

Offices

Canada: Ulysses Travel Guides, 4176 St. Denis Street, Montréal, Québec, H2W 2M5, ☎(514) 843-9447, ⇰(514) 843-9448, info@ulysses.ca, www.ulyssesguides.com

Europe: Les Guides de Voyage Ulysse SARL, 127 rue Amelot, 75011 Paris, France, ☎01 43 38 89 50, ⇰01 43 38 89 52, voyage@ulysse.ca, www.ulyssesguides.com

U.S.A.: Ulysses Travel Guides, 305 Madison Avenue, Suite 1166, New York, NY 10165, info@ulysses.ca, www.ulyssesguides.com

Distributors

U.S.A.: Hunter Publishing, 130 Campus Drive, Edison, NJ 08818, ☎800-255-0343, ⇰(732) 417-1744 or 0482, comments@hunterpublishing.com, www.hunterpublishing.com

Canada: Ulysses Travel Guides, 4176 St. Denis Street, Montréal, Québec, H2W 2M5, ☎(514) 843-9882, ext. 2232, ⇰514-843-9448, info@ulysses.ca, www.ulyssesguides.com

Great Britain and Ireland: Roundhouse Publishing, Millstone, Limers Lane, Northam, North Devon, EX39 2RG, ☎1 202 66 54 32, ⇰1 202 66 62 19, roundhouse.group@ukgateway.net

Other countries: Ulysses Travel Guides, 4176 St. Denis Street, Montréal, Québec, H2W 2M5, ☎(514) 843-9882, ext.2232, ⇰514-843-9448, info@ulysses.ca, www.ulyssesguides.com

Canadian Cataloguing-in-Publication Data (see p 3)
© March 2005, Ulysses Travel Guides.
All rights reserved.
Printed in Canada
ISBN 2-89464-662-3

Research and Writing	*Artistic Director*	*Photography*
Jill Borra	Patrick Farei (Atoll)	*Cover page*
Alexandra Gilbert		Robert Mullan /
François Henault	*Copy Editor*	Alamy
Pierre Ledoux	Jennifer McMorran	
Amber Martin		*Inside pages*
Jennifer McMorran	*Editing Assistance*	Patrick Escudero
Alain Rondeau	Pierre Ledoux	
	David Sirois	*Illustrations*
		Pascal Biet
Publisher	*Cartographers*	Lorette Pierson
Claude Morneau	Pascal Biet	Vincent Desruisseaux
	André Duchesne	
Production Director	Patrick Thivierge	*Graphic Designer*
André Duchesne		André Duchesne

Acknowledgements

We acknowledge the financial support of the Government of Canada through the Book Publishing Industry Development Program (BPIDP) for our publishing activities. We would also like to thank the government of Québec for its SODEC income tax program for book publication.

Canadian Cataloguing-in-Publication Data

Main entry under title:

Toronto

(Ulysses travel guide)
Includes index.

ISSN 1493-342X
ISBN 2-89464-662-3

1. Toronto (Ont.) - Guidebooks. 2. Toronto (Ont.) - Tours. I. Series.

FC3097.18.T66	917.13'541045	C00-300417-1

Table of Contents

Table of Contents *(continued)*

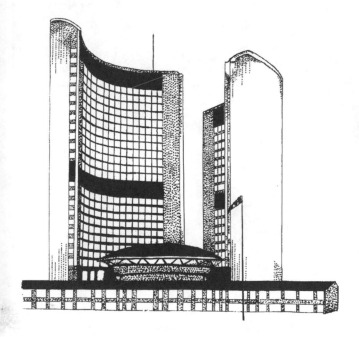

New City Hall

Write to Us

The information contained in this guide was correct at press time. However, mistakes may slip by, omissions are always possible, establishments may move, etc. The authors and publisher hereby disclaim any liability for loss or damage resulting from omissions or errors.

We value your comments, corrections and suggestions, as they allow us to keep each guide up to date. The best contributions will be rewarded with a free book from Ulysses Travel Guides. All you have to do is write us at the following address and indicate which title you would be interested in receiving (see the list at the end of the guide).

Ulysses Travel Guides

4176 St. Denis Street
Montréal, Québec
Canada H2W 2M5

305 Madison Avenue
Suite 1166, New York
NY 10165

www.ulyssesguides.com
E-mail: text@ulysses.ca

List of Maps

Map Symbols

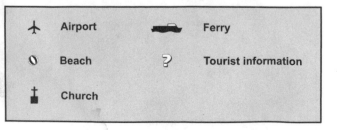

✈ Airport   🚢 Ferry

◐ Beach   ❓ Tourist information

✝ Church

Symbols

≡	Air conditioning
bkfst incl.	Breakfast included
⊗	Fan
⇄	Fax number
⊘	Fitness centre
ℑ	Fireplace
fb	Full board (lodging + 3 meals)
K	Kitchenette
≈	Pool
pb	Private bathroom
ℝ	Refrigerator
ℜ	Restaurant
△	Sauna
✿	Spa
sb	Shared bathroom
☎	Telephone number
🛶	Ulysses' favourite
⊛	Whirlpool

Attraction Classification

★	Interesting
★★	Worth a visit
★★★	Not to be missed

Hotel Classification

$	$50 or less
$$	$50,01 to $100
$$$	$100,01 to $150
$$$$	$150,01 to $200
$$$$$	$200,01 and over

Unless otherwise indicated, the prices in this guide apply to a standard room for two people in peak season.

Restaurant Classification

$	$10 or less
$$	$10,01 to $20
$$$	$20,01 to $30
$$$$	$30,01 and over

The prices in this guide are for a full meal for one person, not including taxes, drinks or tip.

All prices in this guide are in Canadian dollars.

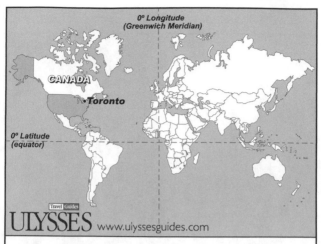

Where is Toronto?

ONTARIO

Capital: Toronto
Population: 11,669,300 hab.
Area: 1,068,630 km²
Currency: Canadian dollar

TORONTO

Population: 2,500,000 inhab.
Metropolitan Area: 5,200,000 inhab.

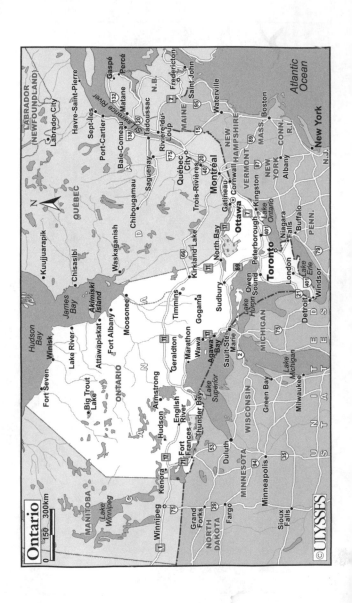

Portrait

Multicultural, vibrant and colourful, the city of Toronto continues to surprise us. Long considered too virtuous, Canada's economic powerhouse is now a metropolis in the true sense of the word, offering a wide range of activities.

For much of the 20th century the words that came most readily to mind in describing the Queen City included "virtuous," "monotonous," "conservative" or, the common moniker, "Toronto the Good." Though Toronto's daily grind is very corporate, once the sun sets the city moves to a different beat, one set by its theatres, bars and restaurants. Over the years, numerous urban renewal projects have revitalized the city's landscape. This revitalization started around the time the new city hall was built, giving Torontonians their first public space with real character and personality.

More recently, revitalization projects, such as the one that has transformed the Wa-

terfront and its green spaces or the creation of the Distillery District, have shown that this is a city that means business. The gentrification of certain neighbourhoods, notably through the construction of massive condominiums, reflects the new standard of living of some of Toronto's residents. The coming years will see the restoration of Union Station, along with the modification and expansion of certain museums and university facilities. The character of Canada's biggest city has been enlivened by the desire of its many ethnic communities to bring a reflection of their countries of origin to their adopted city, creating myriad different neighbourhoods with special colour, taste and charm, exemplifying a Toronto teeming with diversity.

The "Toronto the Good" label dates back to the time when nearly all work and leisure were prohibited on Sundays under the Lord's Day Act, which banned all money-making activity and virtually all social or cultural activities, except, of course, for religious worship. Toronto was also a business-minded and work-oriented place where outdoor cafés were forbidden and most available entertainment was offered in private clubs. This state of affairs, which made Toronto simply too dreary in the eyes of many inhabitants, led much of the cultural community to abandon the city.

For example, the Group of Seven, a famous group of painters formed in the 1920s, showed little interest in the city and concentrated mostly on painting wild landscapes in northern Ontario. Literature was produced only on a small scale. It was a dull, lifeless place, a prisoner unto itself. This reputation continues to cling to the city even today to a certain extent, despite many efforts to get rid of it.

Toronto thrives as Canada's most important financial and industrial centre. Its traditional Anglo-Saxon majority slowly yielded to the transformations brought about by massive immigration from continental Europe after the Second World War, but it was immigration from Asia and the West Indies that really changed the cultural face of Canada's biggest city.

The city of Toronto encompasses the six former municipalities of Toronto, North York, Scarborough, York, Etobicoke and East York, which now form one city. The Greater Toronto Area also includes a wide swath of suburbia beyond the metropolitan boundary. The region's economic and financial might makes it one of the most attractive places in North America for immigrants to settle. Toronto is home to Canada's largest Italian community and to North America's second-largest Chinese community, after San Francisco. It also has substantial Jewish, Portuguese, Ukrainian, Jamaican and Greek communities. This massive influx of immigrants over the last half-century has transformed the face of Toronto, making it not only the largest but also the most culturally diverse city in Canada. You can live this multicultural experience by exploring different areas of the city, where you will discover countless restaurants, cafés and shops. Despite all the changes it has gone through, though, Toronto has kept much of its Anglo-Saxon heritage, a clear reminder of its past.

History

When Europeans discovered the new world, a mosaic of indigenous peoples had already occupied this vast continent for thousands of years. Ancestors of these native peoples had crossed the Bering Strait toward the end of the last Ice Age more than 12,000 years ago,

slowly spreading across the whole continent. During the following millennia, as the glaciers retreated, some of them began migrating to the northern reaches of eastern Canada. At the time of the first intensive European forays into North America, several nations forming part of the Iroquoian and Algonkian language families shared the territory on the northern shore of Lake Ontario, the future site of Toronto.

The city, with its fine location on Lake Ontario, appeared on maps for the first time under the name Tarantou, thought to be a Huron or Mohawk word with several possible meanings, the likeliest of which is "meeting place." This seemed appropriate for the simple trading post located at the beginning of a trail favoured by Aboriginal peoples headed from Lake Ontario to Lake Huron. This trail was part of an efficient, centuries-old communications and trading network. With their tradition as traders, natives in southern Ontario received fur from the Iroquois in exchange for produce from their gardens. Canoes proved to be a suitable form of transport on the lakes and rivers that lay at the heart of this network.

The Meeting of Two Civilizations

During the decades that followed the European discovery of America, the growing fashion

Historical Timeline

1610
French fur-trader Étienne Brûlé sets off to explore the continent's interior and reaches lakes Ontario and Huron.

1645-1655
The powerful Iroquois League of Five Nations annihilates rival Aboriginal nations.

1713
The French, vanquished in Europe, sign the Treaty of Utrecht and surrender control of Hudson Bay, Newfoundland and Acadia to the British.

1720
Ontario's first French trading post is established in present-day Toronto.

1750
The French build Fort Rouillé on the site of the trading post.

1756-1763
The Seven Years' War pits the French and British against each other in Europe.

1763
The French officially lose New France to the British.

1791
The Constitutional Act divides Canada into the provinces of Upper and Lower Canada.

1793
Lieutenant-Governor John Graves Simcoe begins building the settlement of York.

1814
The Treaty of Ghent puts an end to hostilities between the Americans and the British in Canada.

1834
The town of York becomes the city of Toronto, the capital of Upper Canada.

1837
William Lyon Mackenzie spearheads the short-lived 1837 Rebellion in Upper Canada.

1867
The Confederation of the Dominion of Canada is created.

1891
Toronto's population reaches 181,000.

Portrait

1930
Toronto's population passes the 500,000 mark.

1954
Canada's first metropolitan government is created: the Municipality of Metropolitan Toronto.

1959
The opening of the St. Lawrence Seaway boosts Toronto's economic development.

1965
The completion of the new city hall starts a new trend that signals a departure from the city's sometimes-austere architecture.

1970
Toronto becomes Canada's metropolis, overtaking its eternal rival, Montreal, in population.

1976
The CN Tower is built.

1998
Creation of the amalgamated "megacity" of Toronto.

2003
The city of Toronto suffers a major electrical blackout in mid-August.

in Europe for fur hats and clothing meant that enormous profits could be expected from the fur trade, rekindling official French interest in North America. The fur trade required constant links with local suppliers, namely the Aboriginal peoples, and thus a permanent presence was necessary.

Located deep inside the continent, far from both the Atlantic coast and the easily navigable portion of the St. Lawrence River, Toronto was never favoured by the French authorities as a suitable spot for settlement, but was seen rather as a

simple trading post. Ontario was nonetheless crisscrossed early on by French explorers. Starting in 1610, only two years after Québec City was founded, explorer **Étienne Brûlé** set out for the interior of the continent. Like several of his predecessors, Brûlé was looking for a land route that could lead him to the fabulous riches of the Orient. After setting out alone, he became the first European to reach Lake Ontario and Lake Huron.

To do this, he followed a route heavily used by Aboriginals and fur traders. Toward the end of the 17th century, the village of Teiaigon, inhabited by the Mississauga First Nation, was located at the beginning of this route and formed an important meeting place in the fur trade. Noting the importance of this region, French merchants set up a trading post here around 1720, followed in 1750 by a fortified trading site called Fort Rouillé (pronounced rwee-YAY).

The French and the Huron First Nation, who populated the region, reached a deal under which the Hurons agreed to trade exclusively with the French, who in return offered to protect them against their Iroquois enemies living further south. The conflict between Hurons and Iroquois was part of a vast military campaign launched by the powerful **Iroquois Five Nations Confederacy**, which wiped out all of its rivals between 1645 and 1655. The Huron, the Petun, the Erie and the Neutral nations, each comprising at least 10,000 people, nearly disappeared within a decade.

These Iroquoian-speaking nations of southern Ontario found themselves victims of a war for the fur trade monopoly being waged by the European powers through Aboriginal surrogates. The Iroquois Five Nations confederacy, allied with the English, had traditionally lived in areas further south, in what is now the United States, and they sought to appropriate

this lucrative trade for themselves. Meanwhile, France was conquered in Europe, a defeat that would prove costly in the Americas. Under the 1713 **Treaty of Utrecht**, France officially yielded control of Hudson Bay, Newfoundland and Acadia to England. This treaty caused New France to lose strategic military positions, weakening it considerably.

In the following years, the noose tightened around France's possessions in North America. When the **Seven Years' War** (1756-63) broke out in Europe, the American colonies soon figured among the major stakes. In what is now Ontario, French troops managed in the early years to contain the British thrust and to remain in control of navigation on the Great Lakes. The French forces were not very numerous, but they operated from several strategic positions, including Fort Frontenac, at the mouth of Lake Ontario; Niagara, the land link between Lake Ontario and Lake Erie; Detroit, at the tip of Lake Erie; Michili-mackinac, where Lake Michigan and Lake Huron meet; and Fort Rouillé, built at the excellent port at what is now Toronto. Fort Rouillé was destroyed by its commander, Captain Alexandre Douville, in 1759, soon after British troops captured another French stronghold, Fort Niagara. One after another, each of these fortifications fell to the British.

British North America

In the years immediately following the British conquest of Canada, little changed in Ontario. A vast, little-occupied territory, it was populated by Aboriginal peoples and fur traders. The British Crown did not decree any colonization or development plans apart from the fur trade during this period. Ironically, it was the **American War of Independence** (1775-83) that would give birth to Ontario, radically changing the history of Canada at the same time.

In the early years of the conflict that pitted England against insurgents in its 13 southern colonies, British forces established strategic positions in Ontario, from which they launched attacks against the American rebels. Overall, however, the war went against the British troops and their allies, and they finally had to concede defeat. The American Revolution, at least in the beginning, had been a genuine civil war between two factions: the supporters of independence and the Loyalists who wished to maintain colonial ties with the British. More than 350,000 of these Loyalists played an active part, fighting on the British side.

The signing of the Treaty of Versailles (1783), which recognized the British defeat at the hands of the American Revolutionaries, pushed tens of thousands of these Loyalists to seek refuge in Canada. Between 5,000 and 6,000 of them settled on the virgin western lands of what is now Ontario and developed the first permanent colonies in this territory. The majority, however, settled along the St. Lawrence River and Lake Ontario, mainly in the vicinities of Kingston and Niagara, the two biggest towns at that time.

The vast majority of the Canadian population, however, was still French-speaking and Catholic. In response to the rise of pro-independence sentiment in the 13 southern colonies, and to avoid a similar situation amongst these former subjects of the King of France, the British Crown granted them the right to maintain their religion and customs. To ensure the Loyalists were not in the minority, while at the same time upholding the rights of French Catholics, London promulgated the **Constitutional Act of 1791**, dividing Canada into two provinces, Lower Canada (now Québec) and Upper Canada (now Ontario). Lower Canada, with its large French majority, remained subject to French civil law, while Upper Canada, located west of the Ottawa River, was inhabited mostly by Loyalists of British stock and was subject to English common law. The Constitutional Act also introduced to Canada the beginnings of a parliamentary system, with the creation of a House of Assembly in each province.

Portrait

Upper Canada at first chose Newark (Niagara) as its capital. This did not last long, however, for the site was poorly protected and might easily fall should the Americans decide to invade Canada.

It was thus in August 1793 that the attention of **John Graves Simcoe**, the lieutenant-governor of Upper Canada, was drawn to the impressive naval and military possibilities offered by the bay facing Toronto. Accordingly, he decided to build a city near the site of the former Fort Rouillé, at the edge of the Don River, on land that the British had bought from Aboriginal peoples for the sum of 1,700 pounds sterling. Simcoe undertook the construction of York, which was later renamed Toronto.

The site was ideal from a strategic standpoint, but "Muddy York," as it was called because of its location on a muddy plain that descended gradually to the shores of Lake Ontario, was not very hospitable. Furthermore, it was still very sparsely populated. By 1812, the capital of Upper Canada still had only 700 inhabitants and filled a purely administrative role. The main centre of economic activity was Kingston, a dismal little village that had grown quickly following the building of the Rideau Canal. Kingston remained the biggest town in Upper Canada until 1820, but the governor's decision to move the capital to York led the colonial administrators and the small group of intellectuals to head gradually to the new capital, which soon dominated.

The Upper Canadian settlers mistrusted their southern neighbours, who soon justified these fears. In 1812, allegedly fed up with excessive British control over the Great Lakes, the Americans declared war on Britain and, thus, on Canada. Loyalists and their descendants still formed the majority of Upper Canada's population, lending a rather emotional aspect to this conflict. Britain, tied down in Europe by the Napoleonic Wars, could not provide significant aid to its colony.

The strategic location of the new town of York was put to the test by this war. Fort York, located at the entrance to the bay, formed the main defence of Upper Canada against American attacks. At the end of April 1813, an American invasion force landed near the present location of Sunnyside Beach. After a brief skirmish, British troops quickly retreated inside Fort York, but they could not resist the American assault. Before leaving the fort, the British exploded their arms depot at the very moment the Americans captured it, killing General Zebulon M. Pike of the American army. In reprisal, the Yankee troops set fire to the fort and to the parliament at York, located at the foot of Parliament Street, and then sacked the town. This pillaging left Upper Canada's pro-British population with deeply anti-American sentiments, which to a small extent have lasted up to this day. York's Loyalist character was clearly revealed by the choice of street names of the period, including King, Queen, Duke, Duchess, Frederick and Princess. Despite York's overthrow, colonists elsewhere in Upper Canada managed to repulse American attacks and gave the United States of America its first military defeat.

In 1814, the **Treaty of Ghent** ended the hostilities and re-established the pre-war boundaries between Canada and the United States. With the threat of war set aside, York and the rest of Upper Canada underwent a substantial wave of British immigration. The Loyalists, who had made Upper Canada their home since 1783, were joined by large numbers of immigrants, mostly from the British Isles, who were fleeing the recession and unemployment that spread in Britain after the Napoleonic wars. Upper Canada continued to settle its fine agricultural lands. This ever-growing influx of immigrants moving onto nearby lands considerably increased the population of the little town of York. With the development of the hinterland, the town became a centre of economic activity and an important meeting place where area farmers could sell their cattle, poultry, grains and other products at the Weekly Public Open Market, which later became the St. Lawrence Market. Trade developed little by little, and York also became the centre for Upper Canada's banking activities. In 1834, York became the municipality of Toronto, and in less than seven years its population grew from 1,800 to 9,000. When Toronto was created, it was divided into five wards: St. Andrews, St. David, St. George, St. Lawrence and St. Patrick.

The development of new communications links with the outside world in the middle of the 19th century also played an important role in Toronto's economic growth. With the massive arrival of colonists, who cleared and cultivated land in the valley surrounding the town, the fur trade gave way to a new economy based on staples such as wood and grains. Part of this production was exported to Europe in exchange for manufactured goods from Britain, such as farming equipment and clothing. Upper Canada thus needed a way to export its goods quickly and easily. The province's and Toronto's geographic isolation had been made obvious by the War of 1812. Besides rendering the colony vulnerable in wartime, the various sets of rapids that blocked navigation along the St. Lawrence River limited commercial trade with the colony even in peacetime. To open the route to Upper Canada, canals were built in several places, notably at Lachine (1814), Fort Erie (1825) and Welland (1824).

Once the new canals were open, traffic could move freely between Lake Erie and the Welland River, between the Niagara River and Lake Ontario, and also between Toronto and the Atlantic Ocean.

The Family Compact

These major changes had an understandably profound effect on the social structures of Toronto and the rest of Canada. The British government came to the conclusion that the loss of 13 of its colonies (creating the United States) had been caused by the excessive freedom they had enjoyed. Governor Simcoe himself intended to reproduce the British class system in Toronto so as to avoid a second American Revolution. The Constitutional Act of 1791 aimed to restrict the powers of the legislative assemblies elected by the people. Under the terms of this act, the executive functions of government were carried out by a governor appointed by the British government, who in turn would name the members of the Executive Council who were to assist him. The legislature took the form of an elected Legislative Assembly holding very little real power and subject to vetos by the governor and the Executive Council.

The governor surrounded himself with some of the colony's most powerful and influential men. Together they ruled, taking little account of the wishes of the people's elected representatives. This oligarchy became known in Upper Canada as the Family Compact (its Lower Canada equivalent was called the *Clique du Château*). The Grange, a Georgian-style mansion built by the Boulton family on lot number 13 (see p 127) at the beginning of the 19th century, quickly became a symbol of the power of the Family Compact and of the superiority of the British aristocracy. Despite the rebellions of 1837, The Grange remained a seat of political power and a sign of the Toronto elite's deep conviction that everything good in Canada must be British.

Disagreements between the Executive Council and the Legislative Assembly were substantial, and political quarrels became inevitable. The farming and working classes became convinced that the Family Compact was using its political monopoly to assure its economic monopoly. Two political parties emerged, the Conservatives, also known as Tories, who wanted to maintain the status quo, and the Reformists, whose aim was to make the government more democratic. In Upper Canada, as in Lower Canada, reform movements developed. In largely French-speaking Lower Canada, the movement was intensified by the racial element, with parts of the English-speaking minority allied to the ruling class and a

French-speaking majority made up largely of farmers and low-paid workers. French-Canadians chose Louis-Joseph Papineau as spokesman. He took charge of the reform movement and went as far as declaring that authority in Lower Canada should return to the French-Canadian majority.

Similar events were taking place in Upper Canada, despite the absence of intense cultural conflicts. The reformist leader was **William Lyon Mackenzie**, a Torontonian of Scottish descent who launched his first attacks against the government and the Family Compact in his newspaper, *The Colonial Advocate*. He was later elected to the Legislative Assembly, where he immediately attacked government finances. As time went on, Mackenzie's remarks became ever harsher regarding the protectionism and abusive powers of the Family Compact, which finally expelled him from the Assembly for defamation. In 1835, he was elected the first mayor of Toronto, but his increasingly extreme views worried some of his more moderate supporters, who ended up rejecting his program completely. The ideas put forth by Mackenzie were shared by a great number of those who expressed their discontent with the Family Compact, but many were unwilling to break ties with Britain.

With the arrival of a new governor, Sir Francis Bond Head, who had the Assembly completely under his thumb, Mackenzie's more radical supporters lost all hope of achieving change through constitutional means. When Mackenzie learned of this, he decided to launch his revolutionary forces. Unfortunately, despite its leader's enthusiasm, this movement of workers and small farmers was very poorly organized, and its attempt to capture Toronto was put down quickly, with little violence. A vanquished Mackenzie would follow Papineau into exile in the United States, where they would try in vain to reassemble their troops and to win American support.

If the period preceding the Act of Union (1851) was characterized by great canal-building projects and the establishment of various infrastructures destined to bring Toronto into the industrial age (gas, water, electricity, etc.), it was the construction of the railways that took precedence as of the 1850s. The establishment of the railway network was seen then as the solution to Canada's communications problems. The many Irish immigrants who had come to live in Canada toward the 1850s to escape the famine and poverty that raged in their homeland became the biggest immigrant group in Toronto by 1851. Many of them took part in the major construction projects that were undertaken then, including the building of the Grand Trunk Railway, which would link many of the bigger towns in Canada. Although a great many of these Irish immigrants were Ulster Protestants, a certain number were Catholic, and ultimately some of the old battles between Catholics and Anglicans were revived. Irish Catholics were not always made to feel welcome, and rising tensions eventually led to violence. The Orange Lodges, created by Ulster-born Irish, came to the defence of the old Anglo-Protestant social order, joining it in dominating municipal politics up to the end of the 19th century.

Thanks to its exceptional geographic location, Toronto became an important hub of the Canadian railway network. Several other lines linked the American railway network to the major Canadian cities, opening the door to the enormous American market. The building of this complex communication network was joined by increased exploitation of Canadian mines and forests, transforming Toronto and helping develop industries such as steel foundries, rolling mills and locomotive factories. The coming of the railway not only ended the isolation of distant regions but also produced an enormous economic entity in North America, while also creating new markets and new needs.

These enormous infrastructure projects were putting a heavy burden on the public treasury, however. At the same time, the Canadian economy was hard hit by the British decision to abandon its mercantilist policies,

ending the preferential tariff for its colonies. To lessen the impact of this change in British colonial policy, Canada signed a treaty in 1854 allowing free entry of certain goods to the United States, in particular its two most important exports, wood and wheat. But the Canadian economy had barely recovered when the treaty was renounced in 1866 under pressure from American business interests. The loss, first of the colonial preference and then of the reciprocity treaty, left the Canadian economy in bad shape. This gloomy economic climate was both a backdrop to and a major impetus for the birth of the Canadian Confederation.

Confederation

Upper Canada was reshaped under the **1867 Confederation**, becoming a province named Ontario, from an Iroquoian word probably meaning beautiful lakes or beautiful waters, an obvious reference to the province's hydrographic wealth. Three other provinces, Québec (formerly Lower Canada), New Brunswick and Nova Scotia joined this pact, which was soon to unite a vast territory reaching from the Atlantic to the Pacific. The confederation pact established a division of powers between two levels of government, the federal government, based in Ottawa, and the provincial governments, with Ontario choosing

Toronto as its capital. This capital of the former Upper Canada had become an important commercial city over the decades and the province's biggest population centre, with about 45,000 inhabitants. From a political standpoint, the establishment of the federal system turned to Ontario's advantage. In the new Parliament in Ottawa, the number of members representing each province was proportionate to its population. Ontario, the most populous of the Canadian provinces, had much to gain from the parliamentary stipulation of representation by population, while Toronto took control of the natural riches of the province (lumber, minerals). As of the 1860s, Toronto became a powerful economic centre linking north, south, east and west, and through which grain, lumber and minerals for exportation were transported.

From an economic standpoint, Confederation failed initially to provide the expected results. It was not until three decades had passed, characterized by sharp fluctuations, that Ontario really experienced its first great period of rapid economic growth. The foundations for this growth were laid several years after Confederation by Sir **John A. Macdonald**, the federal Conservative Prime Minister re-elected in 1878 after five years out of office. His electoral campaign had centred around his National Policy, a series of measures aimed at protecting and promoting Canada's na-scent industries by means of protective tariffs, the creation of a big internal market unified by a transcontinental railway, and the growth of this internal market by a policy of populating the Prairies through massive immigration. At the same time, the arrival in Canada of the industrial revolution and the use of steam as a power source brought about enormous changes that enabled the city to become the main centre for the manufacture of farm equipment and heavy machinery.

Growth and Internationalization

The beginning of the 20th century coincided with the start of a prodigious era of economic growth, aided by an abundance of raw materials and cheap energy. Substantial mineral deposits, in particular cobalt, nickel, silver, iron and zinc, were discovered in the northern part of the province. These discoveries, together with the development of the railway network, led to the settlement of northern Ontario and contributed markedly to Toronto's prosperity during much of the century, as the north furnished raw materials for the city's growing industries. Of course, this industrialization affected the farming sector, which became more mechanized and forced a portion of the province's rural population to seek work in the city. These discoveries also contributed to the development of heavy industry, which would become the backbone of the entire province's industrial infrastructure.

Thanks to Toronto's geographic location, local industry was able to benefit from the relative proximity of booming new markets in Western Canada, whose development and intense settlement activities created a strong demand for equipment and manufactured goods which were being produced in Canada instead of being imported from Britain. Western development also contributed to the establishment of department stores such as Eaton's in 1869 and Simpson's in 1872. These companies would grow quickly, holding an important place in Toronto and across Canada, thanks to their catalogues and extensive mail order businesses. The national policy of settling Western Canada helped create a new wave of industrialization in Toronto, part of a gradual North American movement favouring the Great Lakes basin, both in Canada and the United States, over the older industrial centres further east.

These transformations led to strong growth in the city's population, which was largely of British descent. In 1871, Toronto had only 56,000 inhabitants, but a mere 20 years later it had grown to 181,000. This growth was caused by a massive rural exodus and also by the arrival of Irish immigrants

who continued to flee famine in their homeland.

This unprecedented economic growth did not favour everyone equally, of course. Industrialization led to the rapid development of sometimes insalubrious neighbourhoods, such as Cabbagetown and the Ward, which became home to large groups of poorly paid workers. Meanwhile, fine mansions were built near the city centre, and wealthy families moved to prime areas of the city. The concentration of industry around the railway lines and port installations would also lead to a radical transformation of the urban landscape. The area just beyond the factories and warehouses that lined the port was soon filled with inexpensive housing built for the numerous workers.

Almost everywhere in the city, red- and yellow-brick houses, gradually replaced old wooden firetraps. As early as 1834, the City of Toronto forbade the use of wood as a structural material, but this did not prevent two devastating fires, the first in 1849, which destroyed St. James Cathedral (see p 114) and the second in 1904. During the 1890s, Toronto became illuminated by electricity. The telephone appeared, and the famous streetcar network, still in use today, was already spreading across the city.

Starting around that time, the City of Toronto began taking over neighbouring villages. The coming of the streetcars gave people greater mobility and enabled them to live away from the city centre. The annexation of surrounding municipalities began with Yorkville in 1883. By 1912, Toronto and many of its suburbs had merged.

"Toronto the Good"

Toronto was achieving a special place among Canadian cities, of which it was then the second biggest. It obtained its famous moniker "Toronto the Good" because of its attachment to the British Empire and its austere values. Even some Torontonians had little admiration for their city, which they themselves considered quite dull. This attribute was reinforced by a 1906 law forbidding any sort of work or entertainment on the Lord's Day, which was scrupulously respected by many inhabitants. Torontonians had to wait until 1950 before they could attend sporting events such as hockey or baseball games on a Sunday. It was also in true British spirit that affluent members of Toronto society formed numerous private clubs and organizations, such as the Albany Club, the National Club, the Royal Yacht Club and the Toronto Cricket Club. All of this proper British living actually held back the Toronto arts scene. Painters and writers did not choose to live in Toronto, nor did they use it in their material. Even though the city has changed enormously since

then, Toronto still has trouble shaking off its reputation as a dull, puritanical city.

During the years before the First World War, immigration to Toronto got a second wind. This time, it was Italians, Jews and Ukrainians who accounted for many of the new arrivals, eventually constituting nearly 13% of the total population. Drawn by the city's flourishing economy, these immigrants established the first ethnic neighbourhoods and slowly transformed Toronto's cultural character.

In 1914, on the eve of the **First World War**, Montréal was the biggest city in Canada, with Toronto still playing a second-string role in banking and some aspects of industry. Toronto grew in importance during the war, which had substantial repercussions on the city's social and economic life. The city used its industrial might to play a major role in the war, with the establishment of munitions factories and meat-packing plants. Due to a serious shortage of male labour, factories turned to female workers, giving women in Canada a social role they had never held before. Even though most of these women returned to traditional roles after the war, their expectations were higher than they had been before. In 1917, even before the war ended, the Canadian and Ontario governments had resolved to give women the right to vote, a longtime demand that had been turned down earlier. As well, the prohibition on the sale and consumption of alcohol in Ontario, a measure that had been intended only for the duration of the war, seemed to have many supporters among the people even afterward. Even as Ontarians prepared to enjoy the exhilarating postwar years, the majority of voters in a 1919 referendum decided to maintain the prohibition on alcohol.

Ontario's economy emerged strengthened from the First World War, and the following decade was marked by steady economic growth that was slowed only by the **Stock Market Crash of 1929** in the United States. During the period between 1920 and 1930, Toronto continued to grow, with new municipalities popping up in the suburbs. The total population was about half a million by then. As elsewhere in North America, Toronto saw the growth of hostility toward immigrants during the 1920s and 1930s. In the postwar years, especially with the effects of the Great Depression, immigrants were less welcome in a place that no longer felt it really needed them. The Canadian Government tightened its borders and set in place a selective immigration process that favoured Americans and British subjects over Jews, Blacks, southern Europeans and eastern Europeans. It even went so far as to impose a tax on all Chinese immigrants to reduce their numbers. When this policy achieved only mixed success, Chinese immigration was simply halted between 1923 and 1947. This wave of xenophobia swept through Toronto along with the rest of Canada, but it seemed to vary according to economic conditions. When things were going well, non-Anglo-Saxon immigrants seemed to be tolerated as long as they were not too visible.

During the period following the 1929 Stock Market Crash, Canada as a whole felt the consequences. Toronto, however, seemed to be less hard hit by the Depression than most other Canadian cities. The wealth and diversity of natural resources available from Ontario's hinterland allowed it to withstand the effects of the American crisis and to maintain a stronger economy, while the rest of the Canadian economy, more highly dependent on export markets, collapsed with the decline in international trade. To deal with the misery afflicting much of the population, the government decided that certain private businesses should set up a scheme to help those who were in the most desperate straits. This slow turn to the left would gradually convert Canada to the welfare state that emerged after the Second World War.

The Postwar Years

Following 10 years of economic crisis, the **Second World War** revived the Canadian economy and revitalized Toronto with the arrival of new technologies such as electronics and avionics. In terms of natural resources, one of the world's richest uranium deposits was discovered in the 1950s near Elliot Lake. These developments were topped off by the 1959 opening of the **St. Lawrence Seaway**, which encouraged exports and developed new markets for Toronto products, and this despite the fact that Toronto's port freezes over in the winter. Toronto would soon increase its control over Canada's service and financial sectors, reducing the gap that separated it from Montréal and taking the lead among Canadian cities. Even though the farming and manufacturing sectors declined in relative importance as production moved toward Asia with its lower costs, any slack was quickly absorbed by the finance, retail, urban development and telecommunications sectors. The provincial and federal governments became more involved in the economy and in social programs, creating a new welfare state. Besides its role as a leading centre of manufacturing and finance, Toronto also housed the national headquarters of many trade unions. The city had been at the centre of trade union development in Canada ever since the beginning of the industrial era, but the years following the Second World War saw unionized labour become a significant economic force.

After 1945, Toronto's population rose again as a new wave of immigrants settled in the city. The end of the war brought optimism and prosperity, while the racism that had marked the 1920s and 1930s disappeared and the country opened its doors once again to immigration. People from Britain and then large numbers of Italians in the 1960s were followed by streams of Germans, Poles and other Slavs, Hungarians, Greeks and Portuguese.

Metropolitan Toronto and the Contemporary Era

In 1951, the greater Toronto area found itself short of revenues. This was felt especially in the suburbs, where the need for services was simply not being met. In response to this situation, Canada's first metropolitan government was created in 1953, the Municipality of Metropolitan Toronto. Made up of people from Toronto and 12 surrounding municipalities, this new council would become responsible for areas such as education, finance, public transit, water management and police services. From the start, it fell under the domination of one **Frederick Gardiner**, a lawyer turned politician known for his aggressive and imposing personality. Upon his arrival at the municipal council, Gardiner had to answer the needs of the whole area surrounding the City of Toronto, which was plagued by problems relating to sewage and water supplies. He also had to look to the problems of Toronto itself, including its serious downtown traffic congestion. This period coincided with a massive move to the suburbs.

One step in the right direction was accomplished with the opening in 1954 of the first phase of Toronto's subway system, the first such system in Canada. But the real solution to the problems faced by many motorists lay not in public transit but rather in the improvement and expansion of the road network. Toronto already had a port and a well established railway network, but it needed new road links to the rest of Ontario. A project to build an expressway crossing the city along Lake Ontario was adopted by the Metropolitan Toronto council just a few months after its creation in 1953. The building of this expressway began in 1954 and continued until 1966. An expressway across the heart of the city did not please everyone, of course, but there was widespread agreement on the need to improve vehicular flow in the city centre. Despite all the opposition to the Gardiner Expressway, only a citizens' coalition formed to protect the Fort York historic site succeeded in having the expressway's route modified. With the refusal of the coalition to have the fort moved to the very shores of Lake Ontario, the metropolitan council resigned

itself to building the highway around the fort. Today, the Gardiner Expressway is in poor shape, with its metal supporting structure rusting away quickly because of the salt used in the winter to melt snow and ice on the roadway. Metal wrapped in epoxy resin is now used to prevent premature rust attacks, but that does not prevent many Torontonians from loathing this expressway, which blocks access to Lake Ontario; in the meantime, it remains a necessary evil.

Starting in the early postwar years, the halo surrounding "Toronto the Good" had begun to tarnish. In 1947, the first cocktail bars began to appear across the city, raising the ire of many citizens. Of far greater importance was the massive influx of immigrants from all over Europe, which accentuated the city's multi-ethnic character. In 1960, Toronto moved a step closer to modern life and greater freedom with the lifting of the Sunday prohibition on activities such as movies, plays and other cultural events. But it was the building of the new city hall, completed in September 1965, that really heralded the winds of change that were blowing over the city. The building, designed by Finnish architect Viljo Revell, broke the conservative shell that had stifled the city. It showed the benefits of modern architecture, perhaps with a little too much enthusiasm. During the following years, a number of historic buildings were demol-

Portrait

Yonge Street

According to the *Guinness Book of World Records*, Toronto is the starting point of the longest street in the world. Yonge Street (pronounced *"young"*), which marked its bicentennial in 1996, stretches 1,896km from the shores of Lake Ontario to the town of Rainy River, in northwestern Ontario. Originally a trail used by the Hurons and then by the French explorer Étienne Brûlé, this road was started in the 1790s under orders from Governor John Graves Simcoe to improve links between the new town of *York* (now Toronto) and Georgian Bay, in case of armed conflict with the Americans. Once the risk of war with the neighbours to the south was eliminated during the 19th century, Yonge Street became a busier artery. Today, it is full of activity and lined with shops of all kinds.

ished, in the name of progress and modernism, to make way for new buildings. Fortunately, some of the developers found themselves facing fierce opposition from citizens who were determined to save these reminders of a not very distant past. Some of the buildings that escaped the wrecker's ball are among the city's finest attractions today; these include Union Station, Old City Hall and Holy Trinity Church. It is ironic to note that Torontonians finally became aware of the architectural value of these old buildings, which add so much to the charm of many urban neighbourhoods, only when faced directly with their demolition.

A certain balance between 19th century conservatism and an enthusiasm for everything new in the 1950s and 1960s was achieved with the election of **David Crombie** as mayor. He would lead the city toward a more harmonious development, setting height limits on new buildings and encouraging the revitalization of many older neighbourhoods through the restoration of old buildings.

Ontario's domination over the Canadian economy became unquestionable in the mid-1970s when Toronto overtook Montréal, its longtime rival, to become the biggest city in Canada. The remarkable performance of the Ontario and Toronto economies depended in large measure on the proximity of the United States. This enormous market absorbed three-quarters of all Canadian exports, and, more importantly, the majority of Canadian subsidiaries of big American companies were established in and around Metropolitan Toronto.

Following its role as a major transport and industrial centre, Toronto turned toward a service economy that grew with the computer age, while its financial power continued to reign as the greatest in Canada. Tourism also began to account for an appreciable portion of the city's economy.

In 1976, Canadian National (CN) built the tower that bears its name in order to resolve communications problems caused by the presence of too many skyscrapers. Emblematic of Toronto, the CN Tower now attracts countless visitors.

Population

During the 1960s, the central area of Toronto began to attract residents back from the suburbs. People moved downtown and restored entire neighbourhoods, some of them endowed with a great many Victorian-style buildings. A good example of this sort of neighbourhood is Yorkville, which briefly was the centre of the local hippie movement before taking on more bourgeois tones.

The prosperity Canada enjoyed up to the 1980s brought in its wake a renewed immigration which had been interrupted by the Depression and the war years. In the quarter-century after the Second World War, nearly two-million immigrants came to live in Ontario, accounting for nearly two-thirds of the Canadian total of new arrivals. Most of these people chose Toronto. No longer did a majority of them come from the British Isles, as had been the case before. Now many of them were people from southern and eastern Europe who headed into exile because of the difficult living conditions following the war in Europe, as well as communism. In just a few decades, Toronto's cultural face became radically transformed by the various ethnic neighbourhoods that contributed to making this city one of Canada's most cosmopolitan. During the 1970s and 1980s, many immigrants from Asia and the Caribbean chose Toronto as their new home.

Chinese immigration was no longer prohibited by Canadian government decree, as it had been between 1923 and 1947, and it bounced back. The influx of this so-called visible minority would change the face of Toronto completely. The city now has seven Chinatowns, which together form North America's second-largest Chinese community after San Francisco's.

Along Dundas Street, between Spadina and Bay, lies a city within a city where one can easily live without speaking a single word of English. Later in the 1970s, many immigrants from the Caribbean and southern Asia added to the mix. Once again, immigration would transform Toronto's image in the space of a decade, giving the city the international flavour of a true metropolis.

The profound changes in Québec that began in the 1960s and gathered steam in the 1970s also contributed to Toronto's changing face. As the French-speaking majority gradually took control of the Québec economy, and as the Québec government passed laws to protect and promote the French language, some big firms that had traditionally operated in English found it too difficult and costly to adjust to some of the changes and chose to move to Toronto. Many English-speaking residents of Québec followed them. This exodus benefited the Toronto economy and greatly strengthened the financial sector.

The Greater Toronto area now has a population of about 5.2 million, making it the biggest city in Canada.

Toronto: City of Neighbourhoods

Toronto is one of North America's most successfully multicul-

tural cities, with immigrants from every corner of the globe managing to blend into its society, while still maintaining their own cultural identity and traditions. It is this harmonious coming together of cultures that makes Canada, and Toronto as its largest, most diverse city, a cultural mosaic, differentiating it from the melting pot which characterizes our neighbours south of the border.

As sprawling as it may seem, Toronto is really a city of neighbourhoods. From Rosedale to Cabbagetown, from the Beaches to Little Italy, from one Chinatown to the next, each of Toronto's neighbourhoods has its own character. While some areas are defined by their architectural eccentricities, the most interesting ones are defined by the people who live in them. Toronto's ethnic diversity is dizzying, with over 70 nationalities speaking more than 100 languages living side by side–and restaurant-goers are all the happier for it!

Chinatown

Toronto's best-known ethnic neighbourhood is Chinatown (see p 123). There are actually seven Chinatowns in greater Toronto, but the most exciting and vibrant is probably the one bound by University, Spadina, Queen and College. During the day, fresh and exotic vegetables line the sidewalks around the intersection of Spadina and Dundas, the area's core, while at night, the bright yellow and

Toronto's Chinatown

The largest, best-established and most visible "minority" in Toronto, people of Chinese origin have been emigrating to Toronto since the mid-19th century. 400,000 members strong, it constitutes one of the largest Chinese communities in North America. The first arrivals, who took up the laundry and restaurant trades, settled on Yonge Street between Queen and King streets. And yet, the first real Chinatown, the heart of the community's commercial and social life, was first established in the Dundas Street area between Bay Street and University Avenue. It encompassed a large concentration of tea shops, restaurants and, above all, laundries, a service indispensable to urban life prior to the invention of the washing machine. Construction of the new city hall in the 1950s forced the community to move west, around the intersection of Dundas Street and Spadina Avenue. This area, the heart of this new and thriving community, remains the hub of Toronto's Sino-Canadian population.

In the 1970s, rising rents forced Chinese newcomers to settle in more remote and modest areas. As a result, the neighbourhood around Gerrard Street and Broadview Avenue became the second Chinatown. During that decade and the following one, the Chinese-Canadian population started to look to the suburbs to the north and west, as did Toronto's other ethnic groups. Chinese neighbourhoods thus flourished in Scarborough and Mississauga, largely due to influx of wealthy immigrants from Hong Kong.

Today, Chinese immigration continues to contribute substantially to the growth of Toronto's population. Though less than a third of the Chinese community now lives downtown, the Spadina Avenue–Dundas Street area remains the economic and cultural heart of the community. It is a bustling beehive of activity seven days a week, practically day and night. Don't miss it.

red lights are reminiscent of Hong Kong. Picturesque, adjacent **Kensington Market** is often associated with Chinatown. The vintage clothing stores and specialty food shops carrying products from Europe, the Caribbean, the Middle East and Asia are veritable must-sees.

Little Italy

Italians make up the city's largest ethnic group, and their spiritual home is Little Italy, located on College Street west of Bathurst, where *trattorias* and boutiques add a bit of Mediterranean flavour to Toronto's scene. In recent years, the area has been redefined by a younger crowd who've marked it as a hip place to be, causing a number of trendy bars and restaurants (not all Italian) to spring up. The result is a vibrant mix of traditional shops and Italian eateries side by side with chic pool halls and cozy wine bars. It's a marvellous spot to sip a cappuccino or try an Italian *gelato*. In the summertime, Little Italy is one of the liveliest night spots in the city, its streets lined with animated outdoor patios that remain busy into the early hours of the morning.

Greektown

Greektown is also known as the Danforth, after the road that runs through it. The area, which runs between Broadview and Coxwell (near the Chester subway stop), is dotted with Greek bakeries (where you'll find the best spinach-and-feta

pies in town), boutiques and *tavernas*. Even the street signs are written in both English and Greek. Some of the smaller, locally owned restaurants are closed in the summer, when their owners return to Greece. In addition to the smaller, traditional places, there are a number of trendy Greek restaurants perfect for a lively dinner out. The Danforth, one of the city's most interesting dining hot spots, has everything from Cuban tapas to Sushi, but the Greeks still dominate when it comes to restaurants, and Greektown, with its late-night fruit markets, specialty food shops, taverns and summer cafés, is a real culinary experience.

Little Poland

Between the Lakeshore and Dundas Street West, Roncesvalles Avenue is known as Little Poland, a pleasant area of grand trees and stately Victorians. This is where you can catch an Eastern European film or savour traditional homemade cabbage rolls and pirogies at one of its many cafés.

Portugal Village

The traditional *azulejos* (ceramic tiles) and a glass of port will make you think you are in Portugal when you visit the area around Dundas Street West, Ossington Avenue, Augusta Avenue and College Street, an area known as Portugal Village. The bakeries here sell some of the best bread in town, while cheese stores, fish markets and lace and crochet shops occupy every other corner.

Little India

Little India, which runs along Gerrard Street between Greenwood and Coxwell has all the character (if less of the chaos) of New Delhi. Strings of coloured lights are draped on restaurant facades, lighting up the street as if every night was a festival. Sari palaces abound, their windows showcasing glittery garments, and supermarkets spill onto the street with baskets full of mustard seeds, pappadams, coconuts and stalks of sugar cane. Everywhere the sound of modern Indian music plunks from scratchy speakers. Unless you're looking for a souvenir gold-coloured Buddha, the main reason for visiting Little India (besides soaking up the atmosphere) is for the food. Every second shop, it seems, is a restaurant, each specializing in a different type of Indian cuisine and most of them offering an all-you-can-eat buffet for around $15.

Caribbean Village

The area around Bathurst Street north of Bloor Street is the commercial district known as the Caribbean Community. Great food shops sell delicious treats, including the savoury patties (pastry turnovers with a spicy meat filling) and *roti* (flat bread with meat, fish or vegetable filling).

The Gay Village

Toronto has the largest population of gays and lesbians in Canada, and is very supportive and accepting of these communities. The Gay Village (affectionately known as the "Ghetto") runs along Church Street between Carlton and Bloor streets. Rainbow flags hang from its lamp posts and gay couples stroll hand in hand. During Toronto's Gay Pride parade and festival at the end of June, the streets of the Village are blocked off for three days and filled with beer tents, vendors and the 700,000 people (both gay and straight) who show up every year. It is definitely one of the city's best parties. Church is lively and bustling, especially in summer, with bars, cafés, restaurants, shops and lots of outdoor patios. Hanlan's Point, on the Toronto Islands, is also a popular gay summertime hangout, and in May, 1999 was officially designated as a clothing-optional beach.

Rosedale

Both of Toronto's most distinguished and affluent neighbourhoods lie just north of the downtown area. Rosedale is bound by Yonge Street to the west, the Don Valley Parkway to the east, Bloor Street to the south and St. Clair Avenue to the north. Rosedale began as the estate of Sheriff William Jarvis, and was so named by his wife Mary after the wild roses that once abounded here. The wild roses and the original house overlooking the ravine are now gone, replaced by a collection of curved streets lined with exquisite residences representing a variety of architectural styles. See also p 154.

Forest Hill

The posh area known as Forest Hill begins north of St. Clair Avenue, extending north to Eglinton Avenue, east to Avenue Road and west to Bathurst Street. Perhaps in keeping with its name, one of Forest Hill's first bylaws back in the 1920s was that a tree be planted on every lot. This haven of greenery is home to some of the city's finest dwellings; many of the loveliest grace Old Forest Hill Road. The community is also home to one of the country's most prestigious private schools, Upper Canada College. See also p 158.

Cabbagetown

Cabbagetown was once described as the "biggest Anglo-Saxon Slum" and was for many years an area to be avoided. The area has been transformed in recent years, however, and is now the epitome of gentrification in Toronto. Its name originated with Irish immigrants who arrived here in the mid-19th century and grew cabbages right on their front lawns. It contains grand trees and quaint small-scale Victorian homes, many of which have historical markers. Winchester, Carlton, Spruce and Metcalfe Streets are all lined with true gems. See also p 142.

The Annex

Extending north and west of the intersection of Bloor Street and Avenue Road to Dupont and Bathurst streets is an area which was annexed by the City of Toronto in 1887, and is now appropriately called The Annex. As this was a planned suburb, a certain architectural homogeneity prevails; even the unique gables, turrets and cornices are all lined up an equal distance from the street. It is now home to university professors and students, journalists and people from all walks of life. The Annex is another of Toronto's restaurant- and shop-lined corridors, perfect for shopping, eating or just strolling along to soak up a bit of the city's atmosphere. See also p 148.

Victorian row houses, Cabbagetown

The Beaches

Last but not least, there are The Beaches (Toronto really does have everything!). Known to locals only as the Beach, this is one of Toronto's most charming neighbourhoods, for obvious reasons–sun, sand, a beach-side boardwalk, classic clapboard and shingle cottages and the open water all lie just a streetcar ride (along Queen Street) away from the hectic pace of downtown. Bounded by Kingston Road, Woodbine Road, Victoria Park Avenue and Lake Ontario, the Beach is more than just a neighbour-hood–it's a way of life. Along the main stretch of Queen Street, there are countless restaurants, cafés and bou-tiques, with everything from designer children's shops to designer pet shops. The side-walks, boardwalk and beach-side bike path are more crowded with in-line skaters, cyclists and dog walkers than the streets are with cars. Trav-ellers will revel in the chance to sunbathe on the hot sand, take a quick dip in the refreshing water or, as the sun sets, do some window shopping and lounge about on a pretty patio. See also p 162.

Politics

In 1953, Toronto and 12 sur-rounding municipalities formed the Municipality of Metropolitan Toronto, Canada's first metro-politan government. When Toronto amalgamated its six former municipalities in 1998 to form a singular City of Toronto, a new City Council was cre-ated, with one councillor per ward, for a total of 58 council-lors plus the mayor of Toronto.

Some years ago, serious fric-tions arose between the muni-cipal government and residents of the Toronto Islands. The islands belong to the city, which rents out parcels of land to the people living there. When the council decided to take back the land and expel residents to make way for a park, residents fought back and eventually won.

Municipal politics in Toronto do not run along party lines, but the city's large population ex-erts considerable influence on the provincial and federal politi-cal scenes, as it accounts for a substantial part of the elector-ate. Toronto has been the capital of Ontario since before Canadian Confederation in 1867.

The Economy

Since the mid-1970s, Toronto has been Canada's biggest city, and it exerts a strong degree of control over the national econ-omy. Although the manufactur-ing sector has lost some ground in recent years, Toronto has maintained a preponderant role due largely to its powerful finan-cial sector. The five biggest Canadian banks have consoli-

All For One...

In January 1998, the six municipalities that made up the Greater Toronto Area were amalgamated to form the "megacity" of Toronto, thus launching a municipal-merger movement that would spread to Ottawa and the Quebec cities of Hull, Quebec City and Montreal. Highly unpopular, this merger was nonetheless imposed by Ontario Premier Mike Harris's Conservative government. The mayor of the former municipality of North York, the colourful Mel Lastman, was elected mayor of the newly amalgamated megacity. He served two terms before being replaced by the current mayor, David Miller.

Portrait

dated most of their head-office operations in Toronto, and most of the big securities firms and insurance companies have their headquarters in the city. The Toronto Stock Exchange plays an important role on North American markets; only the New York Stock Exchange is bigger.

In the manufacturing sector, the automobile industry plays a vital role in Toronto's economy, followed by heavy equipment, iron and steel, chemical products and the dynamic electronics field. Most of the bigger factories are concentrated in the area along Lake Ontario, from Toronto to Hamilton, in what is commonly called the "Golden Horseshoe," Canada's most heavily industrialized area.

This area benefits from easy access to the St. Lawrence Seaway and is served by an extensive railway network, as well as by the fast highways that crisscross Ontario. The tourism industry is also playing a growing role in this future-oriented city.

The Arts

Whether in painting, literature, music or film, Ontario artists have sought over the years to create Canadian-accented works and have managed to differentiate themselves from the undeniably influential English and American artistic movements. This quest has not been easy, although it has been helped by government bodies such as the Canada Council and the Ontario Arts Council, whose role is to subsidize the artistic endeavours of Canadian artists.

A great Canadian cultural centre, Toronto is home to most of Canada's English-language book and magazine publishers and to numerous broadcasters.

Visual Arts

It was not until the 19th century that it became possible to speak of Toronto's art movements. Starting in the early days of settlement, talented painters emerged and found a source of inspiration in the European masters. Their main clients at first were the Church and the bourgeoisie, who encouraged them to produce religious works such as altars and silver carvings or to paint family portraits.

In the early years of the 20th century, some of the great Ontario landscape painters became known for creating genuinely Canadian art. **Tom Thomson**, whose paintings provide a distinctive portrayal of landscapes unique to the Canadian Shield, was an originator of this movement. He died prematurely in 1917 at the age of 40. Nevertheless, his work had an indisputable effect on one of the most notable groups of painters in Ontario, the **Group of Seven**, whose first exhibition

was held in Toronto in 1920. These artists, Franklin Carmichael, Lawren S. Harris, Frank H. Johnson, Arthur Lismer, J.E.H. MacDonald, Alexander Young Jackson and Frederick Varley, were all landscape painters. Although they worked closely together, each developed his own pictorial language. They were distinguished by their use of bright colours in their portrayal of typical Canadian landscapes. Their influence over Ontario painting is substantial, and only a handful of other artists of the same period distinguished themselves from the movement, which modern-day artists view as too conformist.

One artist who has had a great impact on the arts in Toronto is not even Canadian. Scottish sculptor **Henry Moore**'s *The Archer*, dominating Nathan Philips Square, is an early example of public art in Toronto and helped transform the city. Moore has donated his complete works to the Art Gallery of Ontario, whose entrance is marked by his curious *Form*.

Literature

As the largest city in the country, it is no wonder that Toronto is the publishing mecca of English Canada. As home to many of the major publishing companies in the country, and as the forum for the International Festival of Authors, Toronto has a rich literary history.

Toronto's first settlers considered themselves British subjects. These Loyalists had decidedly British concerns and sought to champion them in the literature of their new homeland. The break with the crown and with tradition would have come of its own accord, but the presence of the newly independent Americans south of the border helped things along. In the United States, many authors had established themselves not merely as writers of English, but as American writers. This emancipation drew envy from Toronto writers, and English-Canadian writers in general.

Though Toronto writer **Mazo de la Roche** (1879-1961) is well remembered as an excellent Canadian writer, she nevertheless still called for solid links with the British Empire. Her *Jalna* (1927-1960) novels described life on the outskirts of Toronto.

Toronto writer and journalist **Morley Callaghan** (1903-1990) is known for his novel *That Summer in Paris* (1963), which relates the summer of 1929, that he spent with Ernest Hemingway and other members of the Lost Generation (expatriates in Paris). As a contributor to *The New Yorker* and winner of the Governor General's Award in 1951 for *The Loved and the Lost*, Callaghan often chose to obscure his environment in his fiction, and his work is therefore an exception to the norm of Canadian literature, which is forever striving to establish a Canadian identity. His fiction often depicts the hard anonymous life of city-dwellers, in an effort to promote a stronger social engagement.

The 1970s saw the appearance of modern movements, such as Open Letter in Toronto, seeking to bring new contributions to old ideas.

The city figures prominently as the setting for many works by two of Canada's most eminent writers. The first is **Robertson Davies**, a novelist and playwright, among other things. His *Deptford Trilogy* and *Cornish Trilogy*, both set in Toronto, are analytical and thoughtful looks at the growth of the city from provincialism to sophistication. *The Cunning Man* (1994), the last novel in the latter trilogy, is particularly noteworthy.

The second writer is **Margaret Atwood**, a feminist, satirist, nationalist, poet and novelist who carried modernism into the seventies. Her literary and critical writings have contributed immensely to attempts at defining Canadian culture and literature. Atwood is considered one of the greatest Canadian writers in this country's literary cannon. Her most recent successes were *The Blind Assassin* (2000) and *Oryx and Crake* (2003) (see inset p 40).

Margaret Atwood

A novelist, poet and critic, Margaret Atwood is certainly the brightest jewel in the crown of English-language Canadian literature. Born in Ottawa in 1939, she moved to Toronto with her family at the age of seven. She studied literature at the University of Toronto and later at prestigious Harvard University, in Cambridge, Massachusetts. A great traveller, she has lived and worked in Vancouver, Boston, Montréal and Edmonton, as well as in England, France, Germany and Italy. She has lived in Toronto since 1992.

Atwood's numerous literary and poetic works have been translated into more than 20 languages and are both critically and publicly acclaimed. The quality and precision of her language, which give her words particular resonance, are consistently recognized in all her writings. The prolific author has explored very contemporary issues, depicting them in a satirical and self-deprecating style characteristic of modern fiction.

The quality of her work and her social activism have been rewarded with many literary awards and other honours, including the Governor General's Award (1966 and 1985), the *Los Angeles Times* Prize (1985), the Toronto Arts Award (1986), Ms. Magazine's Woman of the Year (1986), the Ida Nudel Humanitarian Award from the Canadian Jewish Congress (1986), the American Humanist of the Year Award (1987), the Commonwealth Writers Prize (1992), the *Sunday Times* Award for Literary Excellence (1994), and the *Booker Prize* in 2000. Her latest novel, *Oryx and Crake*, was published in 2003 and was well received by critics.

Other widely acclaimed novels include *The Edible Woman* (1969), *Surfacing* (1978), and *The Handmaid's Tale* (1985), which was made into a film, and *Alias Grace* (1996) which was shortlisted for the Booker Prize. Margaret Atwood is a Companion of the Order of Canada.

Toronto is the multicultural capital of English Canada. It is only fitting therefore that many immigrant writers have chosen the city as their home. Sri Lankan–born writer **Mickael Ondaatje** now resides here and his novel *In the Skin of the Lion* (1987) is set in the city. The construction of the Bloor Street viaduct and the Harris Filtration Plant both figure in the novel, making for an interesting read. *The English Patient*, which won the Booker Prize in 1993, is a sequel of sorts to *In the Skin of a Lion*, and was the basis for the 1996 Oscar-winning movie of the same name. Ondaatje's latest novel is *Anil's Ghost* (2000).

Austin Clark is also a resident of Toronto. His novel *The Meeting Point* describes Caribbean life in the city. As for **Timothy Findley** (1930-2002), he was the winner of the Governor General's Literary Award of 1977 for his novel *The Wars*, inspired by the experiences of his uncle as a soldier during the First World War.

Royal Alexandra Theatre

Theatre

Toronto is the theatre capital of Canada and the third-largest centre of English-speaking theatre production in the world, behind only London and New York. Everything goes, from the great classics to experimental works. During much of the 20th century, Toronto offered a rather limited theatrical scene. In 1960, the city had only two professional theatre companies; now there are more than 200 professional theatre or dance companies. Together they put on more than 10,000 performances a year. More than seven million tickets are sold each year to different shows, running the gamut from musicals to dramas to comedies. There is something for everyone. It was not surprising, therefore, when UNESCO named Toronto the world's most culturally diverse city in 1993.

Toronto has numerous theatres, some dating from early in the century. The Royal Alexandra Theatre is a fine example. Saved from demolition by **Ed Mirvish**, the bargain-store king, the theatre was renovated at great expense and returned to its former splendour. Several former factories and fire halls have also been converted to theatres, with seating at the various venues now totalling 43,000. Numerous festivals, among them the Toronto

Fringe Theatre Festival, the Fringe Festival of Independent Dance Artists, Summer Works and the du Maurier World Stage Festival, showcase new local talents as well as many visiting artists.

Film

Throughout the first half of the 20th century, Canadian film making, with a few exceptions, was almost nonexistent. For many Canadians, it seemed futile and almost useless to go up against American films, the most popular and successful in the world. Starting in the 1950s, however, Canadian cinema began to develop and to acquire a certain identity. But it was not until 1963, with the film *Nobody Waved Goodbye*, that Toronto really found a cinematographic identity, at the same time opening the way to a Canadian film making culture. Figures like **Norman Jewison**, best known for having produced films such as *Moonstruck* and *Fiddler on the Roof*, came onto the scene and had an important influence on the Toronto film industry. Canadian cinema is still quite marginal compared to the American monster. Even today, the proportion of Canadian films showing in Canadian movie theatres is only about 2.5% of the total. It is thus not surprising to see Toronto creators such as **Rick Moranis** and **David Cronenberg** drawn to the huge American film industry.

Several younger Toronto film makers continue to work within the Toronto film industry, without hindering their growing recognition within Canada and on the international scene. Films as varied and personal as those of **Atom Egoyan** (*Exotica, The Sweet Hereafter, Ararat*), **Bruce McDonald** (*Roadkill, Route 61, Hard Core Logo*) and **Don McKellar** (*Last Night*) are a great tribute to the ongoing vitality of Toronto cinema.

All the same, Toronto is a very active city in the film area. Nicknamed Hollywood North, Toronto is sought after by many producers for its diversity, the quality of its production centres and the broad range of local talent. Among North American venues, only Hollywood and New York account for more film production. Because of the number and variety of its neighbourhoods, Toronto is able to offer a variety of sites that can stand in for cities such as Boston, New York, Tokyo, Philadelphia and even Vienna. Many American producers have used Toronto for their film shoots because of the financial savings available, since Toronto is a far cheaper place to film in than the United States. The film and television industry contributed $1.1 billion to Ontario's economy in 2000 and is responsible for about 38,000 jobs. More than 1,200 projects were permitted to film on location in Toronto in 2000. Advertising shoots alone bring in $135 million a year. It goes without saying that Toronto's

International Film Festival, which takes place each September, draws countless film-goers. Not only is it a forum for the world film industry, including of course the American colossus, but its Perspective Canada program also showcases new Canadian film talents.

Music

Many musical artists from Toronto have become known on the international scene. Here is a brief retrospective of some of the better-known ones.

Born in Toronto on September 25, 1932, **Glen Gould** was raised in musical surroundings from a very early age. His mother, who was related to Norwegian composer Edvard Grieg, taught him the basics of piano and organ until the age of 10. The young Glen Gould stood out very quickly as an exceptionally gifted pupil who learned musical composition starting at age five. His virtuosity was recognized unanimously during his first public concert, in 1945. Scarcely a year later, he set out as a soloist in a concert at the Royal Academy in London, where he interpreted Beethoven's fourth piano concerto, and he joined the Toronto Symphony at age 14.

Working with the greatest musicians, including Herbert von Karajan, musical director of the Berlin Philharmonic Orchestra, and Leonard Bernstein of the New York Philharmonic Orchestra, Gould stood out on the world scene as one of the most talented musicians of his period. Drawn more by composition and studio recording than by public concerts, Gould decided prematurely to leave the stage after a recital in Los Angeles on April 10, 1964. He devoted the rest of his career to composition and to the recording of numerous works. He died in Toronto on October 4, 1982.

Neil Young was born in Toronto on November 12, 1945. He spent only part of his youth there before moving with his mother to Winnipeg, Manitoba, where he began his career as a musician, eventually moving to California. At first he was a member of various groups, including The Squires, Buffalo Springfield and, most notably, Crosby, Stills, Nash and Young. He began his solo career in 1969, and in 1972 he recorded *Harvest*, his most popular and best-known album.

Toronto's Yorkville Avenue spawned some major talent in the 1960s. Crooner **Gordon Lightfoot** and folk sensations **Ian and Sylvia** are among those who got their start in the clubs and cafés of trendy Yorkville.

The Band is another famous name in the history of rock and roll. Originally from Toronto, The Band rose to popularity in the late 1960s after achieving considerable success on the

Portrait

Toronto music scene. Following successes like the song *The Weight* and the film *The Last Waltz*, The Band split up, though one member, Robbie Robertson has gone on to a successful solo career, which includes the hit albums *Robbie Robertson* (1987) and *Storyville* (1991).

More recently, the **Barenaked Ladies** have made quite a splash, with their music that blends rock, jazz and folk. The **Cowboy Junkies** foursome, who also come from Toronto, had great success with their *The Trinity Session* album, recorded inside Holy Trinity Church just a few steps from the Eaton Centre.

The Toronto music scene has been particularly vibrant since the end of the 1990s. Groups as stylistically varied as **Broken Social Scene**, **Do Make Say Think**, **Ron Sexsmith**, **The Constantines** and **Tangiers** have been garnering critical and commercial success and are even starting to break the all-important American market.

Architecture

The impetus for Toronto's (then York's) founding in 1793 was military. A 10-square-block grid of streets centred around King and Sherbourne streets was quickly laid out east of Fort York and the harbour–thus "Muddy York" was born. York was nevertheless the capital of Upper Canada, and therefore an air of civility was needed. The hastily built wooden structures that lined its streets were just as quickly replaced with refined Georgian edifices. A courthouse, jail, church, post office and harbour were among the permanent fixtures that established their place in this compact new town. The English gentlemen who arrived in this military outpost thus succeeded in turning it into an orderly reflection of the British Empire.

Beyond the compact streets of the town, essentially to the north of today's Queen Street, the governor parcelled off long, narrow park lots to encourage the aristocracy to settle in the colonies. The Georgian period was just ending and the Georgian style, with its formal solidity, was the first architectural style of the new city. It was used for churches, and public and commercial buildings; however, one of the most poignant Georgian legacies in the city today was a private residence, the Grange (see p 127) built in 1817, on park lot 13. The wealthy classes of the Victorian era went on to use Gothic, Italianate, Romanesque and Queen Anne styles to demonstrate their social and economic status.

The use of brick was the subject of the first law passed by the new city of Toronto in 1834. Not only did it lend the city a look of permanence, which in turn inspired confidence in the newly arriving aristocracy, but it was also a cautionary measure. The prevention of fire was a major concern for the new city fathers. To this day, the majority of Toronto's older buildings are made of brick. Nearby clay pits meant that there was an unlimited supply of both red and yellow bricks, the latter being something of a trademark in Toronto architecture. Called "white" in the 19th century, they were an inexpensive alternative to granite and limestone, which had to be imported.

Toronto was busy annexing neighbouring villages in the late 19th century, an action that greatly increased the city's population and also introduced new elements to Toronto's architecture. The addition of Yorkville, Brockton, Riverdale, The Annex, Seaton Village and Parkdale very quickly gave Toronto a large residential area. These areas were characterized by classic, orderly single-detached or semi-detached row houses, often employing Queen Anne and Richardsonian Romanesque styles.

The heavy and bulky lines of Richardsonian Romanesque were popular in the last years of the 19th century. Toronto architect E.J. Lennox used this style, created by American Henry Hobson Richardson, on many of his and the city's most famous buildings, notably the Parliament Building and Old City Hall.

As the 20th century dawned, Toronto City Council chose not to put a height limit on buildings in its downtown area, as was the case in London and Paris. A series of buildings constructed after the 1905 decision were the tallest in the British Commonwealth, the last being the Canadian Bank of Commerce (see p 104) built in 1929 and 34 stories tall.

The most significant developments in Toronto's architecture in the last half of the 20th century were felt in the city's core. Here the International Style was in sharp contrast to the picturesque Victorian city that had remained for the most part intact since its creation. "Form follows function," "less is more" and an emphasis on purism characterize this by-product of the Modern Movement, spearheaded in North America by Ludwig Mies van der Rohe. The Toronto-Dominion Centre (see p 101) is Toronto's "boring box," a stunning building that became a model for glass towers all over the world. It heralded a transformation of Toronto's financial district that was ultimately criticized for its isolation of people from the space that surrounds them. The trend these days has shifted away from these impersonal megatowers. Since the emergence of post modernism, there has been a shift back to the lavish forms of the past. So much so, that not only do new buildings borrow from the past, but often the old buildings are rehabilitated instead of being replaced.

The post-war era was also characterized by a general shift away from the city to newly developed suburbs, where rows of identical houses and trees spelled Utopia. Toronto has its fair share of these, most located a fair distance from downtown. Thankfully the city's original residential areas, somewhere between the new and the old, were starting to lose favour, and provided inexpensive housing for Toronto's growing immigrant communities. These areas have a real sense of character and an address here is almost as coveted as a Rosedale or Forest Hill address.

Recent masterpieces like the CN Tower, SkyDome, the Royal Bank Plaza and the Toronto-Dominion Centre make Toronto's skyline truly unique. Yet it is perhaps the scattered nature of the city's architectural history, with the new embracing the old, that distinguishes this Canadian metropolis. A stroll through Cabbagetown, The Annex, Rosedale and the financial district proves this.

CN Tower

Practical Information

The information
in this chapter will help visitors better plan their trip to Toronto.

The area code for telephone numbers in this guide is 416, unless otherwise indicated (see p 67).

Entrance Formalities

Passport and Visa

A valid passport is usually sufficient for most visitors planning to stay in Canada less than three months; visas are not required by citizens of Western European countries. For a complete list of countries whose citizens require a visa, see the Canadian Citizenship and Immigration Web site (*www.cic.gc. ca*) or contact the Canadian embassy or consulate nearest you. A three-month extension is possible, but a return ticket and proof of sufficient funds to cover this extension may be required.

Caution: some countries do not have an agreement with

Canada concerning health and accident insurance, so it is advisable to have the appropriate coverage. For more information, see the section entitled "Health" (see p 70).

Table of Distances (km)
Via the shortest route

	Hamilton	Kingston	Kitchener-Waterloo	London	Montréal (QC)	New York (NY)	Niagara Falls	Ottawa	Sault Ste. Marie	Sudbury	Toronto	Thunder Bay	Windsor/Detroit (MI)
Chicago (IL)	788	1100	767	661	1383	1294	896	1242	780	1079	855	1058	460
Hamilton		338	69	140	621	765	77	480	748	460	75	1469	318
Kingston			369	451	299	583	408	203	894	609	263	1623	626
Kitchener-Waterloo				110	650	838	156	511	777	490	123	1496	306
London					738	911	227	600	699	572	198	1414	191
Montréal (QC)						618	689	202	1003	700	547	1638	912
New York (NY)							690	719	1498	1212	829	2212	1018
Niagara Falls								544	814	529	144	1534	413
Ottawa									806	508	410	1516	773
Sault Ste. Marie										302	696	723	584
Sudbury											411	1019	751
Toronto												1421	386
Thunder Bay													1310
Windsor/Detroit (MI)													

Example: The distance between Montréal and Toronto is 547km.

© ULYSSES

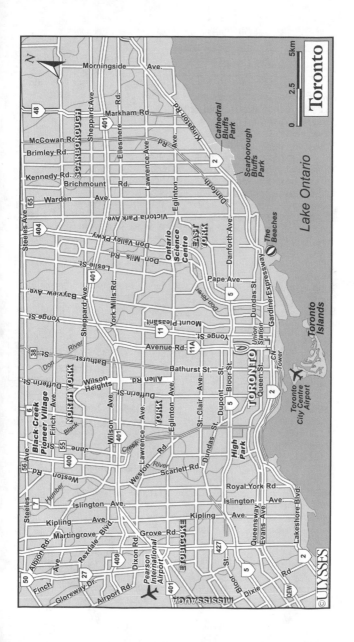

Extended Visits

Visitors must submit a request to extend their visit **in writing** and **before** the expiration of their visitor status or of their visa (the date is usually written in your passport) to a Citizenship and Immigration Canada office. To make a request you must have a valid passport, a return ticket, proof of sufficient funds to cover the stay, as well as the $65 non-refundable filing fee. In some cases (work, study), however, the request must be made **before** arriving in Canada. Contact Citizenship and Immigration Canada at (☎973-4444 or www.cic.gc.ca).

Customs

If you are bringing gifts into Canada, remember that certain restrictions apply:

Smokers (minimum age in Ontario is 19) can bring in a maximum of 200 cigarettes, 50 cigars, 200g of tobacco, and 200 tobacco sticks.

For **wine and alcohol,** the limit is 1.5 litres of wine, 1.14 litres of liquor or 24 x 355ml cans or 341ml bottles of beer. Minimum drinking age in Ontario is 19 years.

There are very strict rules regarding the importation of **plants**, **flowers**, and other **vegetation**; it is therefore not advisable to bring any of these types of products into the country. If it is absolutely necessary, contact the Customs-Agriculture service of the Canadian embassy **before** leaving.

If you are travelling with your **pet**, you will need a health certificate (available from your veterinarian) as well as a rabies vaccination certificate. It is important to remember that the vaccination must be carried out **at least** 30 days **before** your departure and should not have been administered more than one year ago.

Finally, visitors from out of the country may be reimbursed for certain taxes paid on purchases in Ontario (see p 75).

Embassies and Consulates

Canadian Embassies and Consulates Abroad

Denmark
Canadian Embassy
Kr. Bernikowsgade 1,
1105 Copenhagen K
☎ *(45) 12 22 29*
⇻ *(45) 14 05 03*

Germany
Canadian Embassy
Friedrichstrasse 95
10117 Berlin
☎ *(30) 20312-0*
⇻ *(30) 20312-121*

Great Britain
Canadian High Commission
MacDonald House
One Grosvenor Square
London W1X 0AB
☎ *(171) 258-6600*
⇄ *(171) 258-6834*

Netherlands
Canadian Embassy
Sophialaan 7, 2514 JP
PO Box 30820
2500 GV
The Hague, The Netherlands
☎ *(70) 311-1600*
⇄ *(70) 311-1620*

Sweden
Canadian Embassy
Tegelbacken 4, 7th floor,
PO Box 16129
10323 Stockholm, Sweden
☎ *(8)453-3000*
⇄ *(8)24-2491*

United States
Canadian Embassy
501 Pennsylvania Ave. N.W.
Washington, DC
20001
☎ *(202) 682-1740*
⇄ *(202) 682-7726*

Canadian Consulates:
1175 Peachtree St. N.E.
100 Colony Square, Suite 1700
Atlanta, Georgia
30361-6205
☎ *(404) 532-2000*
⇄ *(404) 532-2050*

Three Copley Place, Suite 400
Boston, Massachusetts
02116
☎ *(617) 262-3760*
⇄ *(617) 262-3415*

Two Prudential Plaza
180 N. Stetson Ave.
Suite 2400,
Chicago, Illinois
60601
☎ *(312) 616-1860*
⇄ *(312) 616-1877*

St. Paul Place,
750 N. St. Paul St., Suite 1700
Dallas, Texas
75201-3247
☎ *(214) 922-9806*
⇄ *(214) 922-9815*

600 Renaissance Center,
Suite 1100
Detroit, Michigan
48243-1798
☎ *(313) 567-2340*
⇄ *(313) 567-2164*

550 South Hope St., 9th Floor
Los Angeles, California
90071-2327
☎ *(213) 346-2700*
⇄ *(213) 620-8827*

701 Fourth Avenue South,
Suite 900
Minneapolis, Minnesota
55415-1899
☎ *(612) 333-4641*
⇄ *(612) 332-4061*

1251 Avenue of the Americas
Concourse Level
New York, NY 10020-1175
☎ *(212) 596-1628*
⇄ *(212) 596-1666/1790*

3000 HSBC Center
Buffalo, NY 14203-2884
☎ *(716) 858-9500*
⇄ *(716) 852-4340*

Practical
Information

412 Plaza 600,
Sixth Ave. and Stewart St.
Seattle, WA 98101-1286
☎ *(206) 443-1777*
⇌ *(206) 443-9662*

Foreign Embassies and Consulates in Toronto

Denmark
151 Bloor St. W., Suite 310
Toronto ON M5S 1S4
☎ *962-5661*
⇌ *962-3668*

Great Britain
777 Bay St., Suite 2800
College Park
Toronto, ON M5G 2G2
☎ *593-1290*
⇌ *593-1229*

Germany
77 Admiral Rd.
Toronto, ON M5R 2L4
☎ *925-2813*
⇌ *925-2818*

Netherlands
1 Dundas St. W.
Suite 2106
Toronto, ON M5G 1Z3
☎ *598-2520*
⇌ *598-8064*

Sweden
2 Bloor St. W., Suite 504
Toronto, ON M4W 3E2
☎ *963-8768*
⇌ *923-8809*

United States
360 University Ave.
Toronto, ON M5G 1S4
☎ *595-1700*
⇌ *595-0051 or 595-5419*

Tourist Information

Tourism Toronto
Mon-Fri 8:30am to 5:30pm
Queen's Quay Terminal
207 Queen's Quay W., Suite 590,
Toronto, ON M5J 1A7
☎ *203-2500 or 800-363-1990*
www.torontotourism.com

This location offers friendly staff
and a good selection of pam-
phlets; however, for more
complete information, contact:

**Ontario Travel Information
Centre**
*open year-round, Mon-Fri 10am
to 9pm, Sat 9:30am to 6pm and
Sun noon to 5pm*
lower level of the Eaton Centre at
Queen and Yonge Sts.
☎ *800-668-2746*
www.ontariotravel.net

The **Traveller's Aid Society** *(in
Union Station, on the arrivals
level,* ☎ *366-7788; at Toronto
Pearson International Airport,
Terminal 1* ☎ *905-676-2868,
Terminal 2* ☎ *905-676-2869,
Terminal 3* ☎ *905-612-5890)* is a
volunteer organization that can
provide information about
hotels, restaurants, sights and
transportation.

Getting to Toronto

By Plane

From Europe

Toronto is an air traffic hub in eastern Canada. Air Canada, Air France, British Airways, KLM, Lufthansa, TAP Air Portugal and SwissAir are among the major airlines that offer direct flights to Toronto (Lester B. Pearson International Airport) from major European cities.

From the United States

Air Canada offers direct flights out of Toronto to major US cities. The following American airline companies fly into Toronto's Pearson International Airport: Delta Airlines, Northwest Airlines, USAir, American Airlines and United Airlines.

From Elsewhere in Canada

Air Canada *(☎888-247-2262)*, **Air Transat** *(☎866-847-1112)* and **WestJet Airlines** *(☎888-937-8538 or ☎800-538-5696)* offer flights between Toronto and other Canadian cities.

From Elsewhere

Pearson International Airport is also served by flights on the following airlines: Air Europe, Air Ukraine, Air India, Air Jamaica, Royal Jordanian, Cubana, El Al, Finnair, Guyana, Iberia, Lot Polish Airlines, Pakistan Air, Alitalia and Vasp, among others.

Toronto Pearson International Airport

Toronto Pearson International Airport *(☎247-7678 or 416-AIR-PORT, www.gtaa.com)* welcomes international flights from Europe, the United States, Africa and Asia, as well as domestic flights from the other Canadian provinces. It is the biggest and busiest airport in Canada.

Besides the regular airport services like duty-free shops, cafeteria and restaurants or internet stations, you will also find a currency exchange office. Several car rental companies also have offices at the airport. Shuttle buses run regularly between the airport's three terminals.

For information concerning a flight:

Terminal 1
☎(905) 274-7678

Terminal 2
☎(905) 274-7678

Terminal 3
☎(905) 776-5100

Getting Downtown By Car

The airport lies 27km from downtown Toronto. By car take either Highway 427 south or Highway 409 west to Queen Elizabeth Way (QEW)

Practical Information

east until it joins the Gardiner Expressway. Get off at the York, Yonge or Bay exits for downtown.

Car rentals at the airport

The following car rental companies have counters at the airport:

Avis
Terminal 1
☎*(905) 676-1032*
Terminal 2
☎*(905) 676-1057*
Terminal 3
☎*(905) 676-1034*

Budget
Terminal 1
☎*(905) 676-1500*
Terminal 2
☎*(905) 676-0521*
Terminal 3
☎*(905) 676-0522*

Hertz
☎*674-2020*

Thrifty
☎*(905) 673-8811*

National
☎*(905) 676-2647*

For more information about driving and renting a car, please refer to p 60.

Getting Downtown By Taxi

If you are not renting a car, expect to pay about $45 for a taxi.

Getting Downtown By Shuttle Bus

You can also take advantage of a shuttle bus service called the **Airport Express** *($15.50 one way, $26.75 return;* ☎*905-564-6333 or 800-387-6787; www.airportexpress.com)*, which links the airport with various points throughout downtown, including some of the major hotels. This is an economical way to get into town, and you do not have to be staying at one of the hotels on its route to take the bus. This shuttle offers round-the-clock service from each of Pearson Airport's three terminals to downtown Toronto, and vice versa. From the airport departures are every 20min or 30min; from downtown Toronto, the same schedule applies, with departures from various points such as the Delta Chelsea Hotel, the Sheraton Centre, the Royal York hotel and the Toronto Bus Terminal. The buses are equipped for travellers with disabilities: there is room for two wheelchairs, and braille signage and a visual signboard announce stops.

Getting Downtown By Limousine

Finally, travellers also have the option of taking a limousine to and from the airport: **Official Airport Limousine** *(information:* ☎*905-624-2424 or 800-465-3434)*.

Toronto City Centre Airport

This local airport is located on Hanlan's Point on the Toronto Islands. It is reached by a special ferry at the foot of Bathurst Street, with departures every 15min. For information call ☎*203-6945*.

This airport is served by private flights and by planes from Newark, Montréal, Ottawa and London, Ontario.

By Car

Most people arriving in Toronto by car from east or west will enter the city on Highway 401, which crosses the northern part of the city. Coming from the west, take Highway 427 south to the Queen Elizabeth Way (QEW), continue east to the Gardiner Expressway, and exit at York, Bay or Yonge streets for downtown. Coming from the east, the quickest way to reach downtown is on the Don Valley Parkway; continue to the Gardiner Expressway, then exit at York, Bay or Yonge streets. Those coming from the United States will follow the shores of Lake Ontario on the QEW to the Gardiner Expressway. Rush-hour traffic can be very heavy on Toronto's highways, especially on the Don Valley Parkway.

By Bus

Bus service in and out of Toronto is provided by Greyhound Lines of Canada. There is frequent service to cities both near and far. This is an affordable and convenient way of getting to Toronto if you don't have a car. Note that travel times can be long, however. For example, it takes 6hrs and 45min to reach Toronto from Montréal, 5hrs and 30min from Ottawa, and 5hrs and 15min from Detroit (USA).

Smoking is forbidden on almost all lines and pets are not allowed. Generally children five years old or younger travel for free and people aged 60 or over are eligible for discounts.

The bus station in Toronto is located right downtown. For information call:

Greyhound Lines of Canada
610 Bay St.
(416) 594-1010
www.greyhound.ca

By Train

Via Rail Canada is the only company that offers train travel between the Canadian provinces, and serves many destinations in northern and southern Ontario. This is one of the fastest and most efficient ways

Practical Information

to travel, with several trains running to Montréal, Ottawa, Toronto and Windsor every day.

All VIA trains arrive at Union Station at 65-75 Front Street W., between York and Bay streets. For information on VIA trains call ☎800-361-1235.

An interesting option is Via Rail's overnight train between Montréal and Toronto. Its "Constellation Class" service departs each city at 11pm and arrives in the other at 8am. Sleeping accommodations, showers and breakfast are provided and the return fare ranges from $262 to $383 (plus taxes) if tickets are purchased seven days in advance.

Getting Around Toronto

The City of Toronto consists of six former municipalities which now form one city; the City of Toronto, the Borough of East York and the Cities of York, North York, Scarborough and Etobicoke. The Greater Toronto Area also encompasses municipalities outside Metro Toronto, such as Mississauga and Markham. Toronto is Canada's largest city: the City of Toronto has 2.5 million inhabitants and Greater Toronto has 5.2 million (2001 figures).

The city lies 174m above sea level and covers an area of 624 km².

Toronto's grid system of streets makes it easy to get around. Yonge (pronounced *young*) Street is the main north-south artery and divides the city between east and west. At 1,896km, it is also the world's longest street, running from the shores of Lake Ontario to Rainy River, Ontario.

Street addresses in the city that have the suffix "East" (E.) or "West" (W.) lie east or west respectively of Yonge; 299 Queen St. W. is therefore a few blocks west of Yonge. Toronto's downtown is generally considered to be the area south of Bloor, between Spadina and Jarvis.

By Public Transportation

Toronto's public transportation system is run by the **Toronto Transit Commission**, the **TTC**; it includes a subway, buses and streetcars.

There are three subway lines: the yellow, Yonge– University line is U-shaped and runs north-south, with the bottom of the U at Union Station; the green, Bloor–Danforth line runs east-west along Bloor and Danforth from Kennedy Road to Kipling Road; the blue, Scarborough RT line runs north and east up to Ellesmere Road. There is also the Harbourfront LRT, which runs from Union Station along Queen's Quay to Spadina. The commuter train to

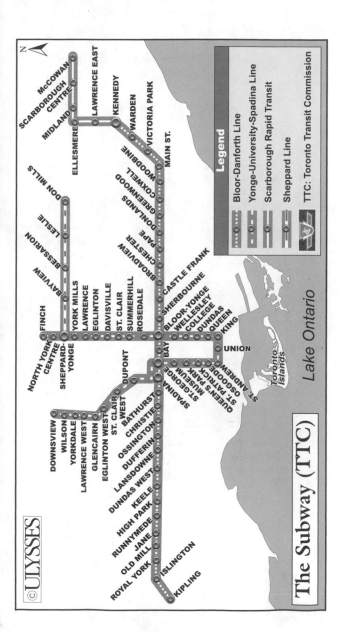

The Subway (TTC)

© ULYSSES

N

Lake Ontario

Toronto Islands

Legend

- Bloor-Danforth Line
- Yonge-University-Spadina Line
- Scarborough Rapid Transit
- Sheppard Line

TTC: Toronto Transit Commission

Toronto On The Rails

In the 1820s, the public-transit situation in Toronto was rather chaotic. Nine independent fare systems and networks, run by four different companies, offered very mediocre service. Commuters had to pay different fares depending on the network used, which did not cover the entire territory and, above all, were not even linked. The biggest company, the **Toronto Street Railway Company**, had antiquated vehicles and refused to service the rapidly developing outlying suburban communities.

Despite these bumpy beginnings, the first horse-drawn street-railway service was introduced on Yonge Street in 1861. Thirty years later, on August 15, 1891, the first electric streetcar went into service on Church Street. In spite of these technological improvements, service remained very shaky and commuters were still dissatisfied.

In the face of growing public pressure, the Ontario government created the **Toronto Transportation Commission** in 1920, which was renamed the Toronto **Transit Commission (TTC)** in 1954. The fleet of streetcars was changed and service was standardized and greatly improved. Urban transport in flourishing Toronto was henceforth on the rails. Today, streetcars are still part of the Toronto landscape and you'll be hard-pressed to find a Torontonian who has never used this means of transportation, which is but a distant memory in most major Western cities.

the eastern and western suburbs is called the GO. It can be accessed from Union Station, at Bay and Front streets. These trains are all safe and clean. Buses and streetcars run along the city's major arteries. You can transfer between buses, streetcars and the subway without another fare, but you will need a transfer, so always take one just in case. Pick up a copy of the TTC's *Ride Guide* for a map of the system. It shows most of the major attractions and how to reach them by public transportation.

Note that the street-level TTC subway signs are small and often sun-bleached, making them somewhat difficult to spot from a distance. Keep your eyes peeled!

The TTC also runs a wheelchair user's service called Wheel-Trans. It costs the same as regular public transit and service is door-to-door. Transportation must be booked one day in advance by calling ☎393-4222.

A **single fare** is $2.25 for adults, $1.50 for students (you must have a TTC student card) and seniors and $0.50 for children under 12. Five adult tickets or tokens cost $9.00, 10 student or senior tokens cost $12, and 10 child tickets or tokens cost $4. If you plan on taking several trips in one day, buy a day pass for $7.50, which entitles you to unlimited travel on that day. Sundays are really

economical, since one day pass can be used by two adults, or by a family (two adults and four children, or one adult and five children). A monthly pass costs $93.50 for adults and $80 for students and seniors.

Bus and streetcar drivers do not give change; you can purchase tickets at subway booths and in certain stores (Shopper's Drug Mart in most malls).

For route and schedule information call ☎393-4636; for fare and general information call ☎393-TONE(8663).

By Car

Toronto is well served by public transportation and taxis, so having a car is not essential to visiting the city, especially since most of the sights are located relatively close to one another, and all of the suggested tours can be done on foot, except the tours of the north, the east and Niagara Falls. Nevertheless, it is quite easy to get around by car. Parking lots, though quite expensive, are numerous in the downtown area. Parking on the street is possible, but be sure to read the signs carefully. Ticketing of illegally parked cars is strict and can be expensive.

Things to Consider

Driver's License: Driver's licenses from Western European countries are valid in Canada

Practical Information

and the United States. While North American travellers won't have any trouble adapting to the rules of the road in Ontario, European travellers may need a bit more time to get used to things. Here are a few hints:

Pedestrians: Drivers in Ontario are particularly courteous when it comes to pedestrians, and willingly stop to give them the right of way. Pedestrian crosswalks are usually indicated by a yellow sign. When driving, check if there is anyone about to cross near these signs.

Driving and the Highway Code: Signs marked "Stop" in white against a red background must always be respected. Come to a complete stop, even if there is no apparent danger.

Traffic Lights: Turning right on a red light after a full stop is permitted unless otherwise indicated; traffic lights are often located on the opposite side of the intersection, so be careful to stop at the stop line, a white line on the pavement before the intersection; a flashing green light is an advance light for left turners.

When a **school bus** (usually yellow in colour) has stopped and has its signals flashing, you must come to a complete stop, no matter what direction you are travelling in. Failing to stop at the flashing signals is considered a serious offense, and carries a heavy penalty.

Wearing of **seatbelts** in the front and back seats is mandatory at all times.

All highways in Ontario are toll-free, and there are no toll bridges. The **speed limit** on highways is 100km/h. The speed limit on secondary highways is 90km/h, and 50km/h in urban areas.

Gas Stations: Like in the rest of Canada, Ontario's gasoline prices are much less expensive than in Europe, and only slightly more than in the United States. Some gas stations (particularly in the downtown areas) might ask for payment in advance as a security measure, especially after 11pm.

Winter Driving: Though roads are generally well plowed, particular caution is recommended. Watch for slippery surfaces and reduced visibility. Gravel is sometimes used to increase traction, so drive carefully.

Streetcars travel in the centre lanes, where they have right of way. When they stop to let off passengers, you must stop as well.

Renting a Car

Packages including air travel, hotel and car rental or just hotel and car rental may offer a better deal than renting a car upon arrival. It is best to shop around. Remember also that some companies offer corporate rates and discounts to auto-club members. Some travel agencies work with major car rental companies (Avis, Budget, Hertz, etc.) and offer good values; contracts often include added bonuses (reduced ticket prices for shows, etc.).

When renting a car, find out if the contract includes unlimited kilometres, and if the insurance provides full coverage (accident, property damage, hospital costs for you and passengers, theft).

Certain credit cards, gold cards for example, cover collision and theft insurance. Check with your credit card company before renting.

To rent a car, you must be at least 21 years of age and have had a driver's license for **at least** one year. If you are between 21 and 25, certain companies will ask for a $500 deposit, and in some cases they will also charge an extra sum for each day you rent the car. These conditions do not apply for those over 25 years of age.

A credit card is extremely useful for the deposit to avoid tying up large sums of money.

Most rental cars come with an automatic transmission, however you can request a car with a manual shift. Special requests must be made for child safety seats and may cost extra.

Car Rental Agencies

For rental agencies at Pearson Airport, please see p 54.

Avis
☎ *800-TRY-AVIS*

BCE Place 161 Bay St.
☎ *777-AVIS (2847)*

Hudson Bay Centre, 80 Bloor St. E.
☎ *964-2051*

Budget
141 Bay St.
☎ *364-7104*

1319 Bay St.
☎ *961-3932*

150 Cumberland St.
☎ *927-8300*

Hertz
128 Richmond St. E.
☎ *363-9022*

Hudson Bay Centre, 80 Bloor St. E.
☎ *961-3320*

Thrifty
Eaton Centre, 220 Yonge St.
☎ *591-0861*

100 Front St. W.
☎ *947-1385*

7 Erskine Ave.
☎ *482-1400*

National Car Rental
Union Station
☎ *364-4191*

Yonge and Bloor Sts.
☎ *925-4551*

Practical Information

Accidents and Emergencies

In case of serious accident, fire or other emergency, dial ☎911.

If an accident occurs, always fill out an accident report. In case of a disagreement as to who is at fault, ask a police officer for assistance. Be sure to alert the car rental agency as soon as possible.

If you are planning a long trip and have decided to buy a car, it is a good idea to become a member of the Canadian Automobile Association, or CAA, which offers assistance through-out Ontario and Canada. If you are a member of an equivalent association in your home country (American Automobile Association, Automobile Club de Suisse, etc.), you can benefit from some of the services of-fered. For more information, contact your association or the CAA in Toronto (☎1-800-268-3750).

By Taxi

Co-op Cabs
☎504-2667

Metro/Yellow Cab Co.
☎504-4141

On Foot

Toronto's underground city, called the **PATH**, is the largest in the country. It weaves its way under the streets from Union Station on Front Street all the way to the Atrium on Bay at Dundas Street. The perfect escape for those cold winter days, it provides access to shops, restaurants, hotels and the subway (see map 63).

By Bicycle

One of the most enjoyable ways to get around in the summer is by bicycle. Bike paths have been laid out to allow cyclists to explore various neighbourhoods in the city. One of the most interesting paths is the **Martin Goodman Trail**, which runs along the shores of Lake Ontario from High Park to the Beaches.

There are two free maps of Toronto's bike paths. One is published by the Sports Swap store and is available at the information desks at Toronto City Hall or Metro Hall, as well as at the store:

Sports Swap
2045 Yonge St.
☎481-0249

The other map is published by Metro Parks and Culture and is available at City Hall and Metro Hall (for information: ☎392-8186).

Since drivers are not always attentive, cyclists should be alert, respect road signs (as required by law) and be careful at intersections. Bicycle helmets are mandatory in Toronto.

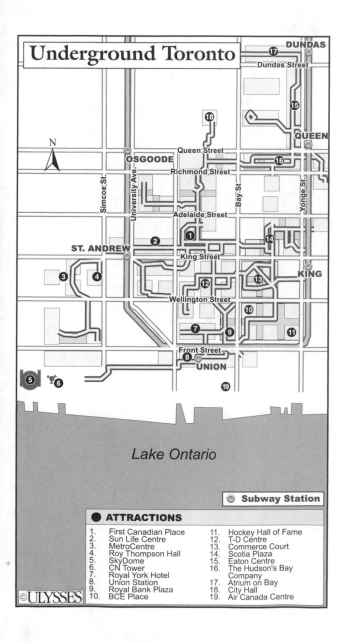

Underground Toronto

DUNDAS

Dundas Street

QUEEN

Queen Street

OSGOODE

Richmond Street

Adelaide Street

ST. ANDREW

King Street

KING

Wellington Street

Front Street

UNION

Lake Ontario

Subway Station

● ATTRACTIONS

1. First Canadian Place
2. Sun Life Centre
3. MetroCentre
4. Roy Thompson Hall
5. SkyDome
6. CN Tower
7. Royal York Hotel
8. Union Station
9. Royal Bank Plaza
10. BCE Place
11. Hockey Hall of Fame
12. T-D Centre
13. Commerce Court
14. Scotia Plaza
15. Eaton Centre
16. The Hudson's Bay Company
17. Atrium on Bay
18. City Hall
19. Air Canada Centre

©ULYSSES

Refer to the Outdoors chapter for rental locations p 175.

In-line Skating

The growing popularity of in-line skating is particularly evident in Toronto. Unfortunately, according to the driving code, in-line skating on the streets of Canadian cities is officially prohibited. It is nevertheless permitted on the city's bicycle paths. In-line skating fans can also flock to the Toronto Islands, where the wide bicycle paths allow for worry-free gliding. The craze over this sport and mode of transport has led to the opening of several specialized boutiques which sell and rent skates and all the necessary equipment that goes with them; some even offer lessons. Refer to the Outdoors chapter for rental locations, p 175.

Guided Tours

Various companies organize tours of Toronto, offering visitors interesting ways to explore the city. Walking tours lead to an intimate discovery of the city's neighbourhoods, while bus tours provide a perspective of the city as a whole. Boat cruises highlight another facet of the city, this time in relation to the lake. Though the options are countless, the following companies are worth mentioning.

Tours on Foot or by Bicycle

A Taste of the World - Neighbourhood Bicycle Tours & Walks
PO Box 659, Station P, Toronto M5S 2Y4
☎ *923-6813*
Culinary, literary and ghostly themed tours of Chinatown, Cabbagetown and the Beaches are offered by Shirley Lum, an energetic Torontonian who will let you in on some little-known secrets of the city's neighbourhoods. The Chinatown tour with dim sum is a favourite.

Royal Ontario Museum
100 Queen's Park
☎ *586-5549*
The ROM offers historical walking tours of the city.

Toronto Historical Board (Heritage Toronto)
205 Yonge St.
☎ *392-6827 ext. 233*
These walking tours are ideal for history buffs, as visitors are lead to some of the city's most intriguing historic sites.

Bus Tours

Gray Line
☎ *594-3310*
Gray Line offers several tours of the city (from 2 to 3.5hrs) as well as an excursion to Niagara Falls. The tour picks up passengers at various downtown points prior to the start of the tour, which officially begins at the bus terminal at Bay and Dundas streets.

The *Maid of the Mist* tourist boat takes its passengers to the turbulent waters of the Niagara River, at the foot of Niagara Falls. *Patrick Escudero*

The gardens that border the buildings of the University of Toronto come to life with vivid colours during the summertime.
-*Patrick Escudero*

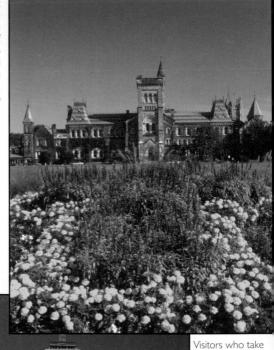

Visitors who take the time to admire the ancient cornices that top the financial district's buildings will discover some beautifully contrasting architectural styles.
-*Patrick Escudero*

Boat Tours

Mariposa Cruise Line
207 Queen's Quay W., Suite 415
Toronto M5J 1A7
☎ *203-0178 or 800-976-2442*
Daily cruises of the harbour offer another perspective of this bustling metropolis. Lunch and dinner cruises are also available.

Great Lakes Schooner Company
249 Queen's Quay W., Suite 111
Toronto M5J 2N5
☎ *260-6355*
This company offers a variety of tours in and around Toronto. You can take an extended cruise on Lake Ontario, or a tour of the harbour aboard a genuine tall ship.

Banking and Currency Exchange

Banks

The majority of banks offer ATM service for cash withdrawals. Most are members of the Cirrus and Interac networks, which allow visitors to make direct withdrawals from their personal accounts. You can use your card as you do normally—you'll be given Canadian dollars with a receipt, and the equivalent amount will be debited from your account. All this will take no more time that it would at your own bank! That said, the network can sometimes experience communication problems that will prevent you from obtaining money. If your transaction is refused by the ATM at one bank, try another bank where you might have better luck. In any case, take precautions so that you do not find yourself empty-handed.

Canadian banks also offer most of the standard services to tourists. Remember to ask about commission fees before beginning any transactions. Long-term visitors are permitted to open a bank account in Canada, provided they have two pieces of identification.

Banks are open Monday to Friday, from 10am to 3pm. Many are also open Thursdays and Fridays until 6pm, and sometimes until 8pm.

Credit Cards

Most credit cards are accepted at stores, restaurants and hotels. While the main advantage of credit cards is that they allow visitors to avoid carrying large sums of money, using a credit card also makes leaving a deposit for car rental much easier and some cards, gold cards for example, automatically insure you when you rent a car. In addition, the exchange rate with a credit card is generally better. The most commonly accepted credit cards are Visa, MasterCard, and American Express.

Practical Information

Exchange Rates*

$1 CAN = $0.81 US	$1 US = $1.22 CAN
$1 CAN = £0.43	£1 = $2.29 CAN
$1 CAN = 0.61 € (euro)	1 € (euro) = $1.63 CAN

*Samples only—rates may fluctuate

Credit cards offer a chance to avoid service charges when exchanging money. By over-paying your credit card (to avoid interest charges) you can then withdraw against it. You can thus avoid carrying large amounts of money or traveller's cheques. Withdrawals can be made directly from an automatic teller if you have a personal identification number for your card.

For lost or stolen credit cards or traveller's cheques:

American Express
☎ *800-221-7282*

MasterCard
☎ *232-8020 or 800-263-2263*

Visa
☎ *800-336-8472*

Diners Club
☎ *800-363-3333*

Traveller's Cheques

Traveller's cheques are accepted in most large stores and hotels; however it is easier and to your advantage to change your cheques at an exchange office. For a better exchange rate, buy your traveller's cheques in Canadian dollars before leaving.

Currency Exchange

Several banks in the downtown area readily exchange foreign currency, but almost all charge a commission unless you're changing cash. There are exchange offices, on the other hand, that do not charge commission, but their rates are sometimes less competitive. It is a good idea to shop around. All banks change US currency, and most of them change British pounds and Euros as well.

Thomas Cook Foreign Exchange
9 Bloor St. W. at Yonge St.
☎923-6549

218 Yonge St. (in the Eaton Centre)
☎979-1590

American Express
50 Bloor St. W. (Concourse Level)
☎967-3411

100 Front St. W. (lower level of the Royal York Hotel)
☎363-3883

Automatic teller machines that exchange currency have been installed at the airport. They are open every day from 6am to 2am and change various foreign currencies into Canadian money. Canadian dollars can also be changed into US dollars, pounds sterling, and Euros.

Currency

The monetary unit is the dollar ($), which is divided into cents. One dollar = 100 cents (¢).

Bills come in 5, 10, 20, 50 and 100 dollar denominations, and coins come in 1, 5, 10 and 25 cent coins, and in 1 and 2 dollar coins.

Europeans may be surprised to hear "pennies" ($0.01), "nickels" ($0.05), "dimes" ($0.10), "quarters" ($0.25), "loonies" ($1), and sometimes even "twoonies" ($2).

Mail and Telecommunications

Mail

Canada Post provides efficient mail service (depending on who you speak to) across the country. At press time, it cost $0.49 to send a letter elsewhere in Canada, $0.80 to the United States and $1.40 overseas.

There are post offices throughout the city. Stamps can be purchased at post offices and from postal counters located in some drug stores and department stores.

General Information
☎979-8822

Selected Post Office Locations

31 Adelaide St. E.
595 Bay St.

Telephone

There are two area codes for the Greater Toronto Area. Downtown Toronto and most of the metropolitan area uses the ☎416 area code, while surrounding cities like Ajax, Kleinberg, Malton, Mississauga and Oakville use ☎905. For the most part, however, there are no long distance charges to these cities. Check in the beginning of a phone book (located

Practical Information

in phone booths) for more precise information.

The area code for telephone numbers in this guide is 416, unless otherwise indicated.

Pay phones can be found everywhere, often in the entrances of some of the larger department stores, and in restaurants. They are easy to use and some even accept credit cards. In Toronto and the surrounding area, a local call costs $0.25 for unlimited time. Have a lot quarters on hand if you are making a long distance call from a public phone. Calling direct from a private phone is less expensive. All numbers beginning with **800**, **877** or **888** are toll-free, usually within Canada and the United States; dial **1** first.

Internet

Thanks to the Internet, keeping in touch with the folks back home has never been so easy. In fact, this popular means of communication is in the process of relegating the good old postcard to the wastepaper basket. All you have to do is obtain an e-mail address before you leave.

Some hotels can also receive and transmit e-mail messages, but generally charge a higher fee than Internet cafés.

For Internet access, Kinko's Canada has a handful of locations in downtown Toronto. They include:

Kinkos
$7.50/hr Internet service
459 Bloor St. W.
☎*928-0110*

Business Hours and Public Holidays

Business Hours

Stores

The law regarding business hours allows stores to be open the following hours:

● Monday to Wednesday from 8am to 9pm, though most stores open at 10am and close at 6pm;

● Thursday and Friday from 8am to 9pm, though most open at 10am;

● Saturday from 8am to 6pm, though most open at 10am;

● Sunday from 8am to 5pm, most open at noon, but not all stores are open Sundays.

It wasn't always this way, however. Toronto used to have a law, The Lord's Day Act, which forbade any businesses from opening on a Sunday!

Emergencies

- Police, ambulance and fire: ☎911
- 24-hour medical emergency: ☎392-2000
- Dental emergency: ☎485-7121 or 967-5649
- Children's Hospital: 555 University, ☎813-1500
- Rape Crisis Hotline: ☎597-8808
- Toronto Hospital (emergencies): 150 Gerrard St. W.,
  ☎340-3944

Practical Information

Public Holidays

The following is a list of public holidays in Ontario. Most administrative offices and banks are closed on these days.

New Year's Day
January 1

Good Friday and/or Easter Monday
dates vary

Victoria Day
3rd Monday in May

Canada Day
July 1

Civic Holiday
1st Monday in August

Labour Day
1st Monday in September

Thanksgiving Day
2nd Monday in October

Remembrance Day
November 11 (only banks and federal government services are closed)

Christmas Day and Boxing Day
December 25 and 26

Climate

Toronto enjoys a relatively mild climate, at least compared to the rest of Canada. In the summer, temperatures can climb to above 30°C, though the average is 23°C (73°F). In the winter, the temperature can drop down around -10 or -15°C, though the average temperature is -6°C; the city is usually hit with two or three big snowstorms per winter.

Weather information is available by calling the following number: ☎661-0123.

Visiting Ontario during the two "main" seasons (summer and winter) is like visiting two totally different countries, with the seasons influencing not only the scenery, but also the lifestyles and behaviour of the local population.

Health

Vaccinations are not necessary for people coming from Europe, the United States, Australia and New Zealand. On the other hand, it is strongly suggested that visitors take out health and accident insurance. There are different types (see below) so it is best to shop around. Bring along all medication, especially prescription medicine. Unless otherwise stated, the water is drinkable throughout Ontario.

In the winter, moisturizing lotion and lip balm are useful for people with sensitive skin, since the air in many buildings is very dry.

During the summer, always protect yourself against sunburn. It is often hard to feel your skin getting burned by the sun on windy days. Do not forget to apply sun screen!

Canadians from outside Ontario should take note that in general your province's health care system will only reimburse you for the cost of any hospital

fees or procedures at the going rate in your province. For this reason, it is a good idea to get extra private insurance. In case of accident or illness, make sure to keep your receipts in order to be reimbursed by your province's health care system.

Insurance

Cancellation

Your travel agent will usually offer you cancellation insurance when you buy your airline ticket or vacation package. This insurance allows you to be reimbursed for the ticket or package deal if your trip must be cancelled due to serious illness or death. Those travelling with children should consider buying this type of insurance.

Theft

Most residential insurance policies protect some of your goods from theft, even if the theft occurs in a foreign country. To make a claim, you must fill out a police report. It may not be necessary to take out further insurance, depending on the amount covered by your current home policy. As policies vary considerably, you are advised to check with your insurance company. European visitors should take out baggage insurance.

Health

This is the most useful kind of insurance for travellers, and should be purchased before your departure. Your insurance plan should be as complete as possible because health care costs add up quickly. When buying insurance, make sure it covers all types of medical costs, such as hospitalization, nursing services and doctor's fees. Make sure your limit is high enough, as these expenses can be costly. A repatriation clause is also vital in case the required care is not available on site. Furthermore, since you may have to pay immediately, check your policy to see what provisions it includes for such situations. To avoid any problems during your stay, always keep proof of your insurance policy with you.

Accommodations

A wide choice of accommodations, including 35,000 hotel

rooms to fit every budget, is available in Toronto. Costs vary depending on the season. Summer is the high season, however, since Toronto is an important city for conventions, it is best to book ahead of time no matter when you plan on visiting. The weekends of the Caribana Festival and the Film Festival are particularly busy, as are Canadian and American holiday weekends. Prices are generally lower on weekends than during the week.

Standards are generally high, as in any world-class city, and many services are available. Prices vary according to the type of accommodation and the quality-to-price ratio is generally good, but remember to add the 7% GST (federal Goods and Services Tax) and the provincial sales tax of 8%. The Goods and Services Tax is refundable for non-residents in certain cases (see p 75). A credit card will make reserving a room much easier, since in many cases payment for the first night is required.

There is a reservation service at the information centre in the Eaton Centre (see p 52); you can also reserve accommodations by calling Tourism Ontario at ☎800-ONTARIO or Tourism Toronto at ☎800-363-1990. Packages that combine accommodations with show tickets are often available when you reserve this way.

Prices and Symbols

All the prices mentioned in this guide apply to a **standard room for two people in peak season**. Prices are indicated with the following symbols:

$	$50 or less
$$	$50,01 to $100
$$$	$100,01 to $150
$$$$	$150,01 to $200
$$$$$	$200,01 and over

The actual cost to guests is often lower than the prices quoted here, particularly for travel during the off-peak season. Also, many hotels and inns offer considerable discounts to employees of corporations or members of automobile clubs (CAA, AAA). Be sure to ask about corporate and other discounts, as they are often very easy to obtain.

The various services offered by each establishment are indicated with a small symbol, which is explained in the legend in the opening pages of this guidebook. By no means is this an exhaustive list of what the establishment offers, but rather the services we consider to be the most important.

Please note that the presence of a symbol does not mean that all the rooms have this service; you sometimes have to pay extra to get, for example, a whirlpool tub. If the symbol is not at-

tached to an establishment, it means that the establishment cannot offer you this service. Please note that unless otherwise indicated, all hotels in this guide offer private bathrooms.

The Ulysses Boat

The Ulysses boat pictogram is awarded to our favourite accommodations and restaurants. While every establishment recommended in this guide was included because of its high quality and/or uniqueness, as well as its high value, every once in a while we come across an establishment that absolutely wows us. These, our favourite establishments, are awarded a Ulysses boat. You'll find boats in all price categories: next to exclusive, high-price establishments, as well as budget ones. Regardless of the price, each of these establishments offers the most for your money. Look for them first!

Hotels

Hotels rooms abound, ranging from modest to luxurious. The vast majority come equipped with a private bathroom.

Bed and Breakfasts

There are several bed and breakfasts in Toronto. Unlike hotels, rooms in private homes are not always equipped with a private bathroom. These establishments generally consist of fewer than 12 rooms, often in beautifully decorated historic homes. It is important to note that bed and breakfasts do not always allow children, and that credit cards are not always accepted. Always check the policy of the individual establishment when making your reservations.

The following associations can reserve bed and breakfast accommodations in the city, whatever your needs.

Bed & Breakfast Associations

Bed & Breakfast Homes of Toronto
PO Box 46093
College Park Post Office
Toronto, ON M5B 2L8
☎*363-6362*

Toronto Bed & Breakfast Inc.
PO Box 269
253 College St.
Toronto, ON M5T 1R5
☎*588-8800 or (705) 738-9449*
⇄*927-0838*

Abodes of Choice Bed & Breakfast Association of Toronto
102 Burnside Dr.
Toronto, ON M6G 2M8
☎*537-7629*
⇄*537-0747*
reservations@abodes-of-choice
.com

Downtown Toronto Association of Bed & Breakfast Guest Houses
PO Box 190, Station B
Toronto, ON M5T 2W1
☎*368-1420*
⇄*368-1653*

Metropolitan Bed & Breakfast Registry of Toronto
322 Palmerston Blvd.,
Toronto, ON M6G 2N6
☎*964-2566*
⇄*960-9529*
www.virtualcities.com

Motels

There are many motels in the area, but they are usually located in the suburbs. Though less expensive than other options, they often lack atmosphere; they are particularly useful when pressed for time, or when driving into the city.

University Residences

Due to certain restrictions, this can be a complicated alternative. Residences are only available during the summer (mid-May to mid-August) and making reservations well in advance is strongly recommended; these can usually be made by paying the first night with a credit card.

This type of accommodation, however, is less costly than the "traditional" alternatives, making the effort to reserve early worthwhile. Visitors with valid student cards can expect to pay approximately $25 plus tax, while rates for non-students are slightly higher. Bedding is included in the price, and there is usually a cafeteria in the building (meals are not included in the price).

Practical Information

Restaurants and Cafés

Prices

Unless otherwise indicated, the prices mentioned in this guide are for a meal for one person, not including taxes, drink or tip.

$	$10 or less
$$	$10,01 to $20
$$$	$20,01 to $30
$$$$	$30,01 and over

For an explanation of the Ulysses boat, which appears next to some of our favourite restaurants and accommodations, please see p 72.

Restaurants

Toronto has a cornucopia of unique restaurants to choose from. The burgeoning of the city's ethnic communities, which have managed to maintain their own cultures and niches within the city, has led to a vibrant restaurant scene with cuisines from cultures the world over. Toronto's dining scene is not only one of the finest in the country, but has myriad unique gems for every budget. The choices are nearly endless, with dining spots specializing not only in Japanese, Vietnamese, Chinese, Italian, Greek and Indian, but in cuisines such as Ethiopian, Mauritian and Sri Lankan, to name a few.

Cafés

In recent years, Toronto has experienced an explosion in café culture, and has embraced the coffee phenomenon wholeheartedly. Everywhere in the city, but particularly in the trendy parts of town, there are cafés serving rich, fresh brews and special coffees from café au lait to iced *mocaccino*. In addition to the ubiquitous java giants such as Seattle-based Starbucks and the home-grown Second Cup, dozens of independent cafés dot the city streets, and it is here that you will find the heart of every neighbourhood. On Queen West, artists, actors and writers linger on sidewalk cafés, and even in the downtown business core office workers spend their lunch hours sipping designer brews. Many cafés serve fresh salads and gourmet sandwiches, although some have only cookies and muffins.

Bars and Nightclubs

Toronto has always had a vibrant underground live music scene that has only become stronger in recent years. On any night of the week there are bands from big names to local acts playing live at one of the city's many notorious watering holes. The club scene has burgeoned of late as well, and in "clubland" downtown clubs with sleek, industrial-looking exteriors and beefy bouncers outside are all the rage. Most bars do not have a cover charge unless a band is playing, but most of the clubs charge $5 to $10 for entry.

The legal drinking age in Ontario is 19; if you're close to that age, expect to be asked for proof. Bars close at 2am and it is illegal to sell alcohol after that time.

Happy Hour

Downtown bars offer two-for-one specials during "Happy Hour" (usually from 5pm to 7pm). During these hours you can buy two beers for the price of one, and other drinks are offered at a reduced price. Some snack bars and dessert places offer the same discounts.

Taxes and Tipping

Taxes

The ticket price on items usually **does not include tax**. There are two taxes, the GST (federal Goods and Services Tax) of 7% and the PST (Provincial Sales Tax), which is 8%. They are cumulative, and apply to most items and to restaurant and hotel bills.

There are some exceptions to this taxation system, such as books, which are only taxed with the GST and food (except for restaurant meals), which is not taxed at all.

Tax Refunds for Non-Residents

Non-residents can be refunded for taxes paid on their purchases made while in Canada. To obtain a refund, it is important to keep your receipts. A separate form for each tax (federal and provincial) must be filled out to obtain a refund. Conditions for refunds are different for the GST and the PST. For further information, call ☎800-668-4748 or visit *www.ccraadrc.gc.ca/visitors*.

Tipping

In general, tipping applies to all table service in restaurants and to both table and bar service in bars and nightclubs (no tipping in fast-food restaurants). The tip is usually about 15% of the bill before taxes, but varies, of course, depending on the quality of service.

Tipping is also standard in taxis (approximately 10% of the fare) and hair salons (10-15%). A $1 to $3 tip is usually given for valet parking, regardless of whether or not you pay a parking fee. In deluxe hotels, housekeeping staff should be tipped approximately $5 to $10

Practical Information

per day, although $2 to $3 per day is fine in a less swanky hotel. As for bell hops, the tip is sometimes included in the hotel rate, (particularly for large groups travelling together), but if it is not, $3 to $5 per bag is appropriate.

Wine, Beer and Alcohol

The legal drinking age in Ontario is 19. Beer can only be purchased at the provincially run "Beer Store," and wine and liquor purchased at the "Liquor Store." Ontario wines can also be purchased at the Wine Rack, a chain of shops that can be found downtown and in some supermarkets. Each location has its own opening hours, but on weekdays and Saturdays most beer stores are open until 9pm or 11pm, most liquor stores until 9pm or 10pm, and all Wine Rack outlets until 9pm. All three are open from 11am to 6pm on Sundays.

Beer

Ontario has a thriving microbrewing industry that produces some fine beers. Among these, be sure to try Sleeman, Upper Canada Brewing Company, Creemore Springs and Amsterdam Brewing. Remember that beer can only be purchased from "Beer Stores".

Wine

Ontario wine has developed quite a good reputation in recent years. Most of it is produced at wineries in the Niagara region. Probably the best-known Ontario vintage is the curious sweet dessert wine called ice wine. Keep an eye out for it; it makes a wonderful souvenir.

Advice for Smokers

As in the United States, cigarette smoking is considered taboo in Toronto and is prohibited in public places. It is illegal to smoke in an office building or in the city's transit system. As of June 1, 2001, smoking has been prohibited in all of Toronto's restaurants and dinner theatres. Smoking is only permitted in fully enclosed smoking rooms and on outdoor patios. The by-law does not apply to bars, however, and as a result, licensed restaurants may choose to classify themselves as a bar, instead of a restaurant. In such cases, remember that minors will be prohibited from entering. Keep in mind that the vast majority of Torontonians are non-smokers, and in general it is not a smoke-friendly city, so be sure to check before lighting up.

Cigarettes are sold in bars, grocery stores and newspaper and magazine shops. The legal age for smoking is 16; however, you must be 19 years of age to purchase cigarettes.

Safety

Violence is far less prevalent in Toronto than in most American cities. In fact, the crime rate here is lower than in any other major North American city. This doesn't mean, however, that people should not take the necessary precautions.

If trouble should arise, remember to call ☎911.

Gay and Lesbian Life

Toronto is a big city and by consequence there are countless bars, restaurants, bookstores and organizations serving the gay and lesbian community. These are mostly concentrated in the part of town known as **The Village**, located along Church Street, north and south of Wellesley Street.

There are two free newspapers that provide information about activities in and around the city. These are distributed throughout downtown in bars and restaurants. The most popular is *XTRA!*, which is published every two weeks; the other is *Fab*.

As far as general information is concerned, the people at *XTRA!*

(☎925-6665) are very friendly and will answer any questions you might have or direct you to someone who can.

Finally, there are two directories of businesses that serve the community. The first one, the *Rainbow Book*, is published by the **519 Community Centre** (*519 Church St.*, ☎392-6874), which organizes various activities and events. The second one, *The Pink Pages*, (*80 Bloor St. W.*, *Suite 1102*, ☎972-7418) is available in bookstores and bars.

Lesbian and Gay Pride Toronto at the end of June is a huge event. There is a host of activities during Pride Week, culminating in Pride weekend, when the streets of the Village are blocked off for three days and filled with beer tents, stages for music and comedy performances, vendors and the 750,000 people (both gay and straight) who show up every year for the festivities and the massive Sunday parade. It is one of the city's biggest parades and one of the largest Gay Pride events in North America, rivalled only by New York's and San Francisco's.

Toronto also puts on an impressive, comprehensive gay and lesbian film festival called **Inside Out** annually at the end of May. For more information on Inside Out, call *XTRA!* (☎925-6665).

Travellers with Disabilities

Tourism Toronto (☎*800-363-1990*) has prepared a brochure, "Toronto with Ease," that provides information on accessibility for travellers who use wheelchairs. It is available by telephone or at their information offices at Queen's Quay (see p 52).

For information on accessible establishments in Toronto, contact:

Beyond Ability International
24 McClure Court,
Georgetown, ON L7G 5X6
☎*410-3748*
www.beyond-ability.com

They can also send you their newsletter "Access World."

Toronto Transit operates a wheelchair-accessible bus (see p 59), and the bus from Pearson International Airport is equipped for persons with disabilities (see p 54).

Finally, for general information, contact the **Centre for Independent Living in Toronto** (☎*599-2458, www.cilt.ca*).

Travelling with Children

Children in Ontario are treated like royalty, and the wealth of activities for children in Toronto is impressive. There is plenty to keep the young busy. See the list of the top Toronto attractions for children on pp 84 and 85. Facilities are available almost everywhere, whether it be for transportation or leisure activities. Generally, children under five travel for free, and those under 12 are eligible for fare reductions. The same rules apply for various activities and shows. Find out before you purchase tickets. High chairs and children's menus are available in most restaurants, and a few of the larger stores provide a babysitting service while parents shop; otherwise, you can contact the Daycare and Babysitting Info Line at ☎392-0505.

Travelling with Pets

Dogs on a leash are permitted in most public parks in the city. Small pets are allowed on the public transportation system, as long as they are in a cage or well controlled by the owner. Pets are generally not allowed in stores, especially not food stores; however, many residents tie their pets up near the entrance while they run in. Pets are not allowed in restaurants, but are sometimes permitted in hotels. Be sure to check when making your reservation.

Identity and Culture Shock

Culture Shock

You're going to visit a new country, get acquainted with different people, taste new flavours, smell unfamiliar scents, see surprising things–in short, discover a culture that is not your own. You'll gain a great deal form this encounter, but it may also shake you up more than you'd think. Culture shock can strike anyone, anywhere… even, sometimes, not so far from home!

All the more reason, if you go to a foreign country, to be on the alert for the symptoms of culture shock. Faced with the different ways of doing things in the new culture, your usual reference points may prove of little use to you. The language may be unfamiliar to you, beliefs may strike you as impenetrable, customs incomprehensible, people unapproachable… and some things might seem unacceptable from the outset. Don't panic, humans can display great adaptability. But to do so, they must be given the means.

Remember that cultural diversity is a treasure! Instead of searching for your usual touchstones, put yourself in the shoes of the people around you and try to understand their way of life. When you stay courteous, unassuming and sensitive, people can be extremely helpful. Respect is the simple key to improving many situations.

Remember that it isn't a question of simply tolerating what seems odd to you. Respect means much more than that. Who knows, trying to understand the why's and wherefore's of different facets of a culture might well become one of the things you enjoy most about travel.

Laws and Customs Abroad

It isn't necessary to memorize the legal code of the country you're going to visit. However, be aware that you are subject to the laws of the land you are in, even though you are not a citizen of that country. Never assume that because something is permissible by law at home, it is automatically legal elsewhere. Also, never forget to take cultural differences into account. Certain gestures or attitudes that seem trivial to you can get you in trouble in other countries. Staying sensitive to the customs of your hosts is the best strategy for avoiding problems.

The Responsible Traveller

The adventure of travelling will probably be an enriching experience for you. But will it be the same for your hosts? The ques-

Practical Information

tion of whether or not tourism is good for a host country is controversial. On one hand, tourism brings many advantages, such as the economic development of a region, the promotion of a culture and inter-cultural exchange; on the other hand, tourism can have negative impacts: an increase in crime, deepening of inequalities, environmental destruction, etc. But one thing is for sure: your journey will have an impact on your destination.

This is rather obvious when we speak of the environment. You should be as careful not to pollute the environment of your host country, just as you wouldn't do at home. We hear it often enough: we all live on the same planet! But when it comes to social, cultural and even economic aspects, it can be more difficult to evaluate the impact of our travels. Be aware of the reality around you, and ask yourself what the repercussions will be before acting. Remember that you may make an impression that is much different than the one you wish to give.

Regardless of the type of travelling we choose, it is up to each and every one of us to develop a social conscience and to assume responsibility for our actions in a foreign country. Common sense, respect, altruism, and a hint of modesty are useful tools that will go a long way.

Miscellaneous

Drugs

Non-prescription drugs are illegal and not tolerated (even "soft" drugs). Anyone caught with drugs in his or her possession risks severe consequences.

Electricity

Voltage is 110 volts throughout Canada, the same as in the United States. Electricity plugs have two parallel, flat pins (generally accompanied by a third, round pin, which is the ground). Adaptors are available here in most hardware stores or Radio Shack stores, found in malls.

Language

Though English clearly predominates in Toronto, more than 100 languages are spoken in the city.

Laundromats

Laundromats are found almost everywhere in urban areas. In most cases, detergent is sold on site. Although change machines are sometimes provided, it is best to bring plenty of quarters ($0.25) with you.

Weights and Measures

Although the metric system has been in use in Canada for more than 20 years, some people continue to use the Imperial system in casual conversation. Here are some equivalents:

Weights
1 pound (lb) = 454 grams (g)
1 kilogram (kg) = 2.2 pounds (lbs)

Linear Measure
1 inch (in) = 2.54 centimetres (cm)
1 foot (ft) = 30 centimetres (cm)
1 mile (mi) = 1.6 kilometres (km)
1 kilometre (km) = 0.63 miles (mi)
1 metre (m) = 39.37 inches (in)

Land Measure
1 acre = 0.4 hectare (ha)
1 hectare (ha) = 2.471 acres

Volume Measure
1 U.S. gallon (gal) = 3.79 litres

Temperature

To convert °F into °C:
subtract 32, divide by 9, multiply by 5.

To convert °C into °F:
multiply by 9, divide by 5, add 32.

Practical Information

Museums

Most museums charge admission; however, permanent exhibits at certain museums are free on Wednesday evenings between 6pm and 9pm. Special rates are offered for temporary exhibits during the same period. Reduced prices are available at any time for seniors, children and students. Call ahead to check.

Newspapers

International newspapers can easily be found in Toronto on newsstands, at Chapters and Indigo bookstores or magazine shops such as The Great Canadian News Company and La Maison de la Presse Internationale. Toronto has four major daily newspapers: the *Toronto Star*, the *Toronto Sun*, the *Globe and Mail* and the *National Post*. The latter two are national papers, with Toronto as their biggest market. The two free weekly arts and entertainment newspapers, *Now* and *eye*, can be picked up in restaurants and cafés or at street-corner stands all over the city.

Pharmacies

Apart from the smaller drug stores, there are large pharmacy chains that sell everything from chocolate to laundry detergent, as well as the more traditional items, such as cough drops and headache medications. Some are even open 24hrs such as the following Shoppers Drug Mart locations:

3089 Dufferin St.
☎ 787-0238

700 Bay St.
☎ 979-2424

2345 Yonge St.
☎ 487-5411

Time Zone

Most of Ontario, including Toronto, is in the Eastern Standard Time zone, as is most of the eastern United States. It is 3hrs ahead of the west coast of the continent. There is a 6hr time difference between Toronto and most continental European countries and 5hrs between Toronto and the United Kingdom. Daylight saving time goes into effect in Ontario on the first Sunday in April and ends on the last Sunday in October. All of Ontario (except the extreme western part) is on the same time.

Exploring

This chapter outlines

10 walking tours as well as two driving tours that lead travellers on a discovery of Toronto and the surrounding areas. The final tour heads straight to magnificent Niagara Falls.

The tours and main attractions described are rated according to a star system so that you'll know what to see, even if you only stay a short while in Montréal.

★	Interesting
★★	Worth a visit
★★★	Not to be missed

The name of each attraction is followed by information in brackets, such as opening hours, address and telephone number.

The admission rate (for one adult) is also indicated. Note that most establishments offer discounts for children, students, senior citizens and families.

Toronto's Top Attractions for Children

Pioneer-living fascinates children, so why not take a trip out to **Black Creek Pioneer Village** (see p 160)?

Underground tunnels and an old-fashioned stable keep younger minds occupied at **Casa Loma** (see p 151).

The opportunities for discovery at the **CN Tower** extend as far as the eye can see, and sometimes that can be all the way to Niagara Falls. The glass floor of the second-floor observation deck is especially mind-boggling for the little ones (see p 90).

Soldiers in full dress, authentic military buildings and the heat of battle make **Fort York** (see p 91) and **Fort George** (see p 168) exciting places for children.

The Harbourfront has something to please everyone. The Milk International Children's Festival, created especially for kids, is an annual celebration of theatre, dance and music. There is also the Craft Studio, where artists can be observed at work (see p 88). Hockey is Canada's national sport, and just about every child has his or her favourite player and team. What better way to please the next "great one" than to take him or her on a tour of the Montréal Canadiens dressing room and let them see the real Stanley Cup!? All this is possible at the **Hockey Hall of Fame** (see p 106).

Sports fans will delight in the opportunity to visit the dressing rooms of the Toronto Blue Jays at the **SkyDome** (see p 89) and the Toronto Maple Leafs and Raptors at the **Air Canada Centre** (see p 90).

Besides the exceptional collections of animals from around the globe, sure to thrill younger animal lovers, the **Toronto Metropolitan Zoo** also has an area called Littlefootland where children can get a closer look at some tamer animals like bunnies, ponies and sheep (see p 164).

Older Children can play detective for a day as they analyze blood and dirt samples and solve a crime at the **Metropolitan Toronto Police Museum & Discovery Centre** (see p 137).

Vibrant **Nathan Phillips Square** is the setting for all sorts of concerts, markets and a skating rink in winter (see p 121).

Ontario Place is an obvious thrill for children, in particular the Cinesphere with its exciting line-up of 3-D movies (see p 92). Along the same lines but with dolphins and whales, **Marineland** (see p 172) is sure to please the young ones.

Fun and discovery are paramount at the **Ontario Science Centre**; one of the biggest crowd-pleasers is definitely the static ball that makes your hair stand on end (see p 153).

Paramount Canada's Wonderland is another full-day activity that no child will refuse (see p 160).

There are samples at the **Redpath Sugar Museum**, where kids can see how the sweet stuff is made (see p 88).

Riverdale Farm is close to downtown and there is no admission fee. Children will love the friendly barnyard animals (see p 145).

Wonderfully mysterious things like dinosaurs and mummies are just some of what the **Royal Ontario Museum (ROM)** has to offer (see p 135).

The beach, seagulls, ducks, Far Enough Farm and the Centreville Amusement Park make the **Toronto Islands** the perfect escape for parents and kids (see p 92).

The **Lorraine Kimsa Theatre for Young People** puts on productions just for children (see p 111).

Exploring

Tour A: The Waterfront

Being near a major body of water often determines the location of a city, and Toronto is no exception. For many years, however, the City of Toronto neglected its waterfront. The Gardiner Expressway, the old railway lines and the numerous warehouses that disfigured the shores of Lake Ontario offered few attractions in the eyes of residents. Fortunately, large sums of money were spent to return this area to life, and it is now home to a luxury hotel, many shops and numerous cafés bustling with constant activity. Today, the Waterfront is a vibrant area, with cultural and artistic events held at the Harbourfront Centre, shoppers taking in Queen's Quay terminal's shops and strollers using the walkways along Lake Ontario. A project is currently under way to further develop green spaces of the area.

The tour makes its way from east to west along Toronto's waterfront, from the factory yards to the mega-development project of Ontario Place. Start at the corner of Queen's Quay East and Cooper Street, at the Redpath Sugar Museum.

● ATTRACTIONS

1. Redpath Sugar Museum
2. Harbourfront Centre
3. Queen's Quay Terminal
4. Power Plant Contemporary Art Gallery
5. Du Maurier Theatre Centre
6. York Quay Centre
7. Harbourfront Antique Market
8. SkyDome
9. Air Canada Centre
10. CN Tower
11. Fort York
12. Ontario Place
13. Cinesphere / IMAX Cinema
14. HMCS Haida
15. Children's Village

◯ ACCOMMODATIONS

1. Radisson Plaza Hotel Admiral
2. SkyDome Hotel
3. Westin Harbour Castle

● RESTAURANTS

1. 360 Restaurant
2. Captain John's Seafood
3. Hard Rock Cafe
4. Pearl Harbourfront
5. Planet Hollywood
6. Susur
7. The Boathouse Bar and Grill
8. Wayne Gretzky's
9. Whistling Oyster Seafood Cafe

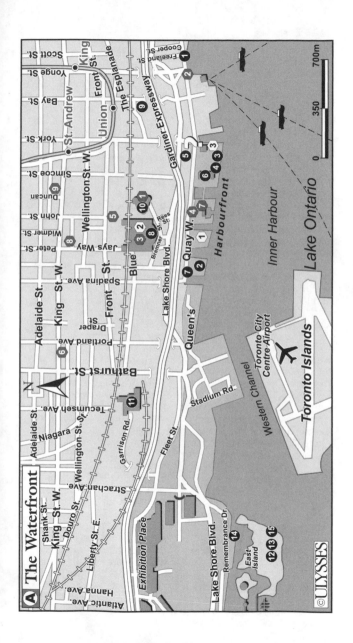

A The Waterfront

Scott St.
King
Yonge St.
Bay St.
York St.
Simcoe St.
Duncan
John St.
Widmer St.
Peter St.
Spadina Ave.
Front St.
Draper St.
Portland Ave.
Bathurst St.
Tecumseh Ave.
Niagara
Shank St.
Douro St.
King St. W.
Wellington St. W.
Adelaide St.
Liberty St. E.
Hanna Ave.
Atlantic Ave.
Adelaide St.

Front St.
The Esplanade
Union
St. Andrew
Wellington St. W.
King St. W.
Jays Way
Blue
Rees St.
Bremner St.
Lake Shore Blvd.
Queen's Quay W.
Gardiner Expressway

Cooper St.
Freeland St.

Harbourfront

Inner Harbour

Lake Ontario

Garrison Rd.
Fleet St.
Stadium Rd.
Strachan Ave.
Exhibition Place
Lake Shore Blvd.
Remembrance Dr.
East Island

Western Channel
Toronto City Centre Airport

Toronto Islands

N

1
2
3
4
5
6
9
10 1
3 2
8
5
6
7
4 3
7
4
1
2
7
6
11
14
12 13 15

0   350   700m

© ULYSSES

The **Redpath Sugar Museum** ★★ *(free admission; call for hours; 95 Queen's Quay E., ☎933-8341)*, a small museum buried within the Redpath Refinery, relates the arduous history of this staple crop. You'll learn about how sugar was one of the first industries that brought African slaves to the Americas, and about production and harvesting methods. Just about everything related to sugar and the Redpath family is presented in this fascinating museum. There are even samples!

A few blocks away, at the foot of Bay Street, a ferry can take you to the Toronto Islands. The dock is just behind the Harbour Castle Westin Hotel. The Toronto Islands are the ideal spot to relax, take a little sun, go for a bike ride, take a stroll, or go for a swim. A walking tour of the islands is outlined on p 92.

A few steps away, at the foot of York Street, is **Queen's Quay Terminal** ★★★ *(207 Queen's Quay W.)*, where boats leave for trips around the bay and the Toronto Islands (the ferries depart from the foot of Bay Street). Queen's Quay is a former warehouse that has been completely renovated and modified to house about 100 restaurants and shops and a theatre devoted exclusively to dance.

The Pier: Toronto's Waterfront Museum *($8.50; every day 10am to 6pm; 245 Queen's Quay W., ☎338-PIER/7437)* is one of the city's newest cultural heritage attractions. Located in a restored 1930 shipping warehouse, The Pier replaces and far supercedes the old Marine Museum. Young visitors will find steam whistles to pull, along with the Discovery Gallery set up inside the hull of a ship. Other fascinating displays include those on Toronto's changing shoreline and harbour, Lake Ontario shipwrecks and historic battles and a simulated race against famous oarsman Ned Hanlan. Visitors can also watch artisans constructing traditional wooden boats, and even sign up for a course. Finally, you can take one of these boats out for a tour of the harbour. The short waterfront walking tours offered in summer are also interesting.

Harbourfront Centre ★ *(free admission; 410 Queen's Quay W.; ☎973-4000 or 973-3000 for information on special events, www.harbourfront.on. ca)* is a good example of the changes on Toronto's waterfront. It is easily reached by the Union Station trolley running west toward Spadina Avenue. Since the federal government purchased 40ha of land along the shores of Lake Ontario, dilapidated old factories and warehouses have been renovated, turning this into one of Toronto's most fascinating areas. Apart from the restaurants, shops and vistas, the centre hosts a variety of shows and cultural events that are the pride of Torontonians.

From Queen's Quay Terminal, head over toward the lake and the **Power Plant Contemporary Art Gallery ★** *($4, free admission on Wed from 5pm to 8pm; Tue-Sun noon to 6pm, Wed noon to 8pm, closed Mon; 231 Queen's Quay W., ☎973-4949)*, a former power plant (surprise, surprise!) that is devoted to the exhibition and interpretation of modern painting, sculpture, photography, film and videographic work. This is a non-collecting gallery, with continuous travelling exhibits. Next door is the red-brick **Du Maurier Theatre Centre** *(231 Queen's Quay W., ☎973-3000)*, behind which is the **Tent in the Park**, where various concerts and plays are presented all summer long. A little further west is the **York Quay Centre ★** *(235 Queen's Quay W., ☎973-3000)*, with restaurants and other establishments. Don't miss the **Craft Studio** *(free admission; York Quay Centre)*, where you can observe craftspeople working with glass, metal, ceramics and textiles and perhaps make some purchases.

Right near Lake Ontario, sailboats and motorboats can be rented at the **Harbourside Boating Centre** *($50 or more for 3hrs; 283 Queen's Quay W., ☎203-3000)*, with prices varying according to the size and type of boat. Sailing lessons are also offered. In the winter, the bay is transformed into a gigantic skating rink. You can rest at one of the many bars and restaurants of **Bathurst Pier 4**, which has water sports as its theme,

or go on to explore some of the sailing clubs.

The very popular **Harbourfront Antique Market ★★** is open to visitors every day except Monday *(May to Oct, Tue-Sat 11am to 6pm, Sun 8am to 6pm; Nov to Apr Tue-Sat 11am to 5pm, Sun 8am-6pm; 390 Queen's Quay W., ☎260-2626)*. This makes for a most interesting visit. You can spend hours perusing the countless antique shops, each one guarding some treasure or marvel you simply cannot do without.

From Harbourfront Centre, it is just a few steps to the SkyDome and the CN Tower.

SkyDome ★★ *($12.50; guided tours every day 9am to 4pm, tour schedules may vary according to events; 1 Blue Jay Way, ☎341-3663)*, the pride of Toronto, is the first sports stadium in the world with a fully retractable roof. In poor weather, four panels mounted on rails come together in 20min, despite their 11,000 tonnes, to form the SkyDome's roof. Since 1989, this remarkable building has been home to the American League's Toronto Blue Jays baseball team and to the Canadian Football League's Toronto Argonauts.

Depending on the requirements of different sports, the SkyDome can be converted quickly to welcome 52,000 baseball fans or 53,000 football fans. For special events, it can fit up to 70,000 people. For con-

Exploring

certs and other events not requiring as great a capacity, out comes the Skytent, a giant cloth that divides the stadium to improve the sound quality. Finally, no spectator, even those who get stuck in the bleachers, need miss any of the action, thanks to the Jumbotron, an enormous screen 10m high and 33m wide.

Visitors can learn more about the SkyDome's technical aspects by taking a 90min guided tour *(every day; ☎341-2770)*. You will see a collection of objects excavated when the foundations for the new stadium were being dug in 1986, as well as a 15min documentary film on the SkyDome's construction titled *The Inside Story*, which relates, perhaps with a bit too much drama, how architect Roderick Robbie and engineer Michael Allen developed the concept of the retractable roof. The tour also includes a visit to the press box and a peek into one of the corporate boxes; called SkyBoxes by the marketing people, these are rented for a mere $1 million for 10 years, not counting tickets, refreshments or food!

The **Air Canada Centre** *($9.50; hourly tours Mon-Sat 10am to 3pm, Sun 11am to 3pm; 40 Bay St., ☎815-5500)* opened near the SkyDome in the former Postal Delivery Building in early 1999. It is now the home of the Toronto Raptors, one of two Canadian-based teams in the National Basketball Association, and the National Hockey League's Toronto Maple Leafs.

The **CN Tower** ★★★ *(observation deck $20; summer every day 8am to 11pm, rest of year everyday 9am to 10pm, hours of operation are adjusted seasonally, call ahead to confirm times; Front St.W., ☎360-8500 or 888-684-3268)*. No doubt the most easily recognizable building in Toronto, the CN Tower dominates the city from a height of 553.33m, making it the highest observation tower in the world. Originally built by the Canadian National Railway company to help transmit radio and TV signals past the numerous downtown buildings, it has become one of the city's main attractions. To avoid long lines, go early in the morning or late in the day, especially in the summer and on weekends. If the day is overcast, it is best to postpone your visit.

The **Simulator Theatre** *($8)* features two motion simulator rides, and **The Edge Arcade** *($8)*, a virtual games arcade whose name says it all.

You can also climb to the observation deck in an elevator

CN Tower

that lifts you off the ground floor at a speed of 6m per second, equivalent to the takeoff of a jet aircraft. Located 335.25m up and set on four levels, the observation deck is the nerve centre of the tower. The first floor houses telecommunications equipment, while the second floor has an outdoor observation deck and a glass floor for those who are not afraid of heights. The third floor has an indoor observation deck and elevators (for a $2.25 supplement) going to the **Space Deck**, floating 447m up and forming the world's highest public observation post. The view from the top is splendid, of course. On a clear day, you can see over a distance of 160km and even make out Niagara Falls. Finally, the fourth floor has a bar and restaurant with seating for up to 400 people. Because of the great height, you may feel the tower sway in the wind. This is perfectly normal and enhances the resistance of the entire structure.

To continue your tour of the waterfront, head west toward Fort York. By car, you can reach Fort York along Lakeshore Boulevard, turning right on Strachan, right on Fleet Street and left on Garrison Road. Streetcar number 511 along Bathurst Street also provides easy access.

It was on the shores of Lake Ontario, at **Fort York** *($5; summer, Mon-Fri 10am to 5pm, Sat and Sun noon to 5pm; rest of the year, Tue-Fri 10am to 4pm, Sat and Sun noon to 5pm; 100 Garrison Rd., ☎392-6907)* that Toronto was born. Built in 1783 by Governor John Graves Simcoe in response to a looming American threat, Fort York was destroyed by American invaders in 1813 and rebuilt soon afterward. As relations with the United States improved, it gradually lost its purpose. In the 1930s, the city of Toronto renovated it extensively to turn it into a tourist attraction. Nowadays, Fort York is the site of the largest Canadian collection of buildings

Fort York

dating from the War of 1812. A visit includes a tour of the barracks, which are furnished as they were when they housed officers and soldiers. There is also a small museum with a short informative video on the history of the fort. In the summer, guides in period dress re-enact military manoeuvres.

Several years ago, Fort York was at the centre of another battle, this one pitting the City of Toronto against real-estate developers who wanted to move the site to make way for the Gardiner Expressway. The decision to preserve Fort York's authenticity was like a wake-up call for the City, which began to see the importance of preserving the many pieces of history throughout the city, such as its splendid streetcar system. Though the expressway and warehouses that now surround Fort York are rather uninspiring and a far cry from the waterfront location it once enjoyed, it is interesting to see how Toronto has developed from this tiny fort into the sprawling metropolis it is today.

Continuing along Lakeshore Boulevard, head just a little further west, beyond the grounds of the Canadian National Exhibition, to Ontario Place.

Ontario Place ★ *($22 for day pass, or $9 grounds admission only; late May to Sep, 10am to midnight; 955 Lakeshore Blvd. W., ☎314-9900; from late May to early Sep, a bus service links Union Station with Ontario Place)*, designed by Eberhard Zeidler, consists of three islands joined by bridges. Five structures are suspended several metres above the water and bustle with activities for the young and the not-so-young. An enormous white sphere stands out clearly from the other buildings; inside is the **Cinesphere**, an **IMAX cinema** *(☎965-7722)* with an impressive six-storey-high movie screen.

Ontario Place has a marina with a capacity of about 300 boats, centred around the **HMCS Haida**, a Second World War destroyer. If you have children with you, head to the **Children's Village**, with its playgrounds, pool, water slides, waterguns, bumper-boats, Nintendo centre, LEGO creative centre, cinema and other attractions. The not-so young will appreciate the **Forum**, an outdoor amphitheatre with various musical shows each evening.

Take the time to stroll alongside the lake, enjoying the sun and the fresh air. This stretch of the waterfront is a popular stomping ground for Canada geese.

Tour B: The Toronto Islands

Originally, the Toronto Islands were nothing but a sandy peninsula known as "place of trees standing out of the water" by

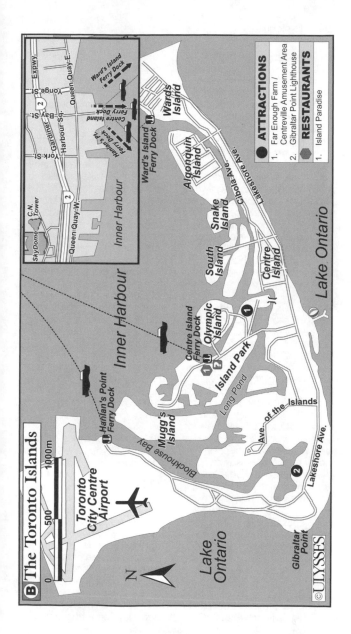

B The Toronto Islands

Lake Ontario

Toronto City Centre Airport

Inner Harbour

Hanlan's Point Ferry Dock

Mugg's Island

Blockhouse Bay

Long Pond

Island Park

Centre Island Ferry Dock

Olympic Island

South Island

Snake Island

Algonquin Island

Wards Island

Ward's Island Ferry Dock

Ave. of the Islands

Lakeshore Ave.

Cibola Ave.

Lakeshore Ave.

Centre Island

Gibraltar Point

Lake Ontario

N

0   500   1000m

C.N. Tower

SkyDome

Queen-Quay-W.

Harbour-St.

Bay-St.

Yonge-St.

York-St.

Gardiner Expwy.

Queen's Q. E.

Hanlan's Pt. Ferry Dock

Centre Island Ferry Dock

Ward's Island Ferry Dock

Inner Harbour

ATTRACTIONS

1. Far Enough Farm /
   Centreville Amusement Area
2. Gibraltar Point Lighthouse

RESTAURANTS

1. Island Paradise

© ULYSSES

the Mississauga First Nation. This sandbar did afford protection to the harbour, however, and thus contributed to the choice of York as the naval and military centre of Upper Canada. A violent storm in 1858 separated the islands from the mainland, and erosion, dredging, landfill and currents have since doubled their size. These 17 islands, only 8 of which are named, are an idyllic collection of paths, beaches and cottages that belong to some 250 families that reside here. There are approximately 1.2 million visitors to this automobile-free environment every year.

A short 10min **ferry ride** from the Toronto Ferry Docks, on Queens Way at the foot of Bay Street, will take you out to the islands *($6, return; open year-round; for general information and schedules ☎392-8193).* Three ferries, each departing from the Mainland Ferry Terminal at the foot of Bay Street, service the three biggest islands, Hanlan's Point, Centre Island and Ward's Island; bridges connect the other islands. Bicycles are permitted on all of these ferries, except, on occasion, the Centre Island ferry, which gets very crowded on weekends. The ferry also runs in the winter (though less frequently), so you can visit the island year-round.

You can explore the islands on foot, by bike, on in-line skates or aboard a trackless train that runs regularly between the Centre Island Dock and Hanlan's Point, offering free historical guided tours along the way. Enjoy the fresh air: the train is one of the only motorized vehicles on the islands.

Winter is actually a lovely time to come over, as spectacular cross-country skiing and snowshoeing trails take the place of walking and jogging paths; there is also some great ice-skating. Summer, of course, remains the busiest time of the year as the paved, scenic trails that criss-cross the islands are the delight of walkers, joggers, in-line skaters and cyclists. Remember that swimming is prohibited in the channels and lagoons. Tennis, frisbee, golf, softball diamonds and wading pools round out the other outdoor possibilities.

Finally, one of the highlights of this urban oasis is certainly the spectacular view of Toronto, sparkling in the distance day and night.

Whatever your mode of transportation, if you have young ones in tow, make your first and second stops at the **Centreville Amusement Area** *(free admission to grounds, charge per ride, day pass)* and **Far Enough Farm** *(late Apr to mid-May, Sat and Sun, mid-May to Sep, every day; ☎203-0405)* respectively. The former is an old-fashioned amusement park built in 1833, one year before the town of York became Toronto. It boasts a classic ferris wheel, bumper cars, a log flume ride and a pretty 1890s merry-go-round. The latter is a petting zoo with barnyard animals, just a short distance beyond the amusement park, where the young ones can enjoy a pony ride.

Centre Island is and has always been the busiest of all the islands. In the 1950s, there were 8,000 people living here. The advent of Toronto Islands Park in the late 1950s and early 1960s, however, led to the demolition of Centre Island's elegant resort hotels, theatres and shops.

The formal **Avenue of the Islands** extends across Centre Island from Manitou Bridge to the pier and the beach. It is lined with flower beds, reflecting pools, fountains and beautiful grassy expanses with signs inviting you to "please walk on

the grass." These vast lawns are perfect for picnics. You can also continue to the end of the pier for an expansive view of Lake Ontario. From the pier, follow the water and the beach to the west towards Hanlan's Point. Continue past the filtration plant and the Island Science School, where, incidentally, children can learn about life on the islands. The **Gibraltar Point Lighthouse** is the next big landmark. Built in 1806, it is Toronto's oldest remaining structure. Another sandy beach skirts the water's edge near the lighthouse, while just beyond it the trail forks. Keep left, close to the water, as you make your way to Hanlan's Point.

Hanlan's Point was originally known as Gibraltar Point and was the nucleus of York's (Toronto's) military defence system. It was renamed when the Hanlans moved here in 1862. Their son Ned went on to become a championship rower. Landfill and bulldozing for Toronto Island Airport obliterated the little resort and the baseball stadium in which Babe Ruth hit his first professional home run. The beach and spectacular sunsets of Hanlan's are only slightly marred by the occasional passing plane. Aviation buffs might be interested to know that the airport's former terminal, which now houses its administrative offices, was recently declared a national historic site. It is the only such building preserved in Canada. The path ends at the ferry dock.

Gibraltar Point Lighthouse

Exploring

Retrace your steps, keeping to the left, close to the waters of Blockhouse Bay. You'll rejoin the main path again at the lighthouse; however, once at the filtration plant, turn left to follow Long Pond, where rowboats can be rented, and where the annual Dragon Boat Races (see p 242) are held. After passing the Manitou Bridge, you'll soon come upon **St. Andrews-By-The-Lake Church**, built in 1884 as part of the original cottage community. The sailing vessels moored to your left are part of the prestigious Royal Canadian Yacht Club, which is based here. Its presence, along with the Queen City Yacht Club on Algonquin Island, helps maintain the elegant and exclusive resort feeling of this part of the islands. Cross the bridge over to **Algonquin Island** to explore the pretty streets lined with cottages, several of which have been very well maintained. Street names remind visitors and residents alike that the original native inhabitants of this area also regarded the islands as a choice spot to relax.

Finally, make your way out to **Ward's Island**, where you'll not only find more quaint cottages but can also relax on some of the quietest and cleanest beaches on the islands. If you are lucky, one or both of the two small cafés run by island residents may be open. The Rectory Cafe is located close to the ferry dock, while the Waterfront Cafe overlooks the boardwalk and Lake Ontario. The homes on Ward's and

Algonquin are all privately owned, but they sit on land leased from Metro Toronto. The picturesque boardwalk follows the water all the way back to the pier, where you can drop off your rental bike before heading back to the city.

Tour C:
The Theatre and
Financial Districts

Start at the corner of King and John. The stretch of King Street from here to Simcoe Street is also known as Mirvish Walkway, after the father and son duo of discount-store magnates who refurbished the area by saving the Royal Alexandra from the wrecking ball and by filling in the empty warehouses with restaurants for theatre-goers.

The **Princess of Wales Theatre** *(300 King St. W., tickets ☎872-1212)* was built in 1993 expressly for the musical *Miss*

Royal Alexandra Theatre

Ed Mirvish

Ed Mirvish is a man of initiative. He was born in Virginia, but his family moved to Toronto when he was nine years old. When Ed was 15, his father died and Ed took over the management of the family grocery store. Mirvish's subsequent personal retail ventures would prove to be on a much grander scale, however.

Garish yet delightful in all its neon splendour, his flagship **Honest Ed's** *(581 Bloor St. W.)* discount store opened for business more than 40 years ago, and high volume and low markup have since been the foundations of his business. Shoppers profit from "daily door crashers" where 2-litre bottles of Coca-

Cola might sell for 5¢. When zoning laws prevented Mirvish from razing the decaying mansions along Markham Street behind his store, he transformed them into **Mirvish (Markham) Village**. The buildings now house art galleries and bookstores. Mirvish is also known as a philanthropist of sorts. His growing interest in music, ballet and theatre prompted him to save the historic **Royal Alexandra Theatre** in 1963, and to purchase and refurbish the **Old Vic** in London, England. His son David now runs the Royal Alexandra, and the pair built a brand new theatre, **The Princess of Wales Theatre** especially for the musical *Miss Saigon*.

Exploring

Saigon by none other than the Mirvishes. Though no tours are offered, it is worth taking a peak inside at the minimalist decor of moon and stars in the lobby.

Continue to **The Royal Alexandra** ★★ *(260 King St. W., tickets ☎800-724-6420)*. Plastered on the walls of Ed Mirvish's various food empori-

ums between the Princess of Wales and Royal Alexandra is a collection of newspaper articles attesting to the entrepreneur's various exploits. The Royal Alex, as it is more commonly known, was named after the king's consort. This is one of the most important theatres in the city and has been a favourite meeting place of Toronto's elite ever since it opened in 1907. Its rich Edwardian styling and beaux-arts decor of plush red velvet, gold brocade and green marble were restored in the 1960s by Ed Mirvish.

Just a few steps to the east and you'll find yourself in front of he offices of Swiss Reinsurance Company. This edifice is typical of the mini–Classic Revival palaces that were all the rage around 1907 when it was erected. Known as the **Union Building** *(212 King St. W.)*, it originally housed the Canadian General Electric Company.

● ATTRACTIONS

1. Princess of Wales Theatre
2. Royal Alexandra
3. Union Building
4. Roy Thompson Hall
5. Metro Hall
6. CBC Broadcast Centre
7. St. Andrew's Presbyterian Church
8. Sun Life Tower
9. First Canadian Place
10. Toronto Stock Exchange
11. Standard Life and Royal Trust
12. Toronto-Dominion Centre
13. Bank of Nova Scotia
14. National Club Building
15. Bank of Montreal
16. Canada Permanent Building
17. Northern Ontario Building
18. Atlas Building
19. Scotia Plaza
20. Bank of Commerce Building
21. Commerce Court
22. Royal Bank
23. Canadian Pacific Building
24. Trader's Bank
25. Bank of British North America
26. Number 15
27. Original Toronto Stock Exchange
28. Design Exchange
29. Royal Bank Plaza
30. Union Station
31. Royal York Hotel
32. Canada Trust Tower
33. Canada Custom Building
34. BCE Place
35. Marché Mövenpick
36. Hockey Hall of Fame
37. Bank of Montreal
38. Hummingbird Centre
39. St. Lawrence Centre

◐ ACCOMMODATIONS

1. Fairmount Royal York Hotel
2. Global Village Backpackers
3. Hilton Toronto
4. Holiday Inn on King
5. Hotel Victoria
6. InterContinental Toronto Centre
7. Le Germain
8. Strathcona Hotel
9. Travelodge Toronto Downtown West

● RESTAURANTS

1. Acqua
2. Duke of Argyle
3. Epic
4. Fenice
5. Fred's Not Here
6. Friscos
7. Golden Thai
8. Hey Lucy
9. Kit Kat
10. Marché Mövenpick
11. N'Awlins Jazz Bar and Grill
12. Senses
13. Shopsy's Deli & Restaurant
14. Szechuan, Szechuan

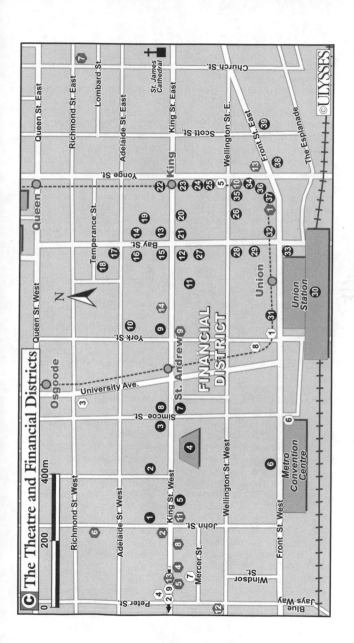

C The Theatre and Financial Districts

© ULYSSES

Across the street rises **Roy Thompson Hall ★★** *($4; 45min guided tours Mon-Sat 12:30pm; 60 Simcoe St., ☎593-4822)*, one of the most distinctive buildings in Toronto's cityscape. The space-age 3,700m² mirrored-glass exterior was designed by Canadian Arthur Erickson and gets mixed reviews, having been compared to an upside-down mushroom and a ballerina tutu. The interior, however, is another story, boasting striking luminosity, a glamorous lobby and exceptional acoustics, which the resident Toronto Symphony and Mendelssohn Choir show off beautifully. Touted as the New Massey Hall while under construction, the hall was ultimately named after newspaper magnate Lord Thompson of Fleet, whose family made the largest single donation.

A large courtyard stretches out to the west of Roy Thompson Hall and is bordered to the west by **Metro Hall** (facing the Princess of Wales), and to the south by **Simcoe Place** (the large square building to the left) and the **CBC Broadcast Centre** *($7; schedule varies; Canadian Broadcasting Centre, 250 Front St. W., ☎205-8605)*. The Broadcast Centre opened in 1992 and quickly took its place on Toronto's skyline with its distinctive red grid-like exterior and angled facades. This is the headquarters of the English networks of the Canadian Broadcasting Corporation and the home of local French radio and television programming. A bright 10-storey atrium is the focus of the lobby; guided tours start here and the **CBC Museum** *(Mon-Fri, 9am to 5pm, Sat 12pm to 4pm; 250 Front St.W.,☎205-5574)* is also located here. Interactive displays highlight the history of radio and television in Canada. The Centre also houses the Graham Spry Theatre, where favourite programs are shown.

Back on King Street, **St. Andrew's Presbyterian Church**, built in 1876, stands on the southwest corner of Simcoe Street. It used to share this intersection with Government House, Upper Canada College, and a rowdy watering hole, leading the corner to be known as "Legislation, Education, Damnation and Salvation." Today, its Scottish Romanesque Revival sandstone exterior contrasts sharply with the steel and mirrored glass that surround it on the way into Toronto's financial district. Ironically, the Sun Life Tower ensured the church's survival by paying some $4 million to build above and below it.

Continue into the heart of Toronto, the **financial district**, which extends between Adelaide Street to the north and Front Street to the south, and between University Avenue to the west and Yonge Street to the east.

The intersection of King and Bay streets is the symbolic and geographical centre of Toronto's financial district. The four corners of this intersection are occupied by four of Canada's five national banks: the Bank of Nova Scotia, on the northeast corner; the Canadian Imperial Bank of Commerce on the southeast; the Toronto-Dominion Bank on the southwest and the Bank of Montreal on the northwest.

Historically, high finance in Toronto has always been centred around this area. It all started at the intersection of Yonge and Wellington in the mid-1800s, when the only form of advertising available to financial organizations was architecture. Image was everything in those days, and a sense of solidity and permanence was achieved through majestic entrance halls, cornices, porticoes and the like. By the early 1900s, the hub of the district had shifted north to King and Yonge, where the sleekness of Art Deco was in vogue. As the district expanded to the west, Bay Street's skyscrapers were built right up against the street, creating a northern version of the Wall Street canyon. In the last two decades, the steel and glass towers have become the centrepieces of vast windswept courtyards. In recent years these concrete parks have been in direct competition with the ever-expanding underground walkway system known as the PATH.

The first tower of steel and mirror, the **Sun Life Tower ★ ★** *(150-200 King St. W.)*, stands opposite St. An-

drew's Church at the corner of Simcoe and King streets. The sculpture in front of it is the work of Sorel Etrog.

Continue along King Street to York Street.

On the northeast corner stands the tower of marble known as **First Canadian Place ★**. Though its stark exterior and squat base are not very appealing, the interior commercial space is bright and airy. The **Toronto Stock Exchange ★ ★** *(free admission; Mon-Fri 9:30am to 4pm, guided tours at 2pm; 130 King St. W., ☎947-4670)* the focal point of Canadian high finance, is located inside. The visitors' centre is on the ground floor of the Exchange Tower, in the reception area. This is one of the more interesting stops in the district as visitors can watch the trading floor from an observation gallery.

Halfway between York and Bay, the **Standard Life** and **Royal Trust** buildings stand on the south side of King Street next to the impressive **Toronto-Dominion Centre ★ ★** *(55 King St. W.)*, on the southwest corner of King and Bay. The work of famous modernist Ludwig Mies van der Rohe, it was the first International Style skyscraper built in Toronto in the mid-1960s. These plain black towers may seem uninspiring, but the use of costly materials and the meticulous proportions have made T-D Centre one of the most renowned forms in Toronto's

Exploring

Street Names

Below is an explanation of the history of Toronto's street names:

Bay: named in 1797 when York's city limits were first extended. The street has an obvious link to the topography of the city, located on the shores of Lake Ontario.

Bloor: named after Joseph Bloor (1788-1862), a brewer who lived at no. 100 on this street. It was the northern boundary of the city for many years. In fact, shortly before being named "Bloor", the street was called "Toll-Gate Road", in reference to the tollgate set up at the corner of Yonge Street, at the city limits.

Church: from 1797, parcels of land were set aside for the building of a church. St. James Church, now St. James Cathedral, was erected here in 1805.

College: this street was originally a private road that led to King's College. Later on, it was rented by the University of Toronto and turned into a public street.

Dundas: named after Sir Henry Dundas, first Viscount of Melville and home secretary from 1791 to 1794. The street was laid out by request of Governor Simcoe in order to link the town of York to two rivers, the Thames to the west and the Trent to the east.

King: named after King George III. It was created by request of Governor Simcoe in 1793.

Queen: named in honour of Queen Victoria (1819-1901) in 1843.

Spadina: this avenue originally served as a private entrance to Dr. W.W. Baldwin's property. The name is derived from the Aboriginal word *espadinong*, which means "little hill."

University: originally known as "College Avenue", it was a private, tree-lined road that linked Queen Street to King's College. In 1888, it was rented by the University of

Toronto and turned into a public street.

Yonge: named after George Yonge, secretary of war from 1782 to 1794, it was one of the first streets laid out in Toronto, by request of Governor Simcoe.

cityscape. The first phase of construction dates between 1963 and 1969, when two towers, 46 and 56 storeys high, were erected. These modern towers gave rise to the construction of other buildings of this type in Toronto's city core and elsewhere in Canada. In the 1970s and 1980s, three other towers (not designed by Mies van der Rohe) were built between King and Wellington streets West.

Stroll along Bay Street to see the beautiful Art Deco facade of the **Old Toronto Stock Exchange** *(234 Bay St.)*, which has been cleverly preserved and blends well with the surrounding skyscrapers. Its mural on the theme of "work" is especially interesting.

Continue a little further north along Bay Street.

Occupying the northeast corner and extending along King is the **Bank of Nova Scotia** ★ *(44 King St. W.)*, built between 1949 and 1951 using Art Deco plans that had been shelved before the war. Heading north up Bay, you will come to the unassuming Neo-Georgian **National Club Building** *(303 Bay St.)*. The club was founded in 1874 to promote the Canada First movement, which challenged the notion of a union with the United States. On the west side of Bay is the former Trust and Guarantee Co. Ltd, now the **Bank of Montreal** *(302 Bay St.)*. A few steps farther north is the **Canada Permanent Building** ★★ *(320 Bay St.)*. The splendour of the vaulted entrance and coffered ceiling seem to flout the hard times that were being ushered in in 1929, when the building was going up. The lobby is a triumph of Art Deco styling; don't miss the bronze elevator doors portraying figures from antiquity.

North of Adelaide, on the left, is the **Northern Ontario Building** *(330 Bay St.)*, a classic 1920s skyscraper. The **Atlas Building** ★ *(350 Bay St.)* is next up the block. Its small lobby is decked out in lovely brass work.

Retrace your steps and continue along King Street West.

Exploring

Turn left on Adelaide Street. Cross the back courtyard of the reddish trapezoid known as the **Scotia Plaza ★** *(30 King St. W.)* and walk through the lobby back to King Street. The facade of the Bank of Nova Scotia (see above) is visible inside this more recent addition, which fits into the surroundings harmoniously.

You will come to the **Canadian Imperial Bank of Commerce ★★** *(25 King St. W.)*, built between 1929 and 1931. With its 34 storeys, it was once the tallest building in the British Empire. Today, this handsome Romanesque Revival–style tower meshes well with its modern backdrop, Commerce Court. Step into the main hall to admire its stunning coffered ceiling, gilded moulding and wrought-iron details.

Nearby is the grand former head office of the **Royal Bank** *(2 King St. E.)*, now a retail store. Designed by Montréal architects Ross and Macdonald, it features classic Greek styling. Across King Street stands the **Canadian Pacific Building** *(1 King St. E.)*. Continuing down Yonge, you'll come to the **Trader's Bank** *(61-67 Yonge St.)*. With its 15 storeys, it was Toronto's first real skyscraper when it was built in 1905. Ironically, its design sought to reduce the appearance of height in the building. The **Bank of British North America** building *(49 Yonge St.)* stands at the corner of Yonge and Wellington.

Go south on Yonge Street, cross Yonge at Wellington Street and continue west along the latter.

On the south side, at number 15, you'll find the oldest building on this tour. Originally the Commercial Bank of Midland District, then the Merchant's Bank, it is now simply known as **Number 15**, or, depending whom you talk to, Marché Mövenpick (see p 202Greek Revival in style, it was designed in 1845 by the same architect as St. Lawrence Hall (see p 113).

Turn left on Bay Street and walk to Front Street.

The Design Exchange *($8; exhibition hall: Mon-Fri 10am to 6pm, Sat and Sun noon to 5pm; 234 Bay St., ☎216-2160 for information)*, known locally as the DX, houses an exhibition hall, for which admission is charged, and the **Design Effectiveness Centre** *(free, irregular opening hours)*. Exhibits of international and national designers are presented in the restored former Toronto Stock Exchange. Besides the latest in fashion, graphic design and ergonomics, the DX also boasts the original historic trading floor and spectacular murals and friezes.

Head back down Bay to Wellington for the next stop on the tour, the lavish and imposing **Royal Bank Plaza ★★** *(200 Bay St.)*. The gold-enriched mirrored exterior is like a breath of fresh air in the midst of the sober white-collar demeanour of Toronto's financial district, especially at twilight; the gold actually acts as an insulator, keeping the warmth in in the winter and the heat out in the summer. Two triangular towers are linked by a clear glass atrium abounding in lush tropical greenery, below which extends an underground shopping complex.

Make your way towards Front Street and Union Station.

Union Station ★ ★ *(65-75 Front St. W.)* dominates Front Street from Bay Street to York Street. It ranks first among Canadian railway stations for its size and magnificent appearance. It was built in the spirit of the great American railway terminals, with columns and coffered ceilings inspired by the basilicas of ancient Rome. Work on the station began in 1915 but was completed only in 1927. This was one of the masterpieces of Montréal architects Ross and Macdonald. Its facade on Front Street stretches more than 250 m, obscuring the port and Lake Ontario in the background.

The **Royal York Hotel** ★ *(100 Front St. W.)* is a worthy introduction to downtown Toronto for anyone arriving by train at Union Station. Its message to new arrivals is clear: the Queen City is indeed a major metropolis that will play second fiddle to none. This hotel, the biggest in the former Canadian Pacific chain (now owned by Fairmont Hotels and Resorts), has more than 1,500 rooms on 25 floors. Like the station, it was designed by Montréal architects Ross and Macdonald. Here, the château style of the railway hotels is combined with Lombard and Venetian elements.

Exploring

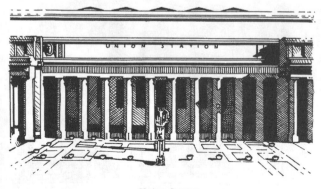

Union Station

Heading south along York Street, you will reach the Air Canada Centre (see p 90, 242). Officially opened in 1999, it now houses the city's hockey team, the Toronto Maple Leafs.

Retrace your steps.

From the Royal York Hotel at the corner of York and Front streets, continue east along Front Street. At the corner of Front and Bay rises the Royal Bank Plaza (see above). Further along, the **Canada Trust Tower** is on the left and the **Canada Customs Building** on the right, at the southwest corner of Front and Bay.

Enter **BCE Place ★ ★** by the courtyard located east of the Canada Trust Tower. BCE Place stretches from Bay Street to Yonge Street and is made up of twin towers linked by a magnificent five-storey glass atrium

supported by an enormous structure of white metal ribs. This bright and airy space is a delightful place to rest for a few moments or grab a bite from the ground-floor fast-food counters. For something unique, head instead to the **Marché Mövenpick** (see p 202), a happy blend of restaurant and market where diners move from stall to stall, choosing the dishes that seem most appealing. The Canadian Chamber of Commerce building, built in 1845, has been well preserved and blends harmoniously into its modern backdrop.

BCE Place also encloses the entrance to the famous **Hockey Hall of Fame ★** *($12; Mon-Fri 10am to 5pm, Sat 9:30am to 6pm, Sun 10:30am to 5pm; 30 Yonge St., ☎360-7765, www. hhof.com)*, a veritable paradise for hockey fans. All sorts of items from the beginnings of

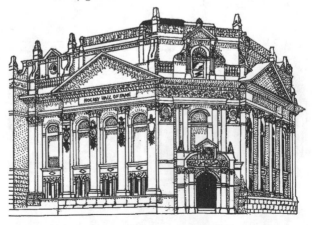

Hockey Hall of Fame

this sport up to the present are on display. The layout includes 17 zones which cover the size of three NHL playing surfaces. Do not miss the WorldCom Great Hall, at the centre of which is the original Stanley Cup, North America's oldest professional sports trophy, donated by Lord Stanley of Preston in 1893. More than 300 plaques pay homage to the various players who have made their mark in professional ice hockey. Once inside the museum you'll see a reconstitution of the Montréal Canadiens' dressing room as well as some of hockey's most exciting moments on video screens. Other exhibits present the evolution of hockey equipment through the decades, with goaltender's masks, hockey sticks, skates and sweaters bequeathed by the greats of the game.

Gooderham Building

Exit BCE Place onto Yonge Street.

At the corner of Yonge and Front Streets is the old building of the **Bank of Montreal ★★**. The Hockey Hall of Fame is actually located in this building, though the only entrance is through BCE Place. Built in 1886 by architects Darling and Curry, the Bank of Montreal building is one of the oldest 19th century structures still standing in Toronto. Designed during a prosperous and optimistic period, its architecture conveys a sense of power and invulnerability that was typical of the era, with imposing masonry, splendid porticoes and gigantic windows. Until the construction of a new building in 1982, this was the Bank of Montreal's headquarters in Toronto. At the southeast corner of Yonge and Front streets is the **Hummingbird Centre**, formerly known as the **O'Keefe Centre**. With 3,200 seats, it is one of Toronto's most important theatre, ballet and opera centres. One block east, the **St. Lawrence Centre** also serves as a site for many concerts and plays each year. Despite its imposing facade, it has a very intimate interior.

The mural of the Gooderham Building to the east is the starting point of the walking tour of the Old Town of York. It is the work of Alberta-born Derek Besant who created it in 1980, simply naming it *Flatiron Mural*.

Exploring

Tour D:
Old Town of York

It was in the rectangular area formed by George, Berkley, Adelaide and Front streets that Commander John Graves Simcoe of the British army founded the town of York, better known today as Toronto, in 1793. This area near Lake Ontario was for many years the business centre of the growing city. At the end of the 19th century, economic activity slowly moved toward what is now known as the financial district (see p 100), leaving behind a partially deserted area. Like Harbourfront (see p 88), the St. Lawrence district has undergone major renovations over the last couple of decades, financed by the federal, provincial and municipal governments. Today a cheerful mixture of 19th- and 20th-century architecture characterizes an area where the city's various socioeconomic groups cross paths.

Beyond Berczy Park is the amusing *trompe l'oeil* fresco painted on the back of the **Gooderham Building** ★ *(49 Wellington St.).* This mural, created by Derek Besant in 1980, has become a well-

● ATTRACTIONS

1. Gooderham Building
2. Beardmore Building
3. St. Lawrence Market
4. Farmer's Market
5. St. Lawrence Neighbourhood Condominiums
6. Lorraine Kimsa Theatre for Young People
7. Canadian Opera Company
8. Distillery District
9. Enoch Turner Schoolhouse
10. Little Trinity Church
11. Bank of Upper Canada
12. Toronto's First Post Office
13. St. Lawrence Hall
14. St. James Park
15. St. James Cathedral
16. Argus Corporation
17. King Edward Hotel
18. Toronto Sculpture Garden
19. Market Square

○ ACCOMMODATIONS

1. Ambassador Inn Downtown Toronto
2. Cawthra Square Bed & Breakfast
3. Hostelling International
4. Novotel
5. Quality Hotel Downtown
6. Royal Meridian King Edward (R)

(R) Property with restaurant (see description)

● RESTAURANTS

1. Biaggio Ristorante
2. Bombay Palace
3. Café du Marché
4. C'est What
5. Hiro Sushi
6. Le Papillon
7. The Old Spaghetti Factory
8. Young Thailand

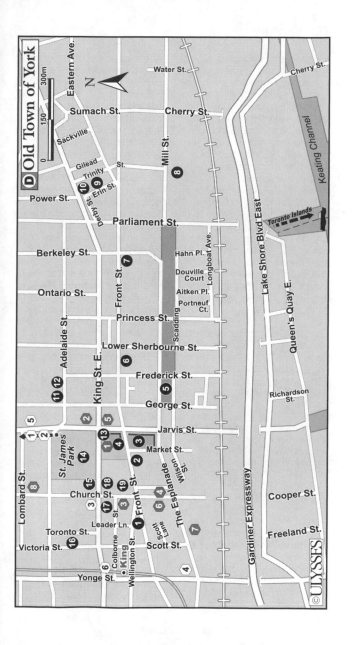

Eastern Ave.

Water St.

Cherry St.

Sumach St.

Cherry St.

Sackville

Mill St.

Gilead St.

Trinity

Erin St.

⑩

⑨

Power St.

Derby St.

Parliament St.

Toronto Islands

Berkeley St.

Hahn Pl.

Front St. ⑦

Douville Court

Longboat Ave.

Ontario St.

Aitken Pl.

Portneuf Ct.

Princess St.

Scadding

Lower Sherbourne St.

King St. E.

⑥

Frederick St.

Adelaide St.

⑤

Lake Shore Blvd East

Queen's Quay E.

⑪ ⑫

George St.

Richardson St.

① ⑤

② ⑤

Jarvis St.

St. James Park

① ④

③

② ⑬

Market St.

⑭

②

Wilson St.

⑮ ⑱

⑲

④

Gardiner Expressway

Cooper St.

Church St.

③

⑰

③

⑥

⑧

Lombard St.

Leader Ln.

① Front St.

Scott Lane

The Esplanade

⑦

Toronto St.

⑯

Scott St.

Freeland St.

Victoria St.

Colborne St.

① Front St.

④

⑥

King

Wellington St.

Scott St.

Yonge St.

0 150 300m

N

© ULYSSES

known sight in Toronto. Contrary to popular belief, it does not portray the windows of the Gooderham Building but rather the facade of the Perkins Building, located across the street at 41-43 Front Street East. The Gooderham is often called the Flatiron Building because of its triangular structure, recalling the shape of its famous New York namesake, which it predates by several years. The building's shape was dictated by the fact that it sits on a triangular lot at the corner of Wellington Street, which follows the grid pattern established by the British during the founding of York, and Front Street, which runs parallel to the north shore of Lake Ontario.

Built for George Gooderham, a businessman who made his fortune in distilleries, this building stands out for its mural and for its castle-like architecture. It still houses many offices.

Look back now from where you came and contemplate the interesting vista formed by the Flatiron Building framed by the office towers of the financial district and the CN Tower.

Across Front Street, many of the gleaming facades that now harbour shops and cafés are those of one-time warehouses. The **Beardmore Building** *(35-39 Front St. E.)* is one of the more noteworthy of a series of buildings that once formed the heart of the warehouse district in the middle of the 19th century.

At the corner of Jarvis Street is the **St. Lawrence Market** ★★ *(91 Front St. E.)*. Built in 1844, it housed the city hall until 1904, the year Henry Bowyer Lane converted it into a public market. Expanded in 1978, St. Lawrence Market is famed today for the freshness of its fruits and vegetables, fish, meats, sausages and cheeses. Actually, this giant red-brick building completely envelops the former city hall, which is still perceptible in the facade. The best time to go is on Saturday, when the fish is freshest and area farmers arrive at 5am to sell their products across the street at the **Farmer's Market**. The **Market Gallery** on the second floor presents historical and contemporary exhibits on the ever-changing face of Toronto, with photographs, maps and paintings. The collection is part of the City of Toronto archives.

These days, the St. Lawrence neighbourhood is seen as a trendy area to live in. Named after a saint, like many of the working-class neighbourhoods in the area, St. Lawrence was mainly an Irish Protestant area of factories, warehouses, and simple housing. Until recently, these buildings stood neglected, but many have recently been transformed into upscale condominiums and office space. One such project, aptly named the **St. Lawrence Neighbourhood Condominiums** *(along The Esplanade, south of the market)* and completed in 1982, has brought people back

Hogtown

What may be Toronto's most typical Victorian factory stands at the corner of Frederick and Front streets. Built in 1867, the red-brick building with its yellow-brick window arches originally housed the William Davies & Co. pork packing plant, and its operations are what lent Toronto one of its early nicknames, "Hogtown."

to this area. The place looks modern, and its many low-rise buildings blend harmoniously into the current urban landscape.

Walk back up to Front Street East on George Street or Frederick Street.

Toronto's **Lorraine Kimsa Theatre for Young People** *(165 Front St. E.)* is located a few steps to the east. What once provided shelter for the horses of the Toronto Street Railway Co. now sets the stage for excellent theatre productions for young people (see p 239).

The **Canadian Opera Company** *(227 Front St. E.)*, for its part, is located in an old factory built in

1888, which originally housed the Consumers' Gas Company. The lovely brickwork and stepped gables are an excellent example of how magnificent even a factory could be in the Victorian era. The motivation behind this grandeur is the same as that which prompted the opulence of the Old Bank of Commerce and the meticulousness of Toronto-Dominion Centre, both on King: the need to impress the customer. The factory has since been transformed into a rehearsal hall.

Continue along Front Street, turn right on Parliament, then left on Mill Street and walk one block to the Gooderham & Worts Distillery.

The **Distillery District** ★ ★ ★ *(55 Mill St., www.thedistillery district.com)* is a real gem of the industrial era and hasn't lost any of its charm, except perhaps in what lies behind its pretty red-brick exteriors. Set between the Gardener Expressway and the newer real estate developments around St. Lawrence Market, the former **Gooderham & Worts Distillery** has figured in many a movie shoot and is one of the best-preserved collections of Victorian-style industrial buildings in North America.

Upon his arrival in Canada in 1831, James Worts built a grain mill before being joined by his brother-in-law William Gooderham, who invested $3,000 in the growing distillery business; the Gooderham & Worts Dis-

Exploring

tillery produced its first whisky in 1837. In 1859, the construction of the distillery in its present location was the largest industrial project of its time. By 1871, the distillery produced more than half the alcohol in Ontario. Shaken by the First World War, prohibition and the transfer of production of certain products, notably the well-known Canadian Club, the distillery closed its doors in 1990, after 153 years of operation. In 2001, the buildings were purchased by Cityscape Holdings Inc., which came up with an ambitious plan to combine art galleries, artists' studios, theatre companies and restaurants in one location, all the while taking care to preserve the integrity of the architecture.

The new owners pulled off a successful restoration that has made a world of difference to the mood and ambiance of the neighbourhood. Unlike similar projects meant to attract tourists, this one is equally enticing to Torontonians. This is a pleasant place to go out for a meal, or just to wander about the pedestrian zone that surrounds it.

Walk up Trinity Street towards King Street.

Pretty little Trinity Street was once home to many poor Irish Protestant workers, who up until 1848 had to pay to send their children to St. James's school, something that many of them could not afford to do. In 1848, the Ontario government authorized free schooling, and many children that had simply gone without finally had access to free education. In Toronto, however, the city council found the notion too radical. Enoch Turner, a brewer and employer of many of the local residents, thus had Trinity Street School built in 1848 at his own expense. The charming soft yellow- and red-brick edifice was eventually transformed into a Sunday school for Trinity Church (see below) after being absorbed by the city in 1851, which finally conceded and accepted to offer free education. The **Enoch Turner Schoolhouse** ★ ★ *(donations appreciated; Mon-Sat by appointment; 106 Trinity St., ☎863-0010)* is the oldest standing school building in Toronto, and the first free school in the city. It currently houses a small exhibit.

Just up the street, **Little Trinity Church** ★ *(425 King St. E.)* was built for members of the local Anglican community, who could not afford to rent pews at St. James. The church, with its enchanting yet simple Tudor Gothic styling, occupies this corner almost magically.

As you make your way back west along King Street East, you'll pass yet more factories and warehouses that have been rehabilitated as restaurants, cafés and office buildings.

Did you know that Mr. Christie's cookies began in Toronto? Now one of the world's most renowned cookie manufacturers and owned by Nabisco brands, Mr. Christie's first bakery was here on King Street East. The horses that delivered the cookies were stabled at 95 Berkeley Street, just up from King, and the cookies were made farther along King at number 200. The bakery is no more, though; the building now houses the St. James campus of George Brown College.

Up on Adelaide Street stands the town of York's first bank, the **Bank of Upper Canada** *(252 Adelaide St. E.)*. At the time of its completion in 1827 the limestone structure dominated the unpaved streets of "Muddy York," as the town was known; the building certainly must have instilled hope and confidence in the residents of the fledgling city. The bank unfortunately failed in 1866, at which point the Christian Brothers moved in and started a Roman Catholic boys' school, the De La Salle Institute, which lasted until 1916.

At number 260 is **Toronto's First Post Office** ★ *(free admission; Mon-Fri 9am to 4pm, Sat and Sun 10am to 4pm; 260 Adelaide St. E., ☎865-1833)*. This old post office has been designated a national historic site. It was opened in 1843 during the British postal period, which lasted until 1851, when Canada Post came into existence. The place is still a working post office, with a clerk in period dress; besides the regular postal services, you can send a letter sealed with authentic beribboned hot wax.

Back down on King Street, the row of buildings at numbers 167 to 185, though constructed at different times, is the oldest "line" of buildings in Toronto. The yellow brick that you see on the facade of number 150 is common throughout Toronto. Fire ordonnances required the use of brick, and the "white" variety, as it was called at the time, was not only inexpensive because of the nearby clay pits, but was also thought to resemble stone, which was much more costly.

Kitty-corner stands impressive **St. Lawrence Hall** ★ *(157 King St. E.)*, which was Toronto's community centre in the latter half of the 19th century. This Victorian structure was designed for concerts and balls. Among the celebrities who performed here were Jenny Lind, Andelina Patti, Tom Thumb and P.T. Barnum. For several years, St. Lawrence Hall was also home to the National Ballet of Canada. The offices of **Heritage Toronto** *(☎338-3886)* can be found on the third floor of this building. The agency offers heritage and history themed guided tours.

Lovely **St. James Park**, a 19th century garden with a fountain and seasonal flower beds, lies a few steps to the west. While seated on one of its many benches, you can

Exploring

St. James Cathedral

contemplate **St. James Cathedral ★ ★**, Toronto's first Anglican cathedral, at the corner of Church and King streets. Built in 1819 with help from a government loan and with the alms of the faithful, it was destroyed in the 1849 fire that levelled part of the city. The St. James Cathedral you see today was built on the ruins of its predecessor, according to a design by architect Frederich Cumberland, who wanted to invoke religious superiority. It has the highest steeple in all of Canada and the second-highest in North America, after St. Patrick's Cathedral in New York. The yellow brick facade accentuates the gothic shapes of the cathedral, giving it a rather sober character. The interior is far more elaborate. The marble choir stall, where Bishop Strachan is interred, is truly magnificent.

Continue west along King Street, turning right at Toronto Street.

Toronto Street was one of the city's most beautiful streets in the 19th century. Nowadays, some buildings still provide a glimpse of the charm and elegance this street once radiated. Note the **Argus Corporation Building** *(10 Toronto St.)*, with its portico of four symmetrical Ionic columns and its neoclassical architecture resembling a Greek temple. This building served as the Toronto post office, a customs office and a branch of the Bank of Canada before being transformed into offices.

Retrace your steps back to King Street.

The splendid **King Edward Hotel ★★** *(37 King St. E.)* (see p 182), between Church Street and Leader Lane, was designed in 1903 by E.J. Lennox, architect of the Old City Hall (see p 120), Massey Hall (see p 118) and Casa Loma (see p 151). With its Edwardian style, its wonderful mock marble columns on the ground floor and its magnificent dining rooms, the King Edward was one of Toronto's most luxurious hotels for nearly 60 years, until, with the decline of the surrounding area, it fell into disrepair. Today, with the revitalization of the neighbourhood, the King Edward is once again drawing a fashionable clientele with its superb rooms and its two wonderful restaurants.

Return now toward St. James Cathedral, in front of which extends the **Toronto Sculpture Garden**. Walk through the garden and back to Front Street, admiring the various sculptures along the way. Once back on Front, you'll find yourself at **Market Square ★** *(80 Front St. E.)*, right next to the city's first market. Of more recent construction, it was designed to blend in with the historic surroundings. Market Square houses numerous shops and luxury apartments.

Tour E: Queen Street West

This tour starts at the corner of Yonge and Queen streets, where Queen West begins. **The Bay** department store occupies the southwest corner and the whole south side of the street all the way to Bay Street. The building originally housed the Simpson's department store, until hard economic times forced its closure and most Simpson's stores became Bays. Simpson's was the largest retail establishment in Canada in 1907, when the nine-storey addition along Queen was added. The original six-storey building (1895) at Yonge and Queen features some lovely terra cotta decorations. An Art Deco addition in 1928 led to glamorous renovations throughout the store, a fine

Exploring

example being the entrance at Richmond and Yonge.

Head north on Yonge Street. On the left is the exterior of the six-storey shopping mecca, the Eaton Centre; on the right you'll soon come upon two more of To-ronto's majestic theatres, the Elgin and Winter Garden and the Canon.

Before visiting the Elgin and Winter Garden, take a look at the **Bank of Montreal** *(173 Yonge St.)* on the corner. This stylish Edwardian building dates from 1909.

The **Elgin and Winter Garden Theatres ★★** *(1hr tours $7; Thu 5pm, Sat 11am; 189 Yonge St., ☎314-2871)* together form the last operating double-decker theatre complex in the world. Opened in 1914, they began as vaudeville theatres; the Elgin downstairs was opu-lence galore, while the Winter Garden upstairs was one of the first "atmospheric theatres," with trellised walls and columns disguised as tree trunks sup-porting a ceiling of real leaves. After a stint as a movie house, these treasures were restored by the Ontario Heritage Centre and now once again serve as venues for live stage perfor-mances.

Once the biggest vaudeville house in the British Empire, the **Canon Theatre ★**, formerly

● ATTRACTIONS

1. The Bay
2. Bank of Montreal
3. Elgin and Wintergarden Theatres
4. Canon Theatre
5. Massey Hall
6. St. Michael's Cathedral
7. Metropolitan United Church
8. Mackenzie House
9. Eaton Centre
10. Church of the Holy Trinity
11. Old City Hall
12. New City Hall
13. Nathan Phillips Square
14. Osgoode Hall
15. Campbell House
16. CityTV and MuchMusic
17. Black Bull Tavern

○ ACCOMMODATIONS

1. Bond Place Hotel
2. Cambridge Suites Hotel
3. Sheraton Centre Toronto
4. St. Lawrence Residences
5. Toronto Marriott Eaton Centre

● RESTAURANTS

1. Addis Ababa
2. Avalon
3. Babur
4. Barberian's
5. Everest Cafe and Bar
6. Fez Batik
7. Hard Rock Cafe
8. Korean Grill House
9. Little India
10. Mildred Pierce Restaurant
11. Monsoon
12. Peter Pan
13. Queen Mother Cafe
14. Rivoli
15. Salad King
16. Sushi Bistro on Queen
17. Sushiman Japanese Restaurant
18. The Fifth
19. Tiger Lily's Noodle House

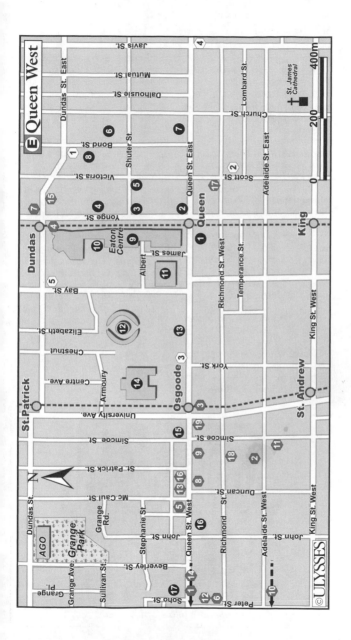

E Queen West

Dundas St. East
Jarvis St.
Mutual St.
Dalhousie St.
Bond St.
Shuter St.
Victoria St.
Yonge St.
Lombard St.
Church St.
Adelaide St. East
Scott St.
Queen St. East
Queen
King

Dundas
Eaton Centre
Albert
James St.
Bay St.
Elizabeth St.
Chestnut
Centre Ave.
Armoury
University Ave.
Osgoode
York St.
Richmond St. West
Temperance St.
King St. West
St. Andrew

St Patrick
Dundas St.
AGO
Grange Park
Grange Ave.
Sullivan St.
Grange Pl.
Beverley St.
Stephanie St.
Grange Rd.
John St.
McCaul St.
St. Patrick St.
Simcoe St.
Duncan St.
Richmond St. West
Adelaide St. West
King St. West
John St.
Queen St. West
Simcoe St.
Soho St.
Peter St.

St. James Cathedral

N

0   200   400m

© ULYSSES

known as the Pantages
(263 Yonge St., ☎364-4100),
had many reincarnations as a
picture palace and then a six-
theatre movie house. In 1988-
89, it was restored to its original
splendour.

*Backtrack down Yonge Street,
turn left at Shuter Street and
walk two blocks to Massey Hall.*

Massey Hall *(178 Victoria St., at
Shuter St., ☎593-4822 or 872-
4255)*, originally Massey Music
Hall, is renowned for its exceptional acoustics. Though the
Toronto Symphony Orchestra
has moved out (see p 240),
Massey Hall is still an impressive
venue for musical acts.

*Two of Toronto's great churches
lie one block to the east.*

Although there were relatively
few Catholics in Toronto in the
19th century, they nevertheless
had **St. Michael's Catholic**
Cathedral *(200 Church St.)* built
between 1845 and 1867. This
building lacks the presence of
the Anglican cathedral or the
nearby United church, and the
sometimes overbearing architecture of Victorian Catholic
churches is evident in the multi-
ple openings of the spire, the
massive dormers and the
polychrome interior. The faux
starred vault was completed in
1870. To the south, facing
Queen Street, the **Metropoli-**
tan United Church ★ (1870) is
seen as a challenge to both the
St. James Anglican (see p 114)
and Roman Catholic cathedrals
and thus represents the commercial and social power of
Toronto's Methodist community (the Methodists, along with
the Congregationalists and two-
thirds of the Presbyterians
formed the United Church in
1925). Due to its grand proportions and location in the
middle of a block-square park, it
dominates the area.

Elgin and Winter Garden Theatres

Continue up Bond Street towards Dundas, stopping in at Mackenzie House along the way.

By 1837, fruitless attempts at establishing responsible government and growing impatience with England had left the Canadian colony in crisis. The colonial emancipation movement was led by Louis-Joseph Papineau in Lower-Canada (Quebec) and by William Lyon Mackenzie in Upper Canada (Ontario). Mackenzie had arrived in Toronto from Scotland in 1820. Before becoming the city's first mayor, he ran a newspaper called *The Colonial Advocate*, which so enraged the Family Compact (see p 20), that his print shop was ransacked and his type dumped in Lake Ontario. After losing the mayorship in 1836, he led an abortive rebellion against the oligarchy, then fled to the United States. **Mackenzie House ★** *($3.50; May to Dec Tue-Sun noon to 4pm, Jan to Apr Sat and Sun noon to 5pm; 82 Bond St., ☎392-6915),* a modest Georgian-style residence built in 1857, was offered to him by a group of followers upon his return in 1859. Heritage Toronto has since restored the house and now maintains a museum here. Guides in period dress re-enact the daily life of a middle-class Toronto household in the 1860s. The odd placement of the house is due to the fact that it was once part of a row of identical residences. It is furnished with antique furniture and also features a reconstruction of Mackenzie's

print shop, complete with the offending printing press. Mackenzie's grandson was William Lyon Mackenzie King, Canada's longest-serving Prime Minister.

Walk along Dundas to Yonge Street and turn left.

Even if you have no desire to go shopping, at least poke your head into the **Eaton Centre ★★**, which runs along Yonge Street between Queen and Dundas. And if you do need something, by all means linger in this glass-roofed arcade, which even a few sparrows consider more pleasant than outside. Here, so-called streets have been stacked five-storeys high and lined with pristine benches and trees. Look up and you will see Michael Snow's exquisite flock of fibreglass Canada geese, called *Step Flight,* suspended over the Galleria. Framed by two 30-storey skyscrapers and two subway stations (Dundas and Queen stations) and occupying 500,000m^2, the Eaton Centre contains more than 320 stores and restaurants, 2 parking garages and a 17-theatre cinema complex. It is also home to the **Thomson Gallery** *(9th floor of The Bay tower at the Eaton Centre),* which exhibits the private collection of the exceedingly wealthy owner of The Bay and the *Globe and Mail.*

Once you've had your fill of the shops, exit the Eaton Centre via Trinity Square, at the northwest corner of the mall.

Exploring

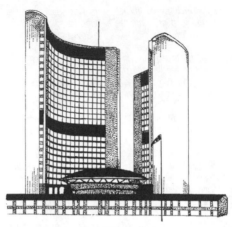

New City Hall

This lovely space was almost never created. The **Church of the Holy Trinity** ★★ (1847), the **Rectory** (1861) and the **Scadding House** (1857) are some of Toronto's oldest landmarks, and the original plans for the Eaton Centre called for their demolition. Fortunately, enough people objected and the huge mall was built around the grouping. Holy Trinity was a gift from an anonymous woman in England who stipulated that free seating be guaranteed in the church. Its excellent acoustics helped create the beautiful music on the Cowboy Junkies album *The Trinity Session*. The rectory and the house of Rev. Henry Scadding, the first rector of Holy Trinity, complete the vista. The latter was moved to make way for the Eaton department store.

Head down James Street towards the back of **Old City Hall** ★★ *(60 Queen St. W.)*, designed by E. J. Lennox in 1889. As you make your way around the building towards the front on Queen Street, look up at the eaves below which the architect carved the letters "E J LENNOX ARCHITECT" to ensure that his name would be remembered. Lennox won a contest to design the building but the city councillors denied his request to place his name on a cornerstone; in retaliation, he had disfigured versions of their faces carved above the front steps so that they would be confronted with their gargoyle-like selves every day! By the time all of these personal touches were revealed, it was too late to do anything about them.

The vast sandstone edifice was built on a square plan around a central square and is probably the most exacting example of the Romanesque style in Canada. The style was developed in the 1870s and 1880s in the United States by architect Henry Hobson Richardson and was based on French Romanesque. It defined itself by heavy, roughly cut stone walls in several colours, round arches and round towers. The numerous vaulted openings are framed by small engaged columns, lending a medieval and picturesque air to buildings of this style. Its elegant clock tower rises above the centre of Bay Street, the hub of high finance in Toronto.

In 1965, the municipal administration of Toronto moved out of its Victorian "old" city hall and into **New City Hall ★★** *(100 Queen St. W.)*, a modernist masterpiece that quickly gained a certain notoriety and is as symbolic of Toronto as the CN Tower. A contest was held to choose an architect and the winner was Finn Viljo Revell, a master of Scandinavian postwar rationalist thinking. Its two curved towers of unequal

length are like two hands protecting the saucer-shaped structure which houses the Council Room.

Stretching out in front of New City Hall is **Nathan Phillips Square ★**, a vast public space named after the mayor of Toronto who blessed Toronto with many new installations at the beginning of the 1960s. A large pool of water straddled by three arches is transformed into a skating rink in the winter. Nearby stands "The Archer," a sculpture by Henry Moore, and the Peace Garden, designed in 1984 by the Urban Design Group. This small green space serves as a frame for the Eternal Peace Flame, which flickers in a half-destroyed shack that reminds us of the effects of war and symbolizes the population's desire for peace.

Cast-iron gates enclose **Osgoode Hall ★★** *(free admission; Mon-Fri 9am to 6pm; 130 Queen St. W., 947-3300)* and its

Exploring

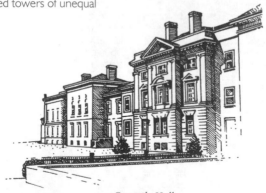

Osgoode Hall

shaded garden, reminiscent of a royal palace of the British Empire, though it was originally built to house the Law Society of Upper Canada and the provincial law courts. Built in stages from 1829 to 1844 by different architects, its facade nevertheless forms a lovely ensemble. Its layout is in the Palladian style, though the decorative elements are those of an Italian Renaissance palace, as was the fashion with London high society at the time. The neoclassical vestibule and the magnificent law library can be visited by checking at the ticket office at the entrance.

Not far from Osgoode Hall, **Campbell House** ★ *(160 Queen St. W.)* was the private club of a select group of Ontario lawyers, the Advocates Society. The house was built in 1822 for Judge William Campbell and is one of the oldest in Toronto. Its brick facade combines traditional Georgian elements with Adamesque fantasy, like the oval bull's-eye window of the pediment, which lightens the structure. The inside, open to visitors, is decorated with lovely woodworking and mantlepieces with delicate trimming typical of the art of the Adam brothers, the Scottish pair who swept Great Britain at the end of the 18th century with their antiquated refinement.

Make your way along Queen Street West, lined with trendy shops, cafés and bars for most of its length. It is also the home

of **CityTV** and **Much Music** *(299 Queen St. W.)*, "the nation's music station". The former Wesley Building was built for a publishing company in 1913-15; note the grotesque readers and scribes that adorn its facade. Renovated in 1986 to accommodate Much Music, the Canadian counterpart to MTV, the building is now a beehive of activity, with "v-jays" often animating their shows right on the sidewalk and a televised fashion-show-cum-dance-party known as the "Electric Circus" every Friday night. Another intriguing feature is the Speakers' Corner video booth, where you can request a video and applaud or criticize whatever cause you like, and maybe even end up on national television.

Stroll along **Queen Street West** ★ ★ and browse through the hip and avant-garde boutiques and bookstores. Queen Street Village, as it is often called, is touted as an "alternative shopping district," and while it has its share of the peculiar and underground, the last few years have seen the opening of several very mainstream clothing stores and cafés. There is something here for both the *artiste* and the conformist in you. Not to mention, when it comes to dining out, there are still as many unpretentious, simple eateries as there are places to see and be seen. There are even a few interesting architectural highlights, as most of these shops and restaurants occupy late-19th-century buildings where Victorian details survive on the upper floors.

The corner of Soho and Queen is often packed with motorcycles, the riders of which congregate at the **Black Bull Tavern** *(298 Queen St. W., 593-2766).* This tavern began as an inn way back in 1833. Today, it boasts one of the most popular terraces in the city and is a great place to have a beer. Number 371-373, now the Peter Pan Restaurant (see p 208), was built in 1890 and originally housed a grocery store. It boasts some lovely stained glass. Numbers 342 to 354 are collectively known as the Noble Block (1888), after Mrs. Emma Noble, a widow who once owned the property.

Queen Street West, west of Spadina, has yet to take on the slick "Queen Street Village" look that characterizes the street for a couple of blocks to the east. The antique and junk shops, used record stores, and independent, family-run businesses still hold sway over the stretch between Spadina and Bathurst, but the territory is slowly being encroached upon by trendy bistros and funky nightclubs. This is certainly not a bad thing, but take this opportunity to stroll the sidewalks of Queen West and experience them before they are transformed forever.

Tour F: Chinatown and Kensington

Toronto has no fewer than seven recognized Chinatowns. The most vibrant and typical of these is explored in this walking tour. While the neighbourhood is presently centred around Spadina and Dundas, it actually started a few blocks east of there, near where New City Hall now stands. The construction of the municipal headquarters and the laying of Nathan Philips Square obliterated most traces of this original Chinatown; a few vestiges do remain, however, making this a good place to begin the tour. If you are setting out to visit this area on a Sunday, get an early start, for Sunday is the day when most Chinese families head out for brunch, though they call it dim sum, and there are no scrambled eggs or baked beans to wade through!

The area just south of the new and old city halls was at one time a staging area for new immigrants to Toronto. Most of the new arrivals from China settled and established their businesses close by, thus founding the city's first Chinatown. At the northwest corner of Nathan Philips Square, if you look hard enough, you can find a

Exploring

small plaque commemorating the first Chinese hand-laundry in Toronto. Walking up Centre Street to Dundas Street, you'll notice that a few Chinese businesses remain.

Textile Museum of Canada ★ *($8; Tue-Fri 11am to 5pm, Wed until 8pm, Sat and Sun noon to 5pm; 55 Centre Ave., ☎599-5321)*, with 11 permanent exhibits, tells you everything you ever wanted to know about textiles from around the world. Costumes, ceremonial cloths, tapestries, fascinating African story-telling cloth and rich embroideries are all on display. Devoted to non-western cultures, most of the exhibits are rather extraordinary.

Walk west along Dundas Street, across University Avenue towards McCaul Street.

St. Patrick's Chinese Catholic Church *(141 McCaul St.)* stands at the corner of McCaul and Dundas streets. The church originally served a mostly Irish congregation, but the parish changed considerably as Chinatown gradually moved westward. The original wooden chapel that stood on this site in the 1860s was one of the first Roman Catholic churches in Toronto. The Romanesque Revival building standing before you today was erected in 1905.

The Art Gallery of Ontario is on the south side of Dundas, just west of McCaul Street.

● ATTRACTIONS

1.	Textile Museum of Canada	5.	Ontario College of Art
2.	St. Patrick's Chinese Catholic Church	6.	Village by the Grange
		7.	Kensington Market
3.	Art Gallery of Ontario	8.	Kiever Synagogue
4.	The Grange		

○ ACCOMMODATIONS

1.	Alexandra Hotel	3.	Grange Hotel
2.	Beaconsfield	4.	Metropolitan Hotel

● RESTAURANTS

1.	Amato	15.	Margarita's Fiesta Room
2.	Bodega	16.	Pho Hung Vietnamese Restaurant
3.	Cafe La Gaffe		
4.	Canteena Azul	17.	Select Bistro
5.	Cities	18.	Squirly's
6.	Citron	19.	Swan Restaurant
7.	Dufflet Pastries	20.	Taro Grill
8.	Epicure Cafe	21.	Tequila Bookworm
9.	Gypsy Co-Op	22.	Terroni
10.	Happy Seven	23.	The Paddock
11.	Lai Wah Heen	24.	Tortilla Flats
12.	Lee Garden	25.	Vienna Home Bakery
13.	Left Bank		
14.	Lotus Garden Vietnamese Vegetarian Restaurant		

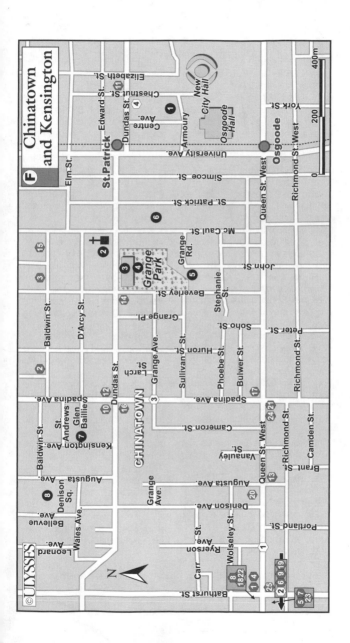

Chinatown and Kensington

F

© ULYSSES

N

Bathurst St.
Leonard Ave.
Wales Ave.
Bellevue Ave.
Denison Sq.
Augusta Ave.
St. Andrews
Glen Baillie
Kensington Ave.
Baldwin St.
Spadina Ave.
D'Arcy St.
Baldwin St.

CHINATOWN

Carr St.
Wolseley St.
Ryerson Ave.
Denison Ave.
Grange Ave.
Augusta Ave.
Vanauley St.
Cameron St.
Spadina Ave.
Bulwer St.
Phoebe St.
Sullivan St.
Huron St.
Grange Ave.
Larch St.
Dundas St.

Queen St. West
Portland St.
Brant St.
Richmond St.
Camden St.
Richmond St.
Peter St.
Soho St.
Stephanie St.
Beverley St.
Grange Pl.

Grange Park
Grange Rd.

John St.
Mc Caul St.
St. Patrick St.
Simcoe St.
Queen St. West
Richmond St. West

University Ave.
St.Patrick
Elm St.
Dundas St.
Centre Ave.
Edward St.
Chestnut St.
Elizabeth St.

New City Hall
Armoury
Osgoode Hall
Osgoode
York St.

8 18 22
11 4
25
2 6 9 19
1
5 7 23
13

0   200   400m

The Art Museum of Toronto was founded in 1900, but was without a permanent home until 1913, when The Grange (see below) was bequeathed to the museum. A new building was added in 1918, and the first exhibition of Canada's renowned Group of Seven (see p 38) was held in 1920 at what was by then known as the Art Gallery of Toronto. A significant chapter in Canada's and Toronto's cultural histories was thus written. In 1966, the museum received provincial support and was officially re-baptized the **Art Gallery of Ontario ★ ★ ★** *($12; Tue-Fri 11am to 6pm, Wed until 8:30pm, Sat and Sun 10am to 5:30pm, closed Mon; 317 Dundas St. W., ☎977-0414).* Successive renovations and additions over the years have each tried to reinvent the AGO, adding new elements and hiding old ones. The Gallery is now laid out in a collection of buildings, which were successfully united in 1989 by architects Barton Myers and Associates, and finally do justice to the splendid treasures they contain, which were donated by wealthy Ontarians over the years.

The 1989 renovations known as Stage III added close to 50% more exhibition space. The permanent collection is now installed chronologically from the 15th century to the present day. It features contemporary art, Inuit sculptures and the beautiful Tanenbaum Sculpture Atrium, where a facade of The Grange (see below) is exposed.

The Henry Moore Sculpture Centre is one of the museum's greatest treasures. Donated by the artist himself, it is the largest public collection of Moore's work in the world. The Canadian historical and contemporary collections contain major pieces by such notables as Cornelius Krieghoff, Michael Snow, Emily Carr, Jean-Paul Riopelle, Tom Thomson and the Group of Seven— Frederick Varley, Lawren Harris, Franklin Carmichael, A. Y. Jackson, Arthur Lismer, J. E. H. MacDonald and Frank H. Johnson. The museum also boasts masterpieces by Rembrandt, Van Dyck, Reynolds, Renoir, Picasso, Rodin, Degas and Matisse, to name a few.

An ambitious 500-million-dollar renovation and extension project called Transformation AGO is currently underway. It represents internationally renowned and Toronto-born architect Frank Gehry's first major project in Canada. The predominantly glass structure incorporates a facade that will allow the street and city to interact with the gallery activity within. A donation from Kenneth R. Thomson of more the 2,000 works, including many by Canadian artists, will fill some of the new space, which represents 20% of the gallery's current surface area.

At press time, plans had just been approved by Toronto's city council. Work is set to begin in spring 2005, with completion expected for spring 2008.

Adjacent to the Art Gallery of Ontario stands its original home, **The Grange** ★ *(admission with AGO; Tue-Fri 11am to 6pm, Wed until 8:30pm, Sat and Sun 10am to 5:30pm, closed Mon; 317 Dundas St. W., ☎977-0414)*. The Georgian-style residence was built from 1817 to 1818 by D'Arcy Boulton Jr., a member of Toronto's ruling elite, the much-reviled Family Compact. The city of Toronto was barely 30 years old at the time, but by 1837, the year of Mackenzie's rebellion, The Grange had become the virtual seat of political power and thus symbolized the oppressive colonial regime in Upper Canada. In 1875, Goldwin Smith, an Oxford scholar, took up residence here. Seen as a liberal intellectual in his day, his suspicion of other religions and races have since revealed him to be a bigot. He nevertheless entertained some very eminent

visitors at The Grange, including a young Winston Churchill, the Prince of Wales (later Edward VII) and Matthew Arnold. When Smith died in 1910, he willed the house to the Art Museum of Toronto, which occupied it for the next 15 years. The gallery then used it for offices until 1973 when its 1830s grandeur was restored and the whole house was opened to the public. It rear facade was integrated into the AGO's sculpture gallery in 1989. This gentleman's house, with its grand circular staircase and fascinating servant's quarters, was one of Toronto's first brick buildings.

The **Ontario College of Art** *(100 McCaul St.)* once occupied the look-alike building east of The Grange. The college's more recent addition faces McCaul Street. Its vibrant interior layout features displays on animation, design, advertising art, tapestry, glassblowing, sculpture and painting.

Exploring

The Grange, Art Gallery of Ontario

Village by the Grange (*78 St. Patrick St.*) is an apartment and shopping complex with ethnic fast-food, shops and minor art galleries. Many rave about this spot's architecture and its hidden treasures, and while there are all sorts of neat things to be seen, smelled, eaten and purchased here, the commercial level is labyrinthine and in need of freshening up, and the fastfood is bit too fast in some places. Nonetheless, it's fine for a quick break or bite to eat.

After an edifying morning of art appreciation, make your way east along Dundas Street into the heart of Chinatown for some food and shopping.

Bright colourful signs, packed sidewalks, Canto-pop piercing the air, racks of roasted ducks, the wonderful scents of fresh fruit or ginseng tea and the pungent odours of durian and fresh or dried fish; Chinatown is a feast for the senses in every way, so by all means, slow down and give yourself the time to soak up the atmosphere. Allow yourself to be drawn in by the marvellous and curious things you see in the shop windows; you won't regret it. Asian grocery stores, herb shops, tea shops and trading companies galore—not to mention the many divine little, and not so little, eateries—ensure that this tour will have something to please everyone! On Sundays, many restaurants serve dim sum (see p 123).

At the **Great China Herb Centre** (*405 Dundas St. W.*), a Chinese doctor may be able to heal what ails you with a wonderful concoction prepared with the mysterious ingredients found in the hundreds of meticulously labelled drawers and jars that line the walls. These are weighed out on an old-fashioned scale and the price is clicked off with amazing rapidity on a real abacus.

The **Tai Sun Co.** (*407 Dundas St. W.*) grocery store has a good selection of vegetables, especially mushrooms. A few doors down is the **Ten Ren Tea House** (*454 Dundas St. W.*), with green tea, black tea and oolong, plus miracle teas that promise to help you lose weight, among other things. You can also pick up a traditional clay teapot, and if you're lucky someone will be performing the ancient tea ceremony. Next door, **WY Trading Co.** (*482 Dundas St. W.*) has a wide selection of the latest Chinese records, CDs and tapes. The **All Friends Bakery** (*492 Dundas St.*) sells sweet and delicious lotus- or ginseng-filled moon cakes that are irresistible.

The wonders continue on Spadina. Note the large yellow building at the southwest corner of Dundas and Spadina; it has a rather curious story. A series of failed businesses came and went, then reports of hovering ghosts finally prompted the building's owners to call in a *feng shui* specialist. *Feng shui*, which means "wind and water,"

he Convention Centre and the other buildings of the financial district are emblems of the economic metropolis that is Toronto. -*Patrick Escudero*

The blue and green spaces of Nathan Phillips Square, with its grassy areas and water fountain, bustles with activity all year long. -*Patrick Escudero*

St. Andrew's Presbyterian Church survived the encroaching skyscrapers of downtown Toronto when the Sun Life Tower was built around it. *-Patrick Escudero*

is an ancient Chinese type of geomancy. An unbalanced alignment of doors and windows, design flaws or an incorrect lot placement can spell disaster for a building's success according to *feng shui*. In this case, the *feng shui* expert found that the billboard on the east side of Spadina just north of Dundas was reflecting negative energy onto the front of the building. A new door was therefore placed on the Dundas side of the building, thus relocating its front facade. Furthermore, the two stone lions on Spadina were put in place to guard the original entrance. The building has yet to house a successful business, and commercial activity here seems limited to the T-shirt and luggage vendor who essentially sells from the street.

On Spadina Avenue, your next stop should be **Dragon City Mall** *(280 Spadina)*, an Asian shopping mall with an interesting food court, among other things. Finally, be sure to stop in at one of the few old shops that have been here since the neighbourhood was almost exclusively Jewish.

Head west of Spadina towards Kensington Market.

Kensington Market ★ ★ ★ is located on Kensington Avenue, one street west of Spadina, between Dundas and Oxford streets. This bazaar epitomizes Toronto's multiethnicity: what began as a primarily Eastern European market is now a wonderful mingling of Jewish, Portuguese, Asian and Caribbean cultures. The lower half of Kensington is mostly vintage clothing shops, while the upper portion boasts international grocers peddling fresh and tasty morsels from all over the world. Perfect for picnic fixings!

The run-down, yet jazzed-up old Victorian row houses and the sidewalks along Kensington from Dundas to St. Andrews are a gold-mine to those for whom all things old are like gold. Used Levi's, leather bomber jackets, sheepskin coats and psychedelic polyester shirts can all be bought for great prices. **Courage My Love** *(14 Kensington Ave.)* and **Exile** *(62 Kensington Ave.)*, carry some unique merchandise. Besides the opportunity to complete your retro wardrobe, this part of Kensington also conceals treasures like incense, natural oils and exotic art.

Making your way north, you'll enter the more edible part of Kensington, where the treasures are just as exotic, if not more so! Creameries, fish markets, meat markets, cheese markets and spice markets fill the air with a bouquet of aromas. The window of **Global Cheese Shoppe** *(76 Kensington Ave.)* offers a sampling of the great prices and great selection inside. **Mendel's Creamery** *(72 Kensington Ave.)*, a veritable institution next door, sells great dill pickles, pickled herring and a wide variety of cheeses. Up on Baldwin Street, the catch of the

Exploring

day at the **Madeiro Fish Market** often comes from West Indian waters.

Turn left on Augusta Avenue, then take the first street on the right to Bellevue Avenue.

Built in 1927, the **Kiever Synagogue** ★ *(25 Bellevue Ave.)* is one of the last synagogues in this area that still has regular services. At one time there were as many as 30 temples in this neighbourhood. Its geometric stained-glass windows provide inspiration to the Congregation Rodfei Sholom Anshei Kiev, which means Men of Kiev, as well as visitors.

Return to Augusta Avenue and turn left.

Around Baldwin Street, the sights and sounds of Portugal become ever more present, with its bakeries, restaurants and fish shops. To be sure you don't miss anything wander up to Oxford. Finally, make your way back to Spadina along Nassau Street, where still more unique shops and shopkeepers vie for your attention and your dollars.

Perhaps you have gathered the fixings for a fine homemade meal along this tour; if not, take a walk along Baldwin Street through Chinatown's residential area. Keep an eye out for the distinctive red and yellow banners on some of the houses, as well as the small medallions placed here and there on their facades to ward off the negative energy. This street is home to some fantastic little bistros and restaurants. See "Restaurants," p 209.

Provincial Parliament

★★★

Tour G: Queen's Park and The University of Toronto

Each of Canada's 10 provinces has its own legislative assembly. Ontario's is located in the **Provincial Parliament ★★** *(1 Queen's Park)*, located at the centre of Queen's Park in the middle of University Avenue. The red sandstone building (1886-1892) was designed in the Richardsonian Romanesque style (see Old City Hall, p 120) by architect Richard A. Waite of Buffalo, who is also responsible for several other Canadian buildings, including the old headquarters of the Grand Trunk Railway on McGill Street in Montreal (the Gérald-Godin building). Notice the amusing crowning towers of the central part of the parliament; they exhibit the inventiveness of 19th century architects, who were preoccupied with eclecticism and the picturesque. Before entering, take a walk around the building to explore the typical 1890s public spaces with their intricately sculpted dark wood exteriors.

The 40 or so buildings of the **University of Toronto ★★** *(between Spadina Rd. to the west, Queen's Park Cr. to the east, College St. to the south and Bloor to the north)* are spread about a vast and very green English-style campus. Awarded a charter in 1827, the institution didn't really get going until the construction of its first building in 1845 (no longer standing). However, religious rivalries slowed down the progress of the university as each denomination wanted its own institution for higher learning. In the following decade there were six universities, each one barely getting by. It wasn't until partial unification in the 1880s that the campus began to expand. Today, the University of Toronto is one of the most respected institutions of higher learning in North America.

From Queen's Park Crescent West, walk around Hart House Circle.

Among the many university buildings, **Hart House ★** *(7 Hart House Circle)* is particularly noteworthy. Its great hall is the social hub of the university. Donated by the Massey Foundation, Hart House was an undergraduate men's activity centre until 1972, when women were finally allowed to become members. It was designed by architects Sproatt & Rolph in the Gothic style; the Soldiers' Memorial Tower, by the same architects, was added in 1924.

Continue around the circle to King's College Circle.

The lovely Victorian **Students' Administrative Council Building** *(12 Hart House Circle)* was built in 1857. It is often called

Exploring

the Stewart Observatory after one of its reincarnations, but originally housed the Toronto Magnetic and Meteorological Observatory and stood on the other side of the Front Lawn. It was moved and reconstructed in 1908.

The oldest building of the original university is **University College** ★ *(15 Kings College Circle)*, built in 1859 by architects Cumberland and Storm. The result is a picturesque Romanesque Revival ensemble with remarkably detailed stone carving. The Norman portal is particularly magnificent. The Romanesque Revival was something new in Canada at the time and thus was not associated with any specific religious or social movements. It therefore met the needs of university leaders, who wanted to create a secular environment, open to everyone. This philosophy did, however, lead some to refer to University College as the "godless college." **Knox College** *(59 George St.)* has pretty leaded casement windows and a rough sandstone exterior. It is a favourite with movie producers.

The imposing circular hall where King's College Circle joins King's College Road is the university's **Convocation Hall** *(31 King's College Circle)*. Attached to this are the administrative offices of the university, located in **Simcoe Hall** *(27 King's College Circle).*

● ATTRACTIONS

1. The Bay
2. Bank of Montreal
3. Elgin and Wintergarden Theatres
4. Canon Theatre
5. Massey Hall
6. St. Michael's Cathedral
7. Metropolitan United Church
8. Mackenzie House
9. Eaton Centre
10. Church of the Holy Trinity
11. Old City Hall
12. New City Hall
13. Nathan Phillips Square
14. Osgoode Hall
15. Campbell House
16. CityTV and MuchMusic
17. Black Bull Tavern

◯ ACCOMMODATIONS

1. Bond Place Hotel
2. Cambridge Suites Hotel
3. Sheraton Centre Toronto
4. St. Lawrence Residences
5. Toronto Marriott Eaton Centre

● RESTAURANTS

1. Addis Ababa
2. Avalon
3. Babur
4. Barberian's
5. Everest Cafe and Bar
6. Fez Batik
7. Hard Rock Cafe
8. Korean Grill House
9. Little India
10. Mildred Pierce Restaurant
11. Monsoon
12. Peter Pan
13. Queen Mother Cafe
14. Rivoli
15. Salad King
16. Sushi Bistro on Queen
17. Sushiman Japanese Restaurant
18. The Fifth
19. Tiger Lily's Noodle House

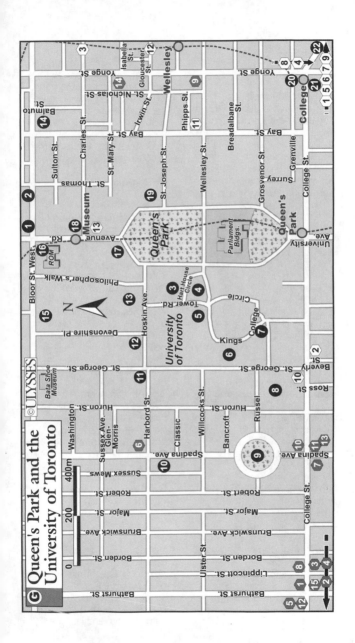

Queen's Park and the University of Toronto

© ULYSSES

0   200   400m

Walk down King's College Road to College Street.

When the University of Toronto was founded in 1827 it sat at some distance from town. Access to the 65ha wooded campus was gained along University Avenue and College Street, both private roads belonging to the university for some time. College was ceded to the city as a public thoroughfare in 1889. Among the huge pavilions that line the street today, the **Koffler Student Services building ★** *(214 College St.)* (1906) is particularly noteworthy. Originally the Public Reference Library, it owes its existence to American philanthropist Andrew Carnegie, who financed the construction of hundreds of public libraries in the United States and Canada.

Continue along College Street to Spadina Avenue, and turn right.

Spadina Avenue is more than 40m across, making it twice as wide as the rest of Toronto's early streets. The avenue was laid out in 1802 by William Warren Baldwin, whose house stood where Casa Loma now reigns. At the time, the road provided an unimpeded view of the lake and the burgeoning town of York to the south. As you look north now, however, you'll notice that the view is now broken by a crescent, in the middle of which stands a richly Victorian Gothic Revival building. This is the original **Knox College** *(1 Spadina Cr.)*, founded in 1844 when Baldwin's granddaughter sold the land to this Presbyterian theological seminary. It was one of the many sectarian schools that would eventually join the University of Toronto. The college relocated to St. George street in 1915 (see further above).

Continue up Spadina to Harbord Street.

The **Ukrainian Museum of Canada (Ontario Branch)** *($2; Mon-Fri 9am to 4pm, Sat and Sun by appt. only; 620 Spadina Ave., ☎923-3318)* presents the colourful heritage of the Ukrainian peoples, who arrived in Canada with the opening of the west. Several stunning traditional costumes and Ukrainian Easter eggs make up part of the display.

Walk east along Harbord Street.

The Athletics Centre and New College are on your right, while further along, at St. George, where Harbord becomes Hoskin, is the **John P. Roberts Research Library** *(130 St. George St.)*. This strange-looking building is often referred to as Fort Book, and some architects say you have to see it from a helicopter to truly appreciate it... go figure!

Across St. George are the towers of the Newman Centre, next to which is **Massey College** *(4 Devonshire Place)*. Built in 1963, the latter successfully marries a medieval atmosphere with modern architecture.

Head over towards **Trinity College** *(6 Hoskin Ave.)*, which blends with Knox College, the Stewart Observatory and Hart House, all to the south (see further above), to create a romantic **ensemble of English Gothic buildings ★**. Designed by architects Darling and Pearson (1925), Trinity boasts a lovely chapel that is the work of Sir Giles Gilbert Scott, well known for his cathedral in Liverpool. These four buildings, with their many stone ribs, leaded windows and peaceful courtyards, were inspired by the pavilions of Oxford and Cambridge.

Immediately to the east, stroll up the winding road called **Philosopher's Walk ★**. The Taddle Creek once flowed where the philosopher now

*Royal Ontario Museum
Facade*

walks, as the sounds of music students practising their scales at the conservatory waft over the clamour of busy Bloor Street. A contemplative stroll next to the newly planted oak trees leads to the Alexandra Gates, which originally guarded the university entrance at Bloor and Queen's Park.

To the left along Bloor, you'll see the High Victorian exterior of the **Royal Conservatory of Music** *(273 Bloor St. W.)*, with its dormers, chimneys and corbels. This building originally housed Toronto Baptist College.

Walk east along Bloor Street and turn left on Queen's Park to the entrance of the ROM.

The **Royal Ontario Museum ★ ★ ★** *($15 Mon-Fri, $18 Sat and Sun; Mon-Thu 10am to 6pm, Fri 10am to 9:30pm, Sat 10am to 6pm, Sun 11am to 6pm; 100 Queen's Park, ☎586-5549 or 586-8000)* is actually two museums in one since admission to the ROM, as it is called, also includes admission to the George R. Gardiner Museum of Ceramic Art. Canada's largest public museum, as well as a research facility, the ROM preserves some six-million treasures of art, archaeology and natural science. Upon entering the impressive vaguely Romanesque style building, visitors' eyes are drawn up to the Venetian glass ceiling, which depicts a mosaic of cultures. The ceiling is the only part of the museum that was not built

Exploring

using materials from Ontario. As you continue into the museum, your gaze will be drawn up once again by the towering totem poles flanking the lobby, one of which is 24.4m tall, its tip reaching just 15.2cm below the ceiling! With exhibits on everything from bats to dinosaurs and Romans to Nubians, your first stop should be the Mankind Discovering Gallery, where the layout and workings of the ROM are explained. Visitors have a somewhat mind-boggling range of choices, including the Dinosaur Gallery, a favourite with amateur palaeontologists of all ages; the Maiasaurus exhibit, an ongoing project where onlookers can observe palaeontologists reconstructing a real dinosaur skeleton; the Evolution Gallery; the Roman Gallery, displaying the largest collection of its kind in Canada; the Textile Collection, one of the best in the world; the East Asian galleries, where you'll find one of the museum's most precious gems: the Chinese Art and Antiquities Collection, containing a Ming Tomb and the Bishop White Gallery, whose walls are covered with Buddhist and Taoist paintings; the Discovery Gallery, a treat for children, with hands-on displays featuring authentic artifacts; the Ancient Egypt Gallery and Nubia Gallery, which boast the consummate and ever-intriguing mummies and ancient relics; the Sigmund Samuel Canadiana Collection of decorative arts, relocated to the ROM from the campus of the University of Toronto; and the last big crowd-pleaser, the Bat Cave, a walk through an all too realistic replica of the St. Clair limestone cave in Jamaica, complete with all too realistic replicas of swooping bats. The possibilities of discovery and exploration at the ROM are endless!

A revitalization project is currently underway. Renaissance ROM aims to increase the volume of the collections on display, upgrade public amenities and develop educational programs for students. Architect Daniel Libeskind came up with the design: a crystal structure of interlocking prismatic forms will hold six new galleries on Bloor Street. The first expansion phase will wrap up in December 2005, while the second, focussing on the renovation of existing facilities, will be completed one year later.

Make your way down Queen's Park to Queen's Park Crescent East.

Note **Flavelle House ★** *(78 Queen's Park)* on the right. Built in 1901 for Joseph Flavelle, this was for many years the grandest of Toronto's mansions. It is now used by the university's faculty of law.

Continue around Queen's Park Crescent to Victoria College and St. Michael's College.

The rich, finely crafted Romanesque-Revival **Victoria College ★** *(73 Queen's Park)* is very inviting for a scholarly building; it is just one of the buildings on the Victoria campus. This grouping, which includes Burwash Hall rimming the site to the east and north, Annesley Hall on Queen's Park and Emmanuel College to the west, is considered one of the finest on the University of Toronto campus.

The collection of buildings that make up the University of St. Michael's College occupy a lovely site at the corner of Queen's Park and St. Joseph Street. This Catholic school was founded by the Basilian Fathers from France; **St. Michael's College** *(81 St. Mary St.)* and **St. Basil's Church** *(81 St. Mary St.)*, both built in 1856, were its earliest buildings. The college was the first to affiliate itself with the University of Toronto in 1881, and thus claims the oldest buildings on campus. They predate University College (see above) by three years.

Walk down Bay Street to College Street.

The **Metropolitan Toronto Police Museum and Discovery Centre** ★ *(free admission, contributions are welcome; Mon-Fri 10am to 4:30pm; police headquarters 40 College St., ☎324-6201)* highlights policing from the era of Muddy York to the days of bicycle-riding cops. Unique exhibits on how to find clues in blood and dirt samples at a crime scene, fingerprinting, famous crimes, old uniforms, a police cruiser and an old-fashioned paddy-wagon will make

super-sleuths out of visitors. Young sleuths can even try to solve a crime.

Eaton's department store was originally located in a collection of individual buildings on Queen Street; then, in 1930, it moved to the Art Deco wonder at the corner of Yonge and College Streets, now called **College Park** *(444 Yonge St.)*. Much of the Art Deco detailing survived the successful transformation into shops, offices and apartments that followed Eaton's relocation when the Eaton Centre was built in 1977. These are visible on the shopping concourse, but above all in the superb seventh-floor concert hall. A pretty pool of water that becomes a skating rink in the winter is located behind it.

Cross Yonge Street, where College Street becomes Carlton Street, and walk over to Church Street.

Toronto's **Maple Leaf Gardens** *(60 Carlton St.)* was home to the National Hockey League's Toronto Maple Leafs for almost seven decades until early 1999. Although the Leafs have since moved to their new home in the Air Canada Centre (see p 90, 242), many fans still associate the heart of their beloved Leafs with the Gardens. The start of the 1931 hockey season forced 700 workers to scramble to finish this yellow-brick box in just over 12 months! Unfortunately the building is closed and tours are no longer available.

Exploring

Tour H:
Bloor and Yorkville

*Start at the corner of Bloor and
University Avenue, known as
Avenue Road north of Bloor.*

The Royal Ontario Museum
(see p 135) lies on the southwest corner; across the street
on the southeast corner is a
neoclassical building originally
known as the **Lillian Massey
Department of Household
Science**, whose mandate was
the education of young women
in the management of a household. More recently, it housed

the Provincial Ombudsmen, but
is now the home of a mam-
moth Club Monaco clothing
store!

Speaking of clothing stores, get
set for a whirlwind shopping
tour of posh Bloor & Yorkville!

This tour covers the area
around Bloor and Yorkville,
two names that are now synonymous with the expensive, the
up-scale and the trendy. The
area north and west of Bloor
and Bedford was once the
Village of Yorkville, incorporated in 1853 and existing as a
separate town until 1883,
when it was annexed to the city
of Toronto. It was a stylish

● ATTRACTIONS

1. Park Plaza Hotel
2. Church of the Redeemer
3. University Theatre
4. Pearcy House
5. ManuLife Centre
6. Holt Renfrew Centre
7. Hudson's Bay Centre
8. Metropolitan Toronto Library
9. Yorkville Public Library
10. Firehall No. 10
11. Hazelton House
12. Heliconian Club
13. Village of Yorkville Park

◯ ACCOMMODATIONS

1. Days Inn - Toronto Downtown
2. Four Seasons Hotel Toronto (R)
3. Hotel Inter-Continental Toronto
4. Howard Johnson Inn Yorkville
5. Marlborough Place
6. Park Hyatt
7. Quality Hotel Midtown

(R) property with restaurant (see
    description)

● RESTAURANTS

1. Allen's
2. Bistro 990
3. Boba
4. Cafe Nervosa
5. Flo's
6. Jacques Bistro du Parc
7. Opus Restaurant on Prince
   Arthur
8. Pappas Grill
9. Sassafraz
10. Serra
11. Swiss Chalet
12. Truffles
13. Yamato

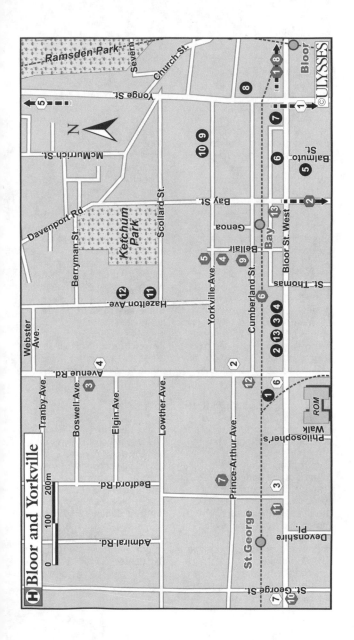

H Bloor and Yorkville

200m

0   100   200m

© ULYSSES

bedroom community that lay within a short distance of the growing metropolis to the south. However, the encroachment of that metropolis eventually saw the transformation of many of Yorkville's and Bloor's loveliest homes into office space and a relocation of the city's elite to more exclusive areas farther north. For the first half of the 20th century, this area was a middle-class suburb. The first signs of the area's trend-setting status began to appear in the postwar era, as the 19th century residences were transformed into coffeehouses and shops, and Yorkville became the focus of Canada's folk music scene. The gentrification of the area took off in the 1970s and 1980s, and on Bloor Street multi-purpose complexes and high-rises have sought to make optimal use of now outrageously high rental costs.

The luxurious **Park Plaza Hotel** (4 Avenue Rd.), built in 1926, stands on the northwest corner of Avenue and Bloor. The rough stone walls, sweeping slate roof and belfry of the **Church of the Redeemer** (162 Bloor St. W.) occupy the northeast corner. Rising behind it is the **Renaissance Centre**, which, though it dominates the church, also gives it a commanding presence over this busy corner. The **Colonnade**, to the east, was the first building on Bloor to combine commercial, residential and office space.

The stretch of Bloor Street from Queen's Park–Avenue Road to Yonge Street is a collection of modern office buildings, shopping malls and ultra-chic boutiques and galleries including such notables as Holt Renfrew, Chanel, Hermès, Tiffany's and Hugo Boss. According to some, Bloor Street is Toronto's Fifth Avenue, so make your way along it as quickly or as leisurely as you wish (see "Shopping" p 249). Most of Bloor Street's facades are clearly more recent additions, though some have been preserved and jazzed up in keeping with the chic boutiques that have moved in. The curved facade of the former **University Theatre** (100 Bloor St. W.) and the modest redbrick Neo-Georgian facade of **Pearcy House** (96 Bloor St. W.) are all that remain of two interesting buildings, which now house a new condominium development.

East of Bay Street is the **ManuLife Centre** (55 Bloor St. W.), which combines residential, office and commercial space. Streetfront shops line the sidewalk under the Centre's curious cantilevered overhang. Across Bloor Street is the **Holt Renfrew Centre** (50 Bloor St. W.), home to this classy department store as well as a shopping mall. Finally, the **Hudson's Bay Centre** (2 Bloor St. E.) occupies the busy corner of Bloor and Yonge.

At Yonge Street, turn left and head towards the trendy Yorkville area.

Before hitting the shops, you'll come upon the **Metropolitan Toronto Library** *(789 Yonge St.)* on the corner of Yonge and Asquith, a large building of brick and glass that is very popular with Torontonians. It does not look like much from the street, but inside, a profusion of plants and bright spaces make it feel just like home. The building was designed by architect Raymond Moriyama in 1973.

Heading west along Yorkville Avenue now, you'll come to the grand **Yorkville Public Library** *(22 Yorkville Ave.)* built in 1907 and remodelled in 1978. The bold porticoed entrance still dominates the facade just as it did when this library served the Village of Yorkville.

Right next door is the old **Firehall No. 10 ★** *(34 Yorkville Ave.)*, built in 1876 and then reconstructed (except for the tower, used to dry fire hoses) in 1889-90. This red- and-yellow-brick hose house once served the village of Yorkville and is still in use. The coat of arms on the tower was salvaged from the town hall; the symbols on it represent the vocations of the town's first councillors: a beer barrel for the brewer, a plane for the carpenter, a brick mould for the builder, an anvil for the blacksmith and a bull's head for the butcher.

As you browse through the shops, take a look at the Georgian-style houses at **numbers 61-63** and **77**, the Queen Anne porch of **number 84**, the Victorian house that once served as the Mount Sinai Hospital at **number 100** and finally the jazzed-up row of Victorian houses at **numbers 116-134**.

An exceptional collection of galleries, shops and cafés lines Yorkville, Hazelton and Cumberland. More architectural gems, too numerous to list, remain on Hazelton Avenue. These have all been faithfully restored, some so well that they look like new buildings; nevertheless, the results are aesthetically pleasing and worth a look. Of particular note are **Hazelton House** *(33 Hazelton Ave.)*, which originally housed the Olivet Congregational Church at the end of the 19th century and now contains shops, galleries and offices, and the Carpenter Gothic–style **Heliconian Club**, a women's arts and letters club founded in 1909.

After exploring Hazelton Avenue, continue along Yorkville and turn left on Avenue Road.

If you have the time and the inclination you can explore the many lovely houses west of Avenue Road, between Avenue and Bedford roads. For the most part, they remain residential and the area is therefore indicative of what Yorkville was like before the developers and trendsetters moved in.

Exploring

The north side of Cumberland Street, between Avenue Road and Bellair Street, is lined with fancy boutiques and galleries, while the south side has recently been transformed into the **Village of Yorkville Park** ★★. This urban park, which lies over a subway station, is an uncommon demonstration of urban ecology, local history and regional identity. It is divided into 13 zones, each representing a different part of the province's geography. The huge boulder toward the centre is native Canadian Shield granite. For more information on the park's layout, see p 174.

Looking south as you traverse the park, you can peer across

the parking lot and through the facades of the University Theatre and Pearcy House (see above).

Tour I: Cabbagetown

Historically, Cabbagetown was delimited by the Don Valley, Parliament Street, Queen Street and Carlton Street. Nowadays, however, when people talk of Cabbagetown, they are most often referring to the community around Parliament Street (its commercial artery), which extends east to

● ATTRACTIONS

1. Regent Park
2. Spruce Court Apartments
3. 397 Carlton
4. Riverdale Park
5. Witch's House
6. Riverdale Farm
7. Necropolis Chapel
8. Owl House Lane
9. Wellesley Street
10. St. James Cemetery
11. St. James-the-Less Chapel
12. St. Enoch's Presbyterian Church
13. Metcalfe Street
14. Carlton Street
15. Parliament Street
16. Hotel Winchester
17. Ontario Street
18. First Church of the Christian Association
19. Allan Gardens Conservatory

◐ ACCOMMODATIONS

1. 1871 Historic House Bed & Breakfast
2. Aberdeen Guest House
3. Banting House
4. Homewood Inn
5. Mulberry Tree
6. Selby Hotel
7. Toronto Downtown Bed and Breakfast

● RESTAURANTS

1. Keg Mansion
2. Mocha Mocha
3. Myth
4. Pan on the Danforth
5. Peartree
6. Provence
7. Rashnaa
8. Timothy's Tikka House

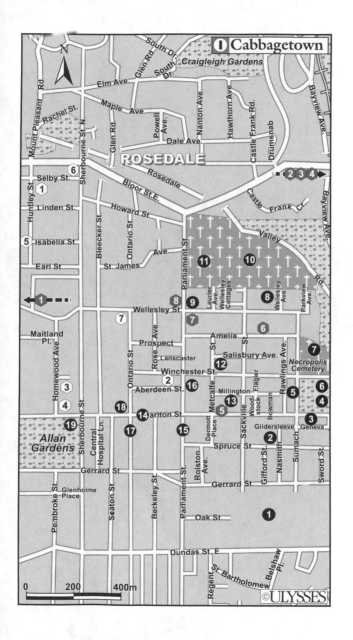

Cabbagetown

Craigleigh Gardens

Mount Pleasant Rd.

South Dr.

Glen Rd. South Dr.

Elm Ave.

Rachel St.

Maple Ave.

Powell Ave.

Nanton Ave.

Hawthorn Ave.

Castle Frank Rd.

Drumsnab

Bayview Ave.

Dale Ave.

ROSEDALE

Selby St.

Sherbourne St. N.

Glen Rd.

Rosedale

Bloor St. E.

Castle Frank Cr.

Bayview Ave.

Linden St.

Howard St.

Bleecker St.

Ontario St.

Huntley St.

Isabella St.

Earl St.

Ave.

St. James

Valley

Rd.

Parliament St.

Laurier Ave.

Wellesley Cottages

Wellesley Ave.

Parkview Ave.

Wellesley St.

Maitland Pl.

Homewood Ave.

Ontario St.

Rose Ave.

Prospect

Lanscaster

Winchester St.

Aberdeen St.

Sherbourne St.

Central Hospital Ln.

Carlton St.

Amelia

Salisbury Ave.

Metcalfe

Sackville

Wood-stock

Bowman

Rawlings Ave.

Flagler

Necropolis Cemetery

Millington

Dermott Place

Gerrard St.

Gildersleeve

Gifford St.

Nasmith

Sumach

Sword St.

Geneva

Allan Gardens

Pembroke St.

Glenholme Place

Seaton St.

Berkeley St.

Rolston Ave.

Parliament St.

Spruce St.

Gerrard St.

Oak St.

Dundas St. E.

Regent St.

St. Bartholomew

Belshaw Pl.

0   200   400m

©ULYSSES

the Don Valley, and north and south between Gerrard and Bloor streets. It was here that the poorest of the Irish immigrants—those who planted cabbages in their front lawns, thus giving the area its name— settled in the 1840s. These tiny, once run-down Victorians have now been gentrified, making this a lovely area for a stroll.

The land was originally set aside by Governor John Graves Simcoe as a government reserve, but was opened to subdivision in 1819. More than a century later, this working-class neighbourhood was seen as a dispensable slum when townplanners, keen on the new concept of urban renewal, razed most of the houses south of Gerrard Street and replaced them with government-subsidized housing called Regent Park. Though the area is now considered an architectural failure by many, a revitalization project involving local citizens is currently under way.

Start on Gerrard Street in front of **Regent Park**. The buildings to the south of Gerrard are actually those of the Regent Park North public housing development; Regent Park South lies south of Dundas Street. Built in 1947 and 1957 respectively, the two-phase project is one of Canada's oldest such developments. Its design, based on the modernist principles of Le Corbusier and others, sought to protect residents from the surrounding slums and provide them with

their own streets and parks, in effect, with their own little community. In reality, however, as Robert Fulford a respected Toronto journalist points out, the design isolates residents and singles them out as second-class. The revitalization project aims to reintegrate Regent Park into its neighbourhood by restoring street patterns and redesigning its parks and housing. Regent Park is worth a look, if only as a point of reference as you continue your tour through the charming Victorian neighbourhood that it partially replaced.

Make your way into the original Cabbagetown along Sackville Street.

The area to your left as you head north on **Sackville Street** was once occupied by the Toronto General Hospital. From 1855 to 1913, when it was demolished and rebuilt on University Avenue, the hospital covered 1.6ha. Trinity College Medical School established itself close by in 1871 at 41 Spruce Street; the school was later absorbed by the University of Toronto. The red- and yellow-brick building has now been incorporated into a residential complex known as Trinity Mews. The house at number 35 was originally inhabited by Charles B. Mackay, a customs clerk, and later by the Dean of Medicine of Trinity. It is still surrounded by its original fence, built in 1867.

Turn back and head east along Spruce Street to Sumach Street.

At the corner of Sumach are the **Spruce Court Apartments**. This was the city's first low-income housing project, and a successful one at that, with grassy courtyards, individual entrances and a very human scale. Spruce Court is now a residential cooperative.

Walk up Sumach and turn right on Carlton Street.

The dignified Italianate villa at **397 Carlton** was built in 1883. At the time, the house stood alone on this block in an area that was still very much "the country." A sense of that rural atmosphere remains in the lovely expanse of green called **Riverdale Park ★★**, which unfolds north of Carlton Street.

Walk north through the park and note the classic gingerbread house to your left at 384 Sumach Street. It has come to be known as the **Witch's House ★** and anyone who has read Hansel and Gretel will know why.

Riverdale Park once covered 66ha on both sides of the Don River. In 1898, Riverdale Zoo opened here with just two wolves and a few deer. The elephants and polar bears that were eventually added needed more space and in 1978, were moved to the brand new Toronto Metropolitan Zoo (see p 164) in Scarborough. The Riverdale facilities have since been home

to the ponies, roosters and other barnyard critters of **Riverdale Farm ★★** *(free admission; 201 Winchester St., ☎392-0046)*, and will delight children. The zoo's original stone gates on Winchester Street now lead to the farm.

North of Winchester Street extends another expanse of green. The **Necropolis** is one of Toronto's oldest non-sectarian burial grounds. It dates from the early 1850s and is the final resting place of William Lyon Mackenzie, the city's first mayor and leader of the rebellion of 1837 (see p 119) and George Brown, one of the fathers of Canadian Confederation. This city of the dead is ironically also a vibrant garden of sorts with an impressive collection of rare and exotic trees, shrubs and plants. Its most stunning feature, however, is its mortuary chapel, the **Necropolis Chapel ★★**, built in 1872. This wonderfully preserved High Victorian Gothic grouping is a true gem, with its patterned slate roof, tracery, ironwork and vine-covered exterior.

Cow

Exploring

*Continue up Sumach and turn
right on Amelia Street.*

In the mid-1850s some rather
unsavoury elements contributed to Cabbagetown's bad
reputation: the Don River and
the new Necropolis were both
seen as threats to the water
supply, while the Peter R. Lamb
& Company factory buildings
which once stood here were
probably something of an eye-
sore, not to mention the stench
that surely emanated from the
production of glue, blacking,
ground bone and animal char-
coal that went on here. Development in the area only started
in earnest in the 1880s, when
the factory burned down
around the same time a second
wave of immigrants from the
British Isles hit Toronto.

The houses along **Wellesley
Street** ★ were all built in the
1880s and 1890s for these new
arrivals, who were generally
better-off than those immigrants who settled a few blocks
to the south in the original
Cabbagetown. Many of these
houses display either the Toronto Bay-n-Gable or the later
Queen Anne style. The former
applies to double and row
houses and appeared all over
the city toward the end of the
19th century. Its picturesque
pointed gables, decorative
bargeboards and polygonal bay
windows are signatures of
Toronto architecture. The
latter is more elaborate, with
towers, turrets, gables, dormers, bay windows and a com-
bination of textures and materi-

als, and is most often found on
single detached dwellings.

One of the best examples of
Toronto Bay-n-Gable style
stands at **398 Wellesley
Street** ★. The Queen Anne
style is represented by a simple
condominium development at
the end of **Owl House Lane**.
The namesake house is adorned with a small owl and was
once lived in by artist C. W.
Jefferys.

Continuing along Wellesley
Street you'll notice a row of
simple gabled cottages running
up a dead-end street called
Wellesley Cottages. These
former working-class dwellings
are now modernized and highly
coveted properties. Continue
up to **Alpha Avenue,** where
another row of low-slung cottages, these ones with mansard
roofs, have been brightly revitalized.

Back on Wellesley Street, you'll
soon come to the most typical
Queen Anne house in the area
at **number 314** ★. A variety of
materials and a delightful ar-
rangement of shapes and orna-
ments bear witness to the fact
that the original owner was a
stone-cutter.

Extending north and west of the
corner of Parliament and
Wellesley streets is **St. James
Cemetery** ★, Toronto's second
Anglican cemetery, laid out in
1845. The wooded roads of
this tranquil spot lead to the
final resting places of Toronto's
elite, many of whom erected

some of the city's most elaborate monuments to the dead. Heritage Toronto has a list of the most prominent ones. Besides these, the cemetery also harbours what is considered one of the most praiseworthy church buildings in the country, **St. James-the-Less Chapel** ★★★ *(625 Parliament St.)*. Its sharp, lofty spire, severe roof line and diminutive base are simple but superb.

Make your way south along Parliament, Cabbagetown's main commercial artery. Turn left on Winchester and walk to Metcalfe Street.

Metcalfe Street ★★★ is perhaps the prettiest and most emblematic street of Cabbagetown. Lofty trees form a canopy over the street, which is lined with elegant iron fencing and rows of late-Victorian houses.

Victorian row houses, Cabbagetown

At the corner of Metcalfe and Winchester is the former **St. Enoch's Presbyterian Church** *(180 Winchester St.)*, built in 1891 in the Romanesque Revival style. The Toronto Dance Theatre now occupies the building.

A surprising house occupies **37 Metcalfe Street**. Successive additions and classic remodelling transformed an Italianate villa (1875) that fronted on Winchester Street into the neoclassical edifice that now faces Metcalfe.

Making your way down Metcalfe towards Carlton you'll pass a neat Bay-n-Gable row on the right running from number six to 18, and a distinctive string of Queen Anne houses on the left from number one to 15.

Carlton Street ★★ marks the northern boundary of "Old Cabbagetown." Most of the homes here are considerably larger and more opulent than those whose front yards were filled with cabbages. Start around Rawlings Avenue and work your way west. Number 314, with its pretty mansard roof, was built in 1874; number 297 is an oft-photographed, lofty Queen Anne residence; the fine Gothic Revival house at number 295 had one of the first telephones in the city; across the street, numbers 294-300 are fine examples of late Bay-n-Gable; number 286 boasts some lovely ornamenta-

Exploring

tions around its windows and door, and finally, note the decorative carved wooden porch of 280-282 Carlton.

Parliament Street is so named because it runs up from the site of the original Parliament Buildings. It is and has always been the neighbourhood's commercial artery. The Canadian Imperial Bank of Commerce building on the corner of Carlton and Parliament was designed by Darling & Pearson in 1905 in the neoclassical style. Just north of Carlton is an early commercial block whose delightful facade features pretty arched-windows; the shopfront of **number 242** ★ is an original.

Walk up Parliament Street to Winchester Street.

The **Hotel Winchester** *(531 Parliament St.)*, built in 1888, originally housed the Lake View Hotel and was something of an attraction in its glory days, due to a lookout point set up atop the corner tower, which offered a view of the lake.

Turn left on Winchester Street.

The south side of Winchester is lined with some lovely row and single detached houses. The triple Queen Anne house at numbers 7 to 11 stands out for its brickwork (number five was actually rebuilt). The double house at number 13-15 is a typical Second Empire residence, with its imposing central block and decorative dormers.

Turn left and walk down Ontario Street.

Harmonious rows of Bay-n-Gable houses line both sides of **Ontario Street** ★★ between Aberdeen and Winchester. Below Aberdeen on the left, the picturesque pointed arches of the double house at 481-483 are typical Gothic Revival. The simple red-brick Gothic **First Church of the Christian Association** *(474 Ontario St.)* on the right was built in 1905.

Back on Carlton Street, make your way west to the limits of Cabbagetown.

Allan Garden Conservatory ★★ *(free admission; every day 10am to 5pm; 19 Horticultural Ave., ☎392-1111)*, bounded by Jarvis, Gerrard, Sherbourne and Carlton Streets, are old-style gardens set in the middle of a lovely park on the edge of Cabbagetown. Among the garden's six greenhouses is the Palm House, a grand Victorian greenhouse built in 1910. The collection is set on the former estate of George William Allan, a lawyer and former mayor of Toronto who married his way into the Family Compact (see p 20).

Tour J: The Annex

Extending north and west from the intersection of Bloor Street and Avenue Road to Dupont

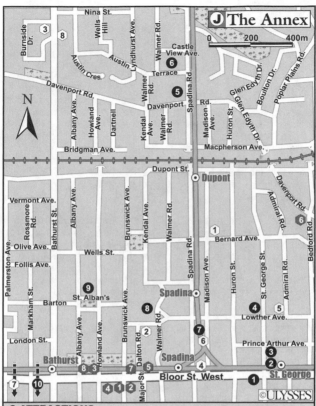

J The Annex

0   200   400m

Nina St.
Burnside Dr.
Wells Hill
Lindhurst Ave.
Walmer Rd.
Castle View Ave.
Terrace
Spadina Rd.
Glen Edyth Dr.
Boulton Dr.
Poplar Plains Rd.
Austin Ter.
Austin Cres.
Davenport Rd.
Albany Ave.
Howland Ave.
Dartnell
Kendal Ave.
Walmer Rd.
Davenport
Rd.
Madison Ave.
Huron St.
Glen Edyth Dr.
Bridgman Ave.
Macpherson Ave.
Dupont St.
Dupont
Vermont Ave.
Rossmore Rd.
Bathurst St.
Albany Ave.
Brunswick Ave.
Kendal Ave.
Walmer Rd.
Spadina Rd.
Bernard Ave.
Admiral Rd.
Davenport Rd.
Bedford Rd.
Olive Ave.
Palmerston Ave.
Wells St.
Follis Ave.
Madison Ave.
Huron St.
St. George St.
Admiral Rd.
Markham St.
St. Alban's
Barton
Albany Ave.
Howland Ave.
Brunswick Ave.
Walmer Rd.
Spadina
Spadina Rd.
Lowther Ave.
London St.
Dalton Rd.
Prince Arthur Ave.
Bathurst
Major St.
Spadina
Bloor St. West
St. George
©ULYSSES

● ATTRACTIONS

1. Bata Shoe Museum
2. York Club
3. Medical Arts Building
4. First Church of Christ Scientist
5. Casa Loma
6. Spadina
7. Spadina Gardens
8. Walmer Road Baptist Church
9. Church of St. Alban-the-Martyr
10. Mirvish Village

○ ACCOMMODATIONS

1. Annex House Bed & Breakfast
2. B & B in The Annex
3. French Connection Bed & Breakfast
4. Global Guest House
5. Lowther House
6. Madison Manor Boutique Hotel
7. Palmerston Inn
8. Terrace House B & B

◆ RESTAURANTS

1. By the Way Cafe
2. Country Style
3. Dooney's
4. Future Bakery and Cafe
5. Korea House
6. Le Paradis
7. Nataraj Indian Restaurant
8. Sushi on Bloor

and Bathurst streets is an area that was annexed by the City of Toronto in 1887, and is now appropriately called The Annex. As this was a planned suburb, a certain architectural homogeneity prevails; even the unique gables, turrets and cornices are all lined up an equal distance from the street. Residents fought long and hard to preserve the Annex's architectural character, and save a few ugly apartment high-rises along St. George Street and Spadina, their efforts have been quite successful. The fact that this area remains essentially as it was about a century ago is a testament to Torontonians' burgeoning awareness of the historical value of their surroundings.

The **Bata Shoe Museum** ★★★ *($6; Tue-Sat 10am to 5pm, Thu until 8pm, Sun noon to 5pm; 327 Bloor St. W., ☎979-7799)* is the first museum of its kind in North America. It holds 10,000 shoes and provides an extraordinary perspective on the world's cultures. The new building was designed by architect Raymond Moriyama to look like a shoe box, and the oxidized copper along the edge of the roof is meant to suggest a lid resting on top. There are four permanent exhibits: "All About Shoes," is touted as a sumptuous feast of footwear with shoe trivia, shoe history and shoes of the rich and famous; "Inuit Boots: A Woman's Art," takes a look at "Kamiks" and the importance of footwear in the Arctic;

"The Gentle Step: 19th Century Women's Shoes" examines the evolution of women's footwear at the dawn of the modern age; "One, Two, Buckle My Shoe" exhibits illustrations of shoes from children's books. Some of the more memorable pieces of footwear on display include space boots of Apollo astronauts, geisha platform sandals and a pair of patent leather beauties that once belonged to Elvis Presley.

The impressive red brick and stone building kitty-corner to the museum, is now home to the **York Club** ★, but was once a private home. It is the most distinguished Richardsonian Romanesque house in Toronto and was built in 1889 for the wealthiest man in the province at the time, George Gooderham. The architect, David Roberts, also designed the distinctive Gooderham Building (see p 108), also known as the Flatiron Building, on Front Street. The York Club moved into the house in 1909, making it the first secular institution tolerated in the area.

Across the street is the **Medical Arts Building** *(170 St. George St.)*, the area's first tall office building, built in 1929. Plans are under way to convert it into a pavilion of the University of Toronto. The remnants of a wall that once surrounded George Gooderham's son's residence just to the north is now part of the Royal Canadian Yacht Club. This "city" clubhouse is of course secondary to the main Toronto Islands location. Another Richardsonian Romanesque masterpiece occupies the northwest corner of St. George Street and Prince Arthur Avenue. With its characteristic wide, round arches and ivy-covered tower, **180 St. George Street** is quite handsome. Up at the corner of Lowther and St. George is the **First Church of Christ Scientist**, the first Christian Science church in Toronto, built in 1916.

Turn right on Lowther and left on Admiral Road.

Admiral Road is a peaceful street with some lovely Annex houses. A grand old tree (since cut down) about halfway up the block from Lowther and the curve of Davenport Road, above Bernard Avenue, explains Admiral's deviation from the strict grid pattern of the surrounding streets.

Turn right at St. George Street and then left on Dupont Street.

Dupont marks the northern boundary of the area annexed by the City of Toronto in 1887. Majestic old trees and typical Annex rows of houses frame this wide avenue.

Head east to Spadina, then turn left and walk beyond the train tracks to MacPherson Avenue. Turn left and then right on Walmer Road, cross Davenport and continue up Walmer Road to Austin Terrace and Casa Loma.

Canadians are known for their reserve, modesty and discretion. Of course there are exceptions to every rule and one of these is certainly **Casa Loma** ★★ *($10; every day 9:30am to 4pm; 1 Austin Terrace, ☎923-1171)*, an immense Scottish castle with 98 rooms built in 1914 for the eccentric colonel Sir Henry Mill Pellatt

Exploring

Casa Loma

(1859-1939) who made his fortune by investing in electricity and transportation companies. Pellatt owned, among others things, the tramways of São Paolo, Brazil! His palatial residence, designed by the architect of Toronto's Old City Hall, E.J. Lennox, includes a vast ballroom with a pipe organ and room for 500 guests, a library with 100,000 volumes and a fascinating cellar. The self-guided tour leads through various secret passages and lost rooms. Great views of downtown Toronto can be had from the towers.

To the east of Casa Loma, atop the Davenport hill and accessible by the Baldwin Steps, is **Spadina** ★ *($5; Tue-Sun noon to 5pm; 285 Spadina Rd., ☎392-6910)*, another house-turned-museum of Toronto's high society. This one is smaller, but just as splendid for those who want to get a taste of the Belle Époque in Canada. It was built in 1866 for James Austin, the first president of the Toronto-Dominion Bank, and the grounds include a solarium overflowing with luxuriant greenery and a charming Victorian garden, in bloom from May to September. The residence has been renovated several times and features several glassed-in overhangs, offering its owners panoramic views of the surroundings, which the natives called *Espanidong*, and the English *Spadina* (the correct pronunciation being *Spadeena*). Heritage Toronto guides have been leading visitors on tours of

the estate since 1982, when the last member of the Austin family left the house.

Return now to the Annex proper by taking Spadina Avenue all the way to Lowther Avenue.

As the main thoroughfare of the Annex, Spadina Avenue was one of the first streets to attract the attention of developers, who put up several rather ugly International Style box-like apartment buildings following World War II. Just south of Lowther, however, is an apartment house that merits our attention. Built in 1906, **Spadina Gardens** *(41-45 Spadina Ave.)* is still the classiest building of its kind on the street, despite more recent attempts to up-stage it.

Continue west along Lowther Avenue, then north up Walmer Road.

The **Walmer Road Baptist Church** *(188 Lowther Ave.)* was once the largest Baptist church in Canada. It was founded by the uncle of artist Lawren Harris, one of the Group of Seven (see p 38). Winding Walmer Road is one of the more picturesque and prestigious-looking streets in the Annex; it also boasts some typical Annex houses like number 53, numbers 83-85 and finally the grand number 109.

Complete your stroll through the Annex by walking west along Bernard Avenue, around the park, along Wells Street and down Howland Avenue to Bloor Street. Only the splendid chancel of the **Church of St. Alban the Martyr** ★ *(just before St. Alban's Sq.)*, what amounts to one quarter of the planned cathedral, was actually completed by the time the money ran out in 1891. This was to be the cathedral church of the Diocese of Toronto, an honour later bestowed on St. James Cathedral (see p 114).

Once at Bloor Street, turn right and walk to Honest Ed's and Mirvish Village (see inset p 97).

Tour K: Rosedale, Forest Hill and North of Toronto

This tour explores two treasures in the vicinity of the Don River, the Ontario Science Centre and Todmorden Mills Park, then heads west into the posh residential neighbourhoods of Rosedale and Forest Hill, before finishing up with a collection of worthy attractions north of the city. It is best followed by car.

Since its opening on September 27, 1969, the **Ontario Science Centre** ★★★ *($12; Jul and Aug, every day 10am to 6pm; Sep to Jun, every day 10am to 5pm; 770 Don Mills Rd.,* ☎*429-4100, www.osc.on.ca)* has

welcomed over 30 million visitors, young and old. Designed by architect Raymond Moriyama, it houses 800 different exhibits. The best part about the centre is its many hands-on exhibits and experiments. These interactive exhibits are spread throughout 12 categories: The Living Earth, Space, Sport, Communication, Food, A Question of Truth, The Information Highway, Technology/ Transportation, The Human Body, Science Arcade, Matter, Energy and Change, and Earth. One of the biggest crowd-pleasers is the electricity ball that stands your hair on end. Scientists at heart also discover the chemistry of cryogenics while the Starlab planetarium transports them to the four corners of the galaxy. They'll learn to make their own paper as well as about the evolution and the impact of the printing press on humanity. The steps involved in making metal objects are described at the foundry on site, and finally the numerous applications of lasers in the modern world are explored. In late 1996, the Science Centre opened its brand new OMNIMAX theatre, which is an improved version of the IMAX. Located at the entrance to the centre, the OMNIMAX seats 320 people under an enormous 24m-wide dome with a powerful hi-fidelity sound system. Admission is separate and reservations are recommended *(tickets:* ☎*696-1000).*

Exploring

Take Don Mills Road south to the Don Valley Parkway south, and take the Todmorden Mills Exit.

Todmorden Mills Heritage Museum ★ *($3; May to Sep, Tue-Fri 11am to 4pm, Sat, Sun and holidays noon to 4pm; Oct to Dec, Mon-Fri 10am to 4pm; 67 Pottery Rd., ☎396-2819)* is an open-air museum with two restored Confederation (1867) houses, a former brewery and the Old Don Train Station, which once served both the Canadian National and the Canadian Pacific railroads. Todmorden Mills on the Don River was once inhabited by settlers from Todmorden Mills in England. The park that surrounds the museum is a lovely spot for a picnic.

Head west into Rosedale at Castle Frank Road.

One of Toronto's most distinguished and affluent neighbourhoods lies just north of the downtown area. **Rosedale** was not always a coveted address; the affluent folk that developers sought to attract here originally found Rosedale "too lonely" and "too far from town." Furthermore it was "too difficult to find domestics" who would go there. It was not until the early 1900s that the majority of the houses were built, for the most part by a nouveau riche middle class, though some eminent surnames did find their way onto the Rosedale rosters, like Osler, Gooderham, Darling and Small.

Rosedale was named by Sheriff Jarvis's wife Mary, who delighted in the roses that grew wild in and around their house, the area's first, Rosedale Villa. Built overlooking the ravine, it was finally demolished in 1905. Following Mary's death in the 1850s, Jarvis laid out Park Road and began dividing up and selling off his domain. The surrounding estates followed suit, and slowly a handful of houses was built. Yet when Rosedale finally took off in the early 1900s, the inclination to sell off land remained as strong with the new arrivals, leading to further subdivisions. As a result, many of Rosedale's houses are built very close together and very near the street. There is also a distinct lack of continuity in the architecture, with houses of different styles located right next to each other. A walk through Rosedale's prettiest streets therefore offers an excellent opportunity to view a wide range of some of Toronto's loveliest residential architecture.

The land north of Bloor Street was claimed by Governor John Graves Simcoe in 1793 when he laid out the town of York. He named it Frank after his infant son and built a house on it which he called Castle Frank. The house burned down in 1829 after having been abandoned by Simcoe when he was called back to England in 1797. This part of Rosedale then passed into the hands of Francis Cayley, who called his rustic

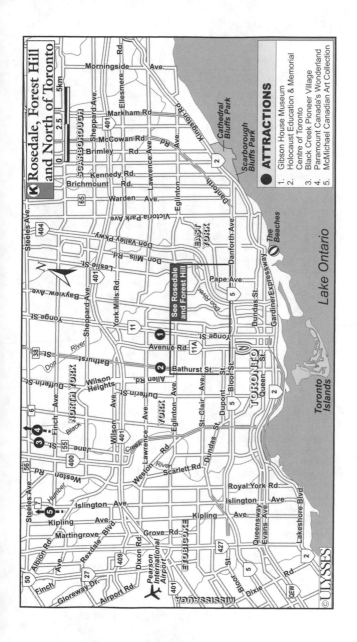

K Rosedale, Forest Hill and North of Toronto

0   2.5   5km

● ATTRACTIONS

1. Gibson House Museum
2. Holocaust Education & Memorial Centre of Toronto
3. Black Creek Pioneer Village
4. Paramount Canada's Wonderland
5. McMichael Canadian Art Collection

Morningside   Ave.

Ellesmere   Rd.

Markham Rd.

401

SCARBOROUGH

McCowan Rd.

Brimley   Rd.

Kennedy Rd.

Brichmount

Warden   Ave.

65

Steeles   Ave.

404

Sheppard Ave.

Bayview Ave.

Leslie St.

401

Yonge St.

York Mills Rd.

11

38

Don   River

Bathurst   St.

NORTH YORK

Wilson
Heights

Allen Rd.

Dufferin St.

Wilson   Ave.

Eglinton   Ave.

Black   Creek

Finch   Ave.

6

55

Jane   St.

400

401

Weston   Rd.

Lawrence   Ave.

Humber River

Scarlett Rd.

56

Weston Rd.

Steeles   Ave.

7

Humber

Islington   Ave.

Kipling   Ave.

Martingrove Blvd.

Grove Rd.

50

Albion Rd.

27

409

Rexdale Blvd.

Dixon Rd.

Gloreway Dr.

Airport Rd.

Pearson International Airport

401

ETOBICOKE

MISSISSAUGA

Royal York Rd.

Islington   Ave.

Kipling   Ave.

Queensway   Evans Ave.

427

Bloor   St.

Dixie   Rd.

Lakeshore   Rd.

QEW

Lawrence Ave.

Dufferin St.

Eglinton Ave.

Dundas St.

St. Clair   Ave.

Dupont   St.

Bloor   St.

YORK

2

Avenue Rd.

See Rosedale
and Forest Hill

11A

Yonge St.

Bathurst St.

1

2

5

TORONTO

Queen   St.

5

2

Toronto
Islands

Don Valley Pkwy.

Don Mills Rd.

EAST
YORK

Pape Ave.

Danforth Ave.

Victoria Park Ave.

Eglinton   Ave.

Lawrence   Ave.

Kingston Rd.

Danforth

Cathedral
Bluffs Park

Scarborough
Bluffs Park

2

The Beaches

Dundas St.

Don River

Gardiner Expressway

5

Lake Ontario

© ULYSSES

49ha estate Drumsnab
(*5 Drumsnab Rd.*). This domain
was slowly parcelled off by land
speculators though the house
(built in 1834 and then added
on to in 1856 and 1908) remains and is the oldest private
residence in Toronto.

*Take Castle Frank Road up to
Elm Avenue.*

Edgar Jarvis, Sheriff Jarvis's
nephew, laid out Elm Avenue
early in the development of
Rosedale. He planted elm trees
and built a fine residence in the
hope of attracting prospective
buyers. His house still stands at
the end of the street. Before
coming to it though, note the
house at 27 Sherbourne Street.
Jarvis succeeded in selling this
lot to the wealthy Gooderham
family (see p 108) of distilling
fame. This house was actually
the second Gooderham man-
sion built on the lot; the first
was demolished.

As you approach Mount Pleasant Road, Branksome Hall
private girls' school is located
on your right. The main building of the school is located on
the other side of Mount Pleasant in the former residence of
Edgar Jarvis, built in 1866. This
fine Italianate house originally
faced Park Road and was Jarvis's
showpiece.

*Head up Mount Pleasant Road
and turn left on South Drive and
left again on Park Road.*

At 124 Park Road stands the
first house built on the land

divided up and parcelled off by
Sheriff Jarvis. When this gra-
cious Georgian house with the
wrap-around veranda was built
in 1855, it only had one storey.

*Continue along Park and turn
right on Avondale Road.*

The area beyond the first intersection on the left marks the
spot where "Rosedale Villa,"
Sheriff Jarvis's house, once
stood. The house was built in
1821 and Jarvis moved in in
1824. He lived here until his
wife's death in 1852. The
house was demolished in 1905.

Crescent Road was one of the
seven curving roads laid out by
Jarvis when his property was
subdivided for development.
Follow it around to the right
and return to Mount Pleasant
Road.

*Take Mount Pleasant Road up to
Mount Pleasant Cemetery.*

The first non-sectarian cemetery in Toronto was Potter's
Field, which lay on the northwest corner of Bloor and
Yonge. The growth of nearby
Yorkville limited the available
space in this cemetery, so the
remains buried here were
transferred to the new Necropolis, next to the Don River (see
p 145). Soon that too proved
too small and thus **Mount
Pleasant Cemetery ★★**
(*bound by Yonge St., Bayview
Ave., Moore Ave. and Merton St.*)
was created in 1876. Its lovely
landscaping quickly made it
something of an attraction in

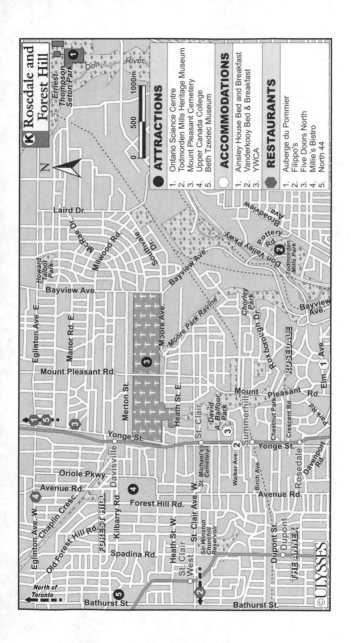

Rosedale and Forest Hill

ATTRACTIONS
1. Ontario Science Centre
2. Todmorden Mills Heritage Museum
3. Mount Pleasant Cemetery
4. Upper Canada College
5. Beth Tzedec Museum

ACCOMMODATIONS
1. Ainsley House Bed and Breakfast
2. Vanderkooy Bed & Breakfast
3. YWCA

RESTAURANTS
1. Auberge du Pommier
2. Filippo's
3. Five Doors North
4. Millie's Bistro
5. North 44

N

0   500   1000m

© ULYSSES

Toronto, and it remains a tranquil and beautiful place for quiet contemplation. It boasts a lovely arboretum with native and introduced species, most of which are identified, as well as some extraordinary architecture. Since it developed from west to east, most of the historic personalities are buried closer to Yonge Street. The notable figures whose final resting places are in Mount Pleasant include William Lyon Mackenzie King, Canada's longest-running Prime Minister; Frederick Banting and Charles Best, who together discovered insulin; Glenn Gould, the world-renowned classical pianist, and Foster Hewitt, the voice of hockey who coined the phrase "he shoots, he scores!" The Eaton and Massey mausoleums are probably the most impressive in the cemetery, the former built with granite imported from Scotland, and the latter designed by E.J. Lennox.

As you continue north from Mount Pleasant towards North York, take a swing through **Forest Hill**, Toronto's other upscale residential neighbourhood.

Take Heath Street to Forest Hill Road and turn right.

The village of Forest Hill was incorporated in 1923 and joined the City of Toronto in 1968. It became a memorable part of Toronto lore in 1982 when the city stopped collecting residents' garbage from

their backyards; the rubbish now has to be left on the sidewalk out front, heaven forbid! Forest Hill has always been the home court of wealthy and influential Torontonians, most of whom reside in stunning Georgian Revival houses set on fittingly leafy lots.

Make your way up Forest Hill Road to Old Forest Hill Road.

On the right side of Forest Hill Road between Lonsdale and Kilbarry roads is one of Canada's most respected private boys' schools, **Upper Canada College**. These hallowed halls have inspired some of Canada's greatest luminaries, including authors Stephen Leacock and Robertson Davies.

Turn left on Kilbarry Road and right on Old Forest Hill Road.

This winding road, which was once a path used by Aboriginals, is lined with some of Forest Hill's most elegant residences. Make your way up to Eglinton Avenue, the northern boundary of Forest Hill. If you feel like doing a bit of shopping, head down Spadina Road towards St. Clair Avenue.

The **Beth Tzedec Museum** *(free admission; Mon, Wed, Thu 11am to 1pm and 2pm to 5pm, Sun by appointment; 1700 Bathurst St., ☎781-3511)* holds several curious and amusing treasures related to the Jewish culture and is certainly worth a visit if you're in the vicinity. It is

Banting and Co.

Frederick Grant Banting (1891-1941) completed his medical studies at the University of Toronto and started a surgical practice in London, Ontario, supplementing his revenue with a post as a medical demonstrator at the University of Western Ontario, in London. On a fall day in 1920, Banting, a surgeon with no previous research experience, read an article on the pancreas. That very night, he jotted down a few ideas about a method that could allow the isolation of the pancreas's anti-diabetic component.

He returned to his alma mater in 1922 to carry out experiments on the pancreas. Under the direction of J.R.R. MacLeod, head of the physiology department at the University of Toronto, Frederick Banting and Charles Best, a graduate student, succeed in isolating insulin before the end of the summer. For his part, Dr. Charles Collip perfected a process through which insulin could be refined and processed in sufficient quantities for clinical trials on humans. The results were invaluable to diabetics, who quite literally experienced a new lease on life thanks to insulin.

In 1923, the Nobel Prize in Physiology or Medicine was awarded to the unassuming Dr. Frederick Banting and his lab director, J.R.R. MacLeod. Because their discovery and the perfecting of the clinical procedure were a team effort, they were anxious to share the honour with their colleagues. Banting thus split his share of the prize money with Best, while MacLeod split his with Collip.

Dr. Banting pursued his research and coordinated national wartime medical-research work. Sadly, his life was cut short by a plane crash in Newfoundland in 1941.

Exploring

located in the modern synagogue of the same name.

*Continue north up Bathurst
Street to Highway 401 and head
east to Yonge Street to visit Gibson House.*

The **Gibson House Museum**
*($3.75; Tue-Fri noon to 4:30pm,
Sat, Sun and holidays noon to
5pm; 5172 Yonge St., ☎395-
7432)* was home to David
Gibson, a local surveyor and
politician, and his family in the
mid-1800s. Gibson was a
staunch supporter of William
Lyon Mackenzie, and was con-
sequently exiled to the United
States in 1837. He built this
house upon returning from
south of the border and finding
his original house burnt to the
ground by Family Compact
supporters. At the time, the
area was farmland with rolling
fields as far as the eye could
see. The house has been restored to that era, and guides in
period dress re-enact the life
and times of the Gibson family.

*Head west on Highway 401, exit
and head north on Bathurst
Street.*

The **Holocaust Education &
Memorial Centre** *(free admission, donations appreciated;
Mon-Thu 9am to 4pm, Fri 9am
to 3pm, Sun 11:30am to
4:30pm; 4600 Bathurst St., ☎635-
2883)* is a moving memorial
that pays tribute to the experiences of European Jews in
World War II. The diorama of
Jewish life in pre-Nazi Europe is
particularly poignant.

*Continue north up Bathurst
Street to Finch Avenue. Head
west on Finch to Jane Street.*

Black Creek Pioneer Village
*($9; May to Dec Mon-Fri 10am
to 5pm, Sat, Sun and holidays
9:30am to 4pm; 1000 Murray
Ross Pkwy., at Jane St. and
Steeles Ave. W., ☎736-1733, from
Finch subway station take bus
60 to Jane St.)* is about 30min
from downtown. Period buildings include an authentic mill
from the 1840s with a 4-tonne
waterwheel that grinds up to
100 barrels of flour a day, a
general store, a town hall, a
print shop and a blacksmith; all
of these are staffed by friendly
animators going about their
business dipping candles, shear-
ing sheep and baking goodies
that you can sample. In the
summer, enjoy a horse-drawn
carriage ride, and in the winter
bundle up for skating, tobog-
ganing and sleigh rides.

*Head north up Jane Street to
Rutherford Road.*

The first one of its kind in the
country, **Paramount Canada's
Wonderland** *(day pass $44.99;
May, and Sep to early Oct, Sat
and Sun 10am to 8pm; Jun to
Labour Day, every day 10am to
10pm; 9580 Jane St., Vaughan,
☎905-832-7000; 30min from
downtown, Rutherford exit from
Hwy. 400 and follow the signs,
or Yorkdale or York Mills subway
then take special GO express bus)*
is the answer if you have a day
to kill and children to please.
Gut-wrenching rides include
the Vortex, the only suspended
roller coaster in Canada, and

the renowned Days of Thunder, which puts you behind the driver's seat for a simulated stock car race. The park also features a water park called Splash Works with 16 rides and slides, and live shows at the **Kingswood Theatre** (☎905-832-8131). Wonderland was recently purchased by Paramount, and Star Trek characters now wander through the park along with more Canadian idols like Scooby Doo and Fred Flintstone. The restaurant facilities may not be to everyone's liking, so pack a lunch.

Kleinberg's McMichael Canadian Art Collection lies about 45min north of downtown Toronto. Take Hwy. 400, then Major Mackenzie Dr. to Islington Ave.

The **McMichael Canadian Art Collection** ★★★ *($12; every day 10am to 4pm; 10365 Islington Ave., ☎905-893-1121 or 888-213-1121)* houses one of the most magnificent collections of Canadian and Aboriginal art in Canada and draws many visitors to the peaceful hamlet of Kleinberg on the outskirts of Greater Toronto. A magnificent stone and log house built in the 1950s for the McMichaels is home to the collection. The McMichaels are great art-lovers, and their personal collection of paintings by the great Canadian masters is at the heart of the museum's collection today. The large, bright galleries present an impressive retrospective of the works of Tom Thomson and the Group of Seven. A visit here allows you to admire and contemplate some of the best works of these artists who strove to reproduce and interpret Ontario's wilderness in their own way. Inuit and other Aboriginal art are also well represented, notably the work of Ojibwa painter Norval Morrisseau, who created his own "pictographic" style.

Exploring

McMichael Canadian Art Collection

Tour L:
Eastern Toronto

The Beaches

We say "Beaches" in the interests of conformity, clarity and perhaps tourism; however, in the interests of historical accuracy it should be noted that longtime residents are almost fiercely attached to what they feel is the neighbourhood's true name, "The Beach." The Beaches extend west from Woodbine Avenue to the R.C. Harris Filtration Plant, and north from the lake to Kingston Road.

In 1853, English soldier Joseph Williams built his domain here and called it Kew Farms. He changed the name to Kew Gardens in 1879, when the farm became a park that was all the rage with weary Torontonians. Soon these same city-dwellers began building cottages here (you'll notice that many of the neighbourhood's present houses are clearly winterized summer cottages). The reason for calling this place The Beaches is probably that in those days there were actually three beaches: Kew Beach to the west, Scarboro Beach Park in the middle and Balmy Beach to the east.

Take streetcar no. 501 east along Queen Street to Woodbine Avenue.

Once at the beach, the fun begins. A pretty wooden boardwalk runs the length of the beach, as does the **Trillium Trail**, a jogging and cycling path. A tennis club, lacrosse club and lawn-bowling club all face the beach. The green space to your left eventually opens up at Kew Gardens, which extends all the way up to Queen Street East. On Lee Avenue, which lines the park to the east, is the house built by Kew Williams, son of Joseph, at number 30.

If the prospect of warm sand, bright sun and a backdrop of sparkling waves carrying sailboats along the horizon appeals to you, then by all means hit the beach! The boardwalk continues all the way to Silver Birch Avenue and the Balmy Beach Canoe Club. From there, let the sand get between your toes and walk the few blocks to the **R.C. Harris Filtration Plant**, one of Toronto's most evocative buildings and revered by some as its most imposing example of "engineering raised to art."

Walk up to Queen Street East and head west to experience a bit more of the "Beaches" way of life, complete with surf shops and sidewalk cafés. There is certainly a lot of window shopping to be done.

At Glen Manor Drive, turn right and walk up to Southwood Drive. Pianist Glenn Gould was a Beaches resident until his late 20s; his parents' house at **32 Southland Drive** is identified by a plaque.

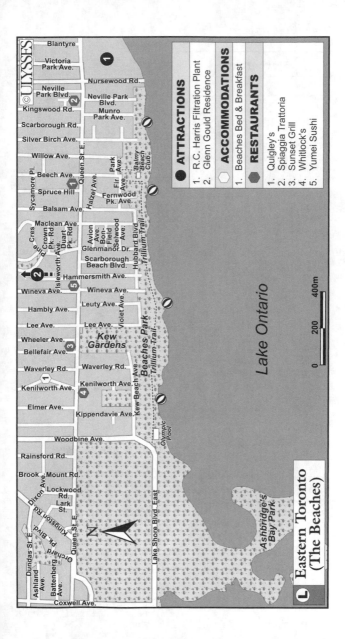

ULYSSES

Eastern Toronto (The Beaches)

Lake Ontario

Ashbridge's Bay Park

0   200   400m

N

ATTRACTIONS
1. R.C. Harris Filtration Plant
2. Glenn Gould Residence

ACCOMMODATIONS
1. Beaches Bed & Breakfast

RESTAURANTS
1. Quigley's
2. Spiaggia Trattoria
3. Sunset Grill
4. Whitlock's
5. Yumei Sushi

Blantyre
Victoria Park Ave.
Neville Park Blvd.
Kingswood Rd.
Scarborough Rd.
Silver Birch Ave.
Willow Ave.
Beech Ave.
Spruce Hill
Balsam Ave.
Maclean Ave.
Crown Pk. Rd
Duart Pk. Rd
Glenmanor Dr.
Scarborough Beach Blvd.
Hammersmith Ave.
Wineva Ave.
Hambly Ave.
Lee Ave.
Wheeler Ave.
Bellefair Ave.
Waverley Rd.
Kenilworth Ave.
Elmer Ave.
Kippendavie Ave.
Woodbine Ave.
Rainsford Rd.
Brook Mount Rd.
Lockwood Rd.
Lark St.
Dixon Ave.
Kingston Rd.
Orchard Pk. Blvd.
Dundas St. E.
Ashland Ave.
Battenberg Ave.
Coxwell Ave.
Queen St. E.
Lake Shore Blvd. East

Nursewood Rd.
Neville Park Blvd.
Munro Park Ave.
Balmy Beach Club
Fernwood Pk. Ave.
Halsey Ave.
Fir Ave.
Park Ave.
Avion Ave.
Fiorn Field Ave.
Selwood Ave.
Hubbard Blvd.
Trillium Trail
Isleworth Ave.
Wineva Ave.
Leuty Ave.
Violet Ave.
Lee Ave.
Kew Gardens
Beaches Park
Trillium Trail
Kew Beach Ave.
Waverley Rd.
Kenilworth Ave.
Olympic Pool

Sycamore Pl.
Cres.

Scarborough

A tour of Scarborough, you wonder? The reputation of this borough of Metropolitan Toronto, sometimes referred to as Scarberia, unfortunately precedes it! So why should you visit it? Well, despite its undistinguished strawberry-box bungalow houses, the city is also • home to Metropolitan Toronto's spectacular zoo and to the majestic gray cliffs that earned it its name (Elizabeth Simcoe, the wife of Lt.-Gov. John Simcoe felt that they resembled those of Scarborough, England).

Four spectacular parks provide access to those fabled grey cliffs known as the Bluffs: Bluffers West Park, Scarborough Bluffs Park, Bluffers Park and Cathedral Bluffs Park. Each park boasts spectacular scenery over Lake Ontario and a wealth of outdoor possibilities.

From the Bluffs take Brimley Road north towards the centre of Scarborough.

Scarborough Historical Museum *($3; Apr to Jun and Sep to mid-Dec, Mon-Fri 10am to 4pm; Jul and Aug, Wed-Sun noon to 4pm; Thomson Memorial Park, 1007 Brimley Rd., ☎338-8807),* an outdoor museum, features historic buildings and a display annex. The Cornell House of 1858 evokes rural life at the turn of the 20th century; the McGowan Log House recreates an earlier time, that of the pioneers in the 1850s, and finally the Hough Carriage Works is an authentic 19th-century carriage shop.

Continuing up Brimley Road, just north of Ellesmere Road, you'll come to Scarborough's town centre. Partly an attempt to shed its unfavourable image, the town centre was conceived in the late 1960s following the unveiling of New City Hall and the birth of Toronto's new public image. Architect Raymond Moriyama designed the exceptional **Scarborough Civic Centre** and thus gave the city core a focal point. Opinions are mixed as to the success of this building, which is nevertheless a lively place with a large square.

To reach the zoo, take McGowan Road up to Finch Avenue and head east. Continue along Old Finch Road to Meadowvale Drive and head south to the entrance.

Finally, for an enjoyable change of scenery just minutes from the heart of downtown Toronto, head to the **Toronto Metropolitan Zoo ★★** *($15; Mar to May, every day 9am to 6pm; Jun to Aug, every day 9am to 7:30pm; Sep and Oct, every day 9am to 6pm; Nov to Feb, every day 9:30am to 4:30pm; 361A Old Finch Ave., at Hwy. 401 and Meadowvale Rd., ☎392-5900, www.torontozoo. com),* where you can see some 4,000 animals from the four corners of the globe and take advantage of this lovely 300ha park. The African pavilion is particularly interesting, since it is

© ULYSSES

L Eastern Toronto (Scarborough)

● ATTRACTIONS
1. Scarborough Historical Museum
2. Scarborough Civic Centre
3. Toronto Metropolitan Zoo

⬡ ACCOMMODATIONS
1. Scarborough's Guild Inn

located in a large greenhouse where the climate and vegetation have been recreated. Canadian wildlife is also well represented, and several species accustomed to the local climate roam free in large enclosures.

★★★

Tour M: Niagara Falls

This tour covers the region to the west of the Niagara River, along the U.S. border. Control over this area was once crucial as far as shipping on lakes Ontario and Superior was concerned, and the two forts that were built to protect it still

stand on either side of the river. Nowadays, however, the region is best known for its wineries and orchards, and as the home of the extraordinary Niagara Falls, which have continued to amaze people of all ages and inspire lovers and daredevils for decades.

★★

Niagara-on-the-Lake

The history of Niagara-on-the-Lake dates back to the late 18th century, when the town, then known as Newark, was the capital of Upper Canada (1791 to 1796). Nothing remains of that time, however,

Exploring

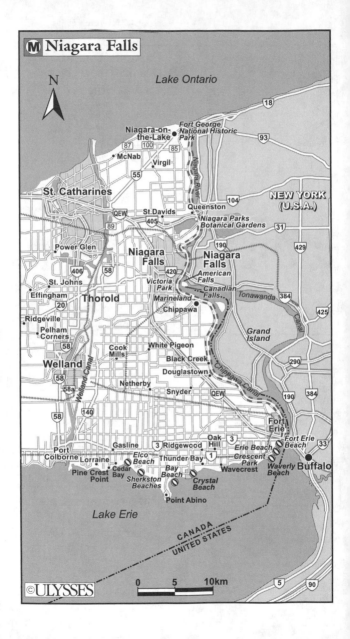

M Niagara Falls

N

Lake Ontario

18

Niagara-on-the-Lake
Fort George National Historic Park
93
87 100 85
McNab
Virgil
55
St. Catharines
104
NEW YORK (U.S.A.)
QEW
St.Davids
Queenston
89
405
Niagara Parks Botanical Gardens
31
429
Power Glen
190
Niagara Falls
Niagara Falls
406
420
American Falls
St. Johns
Victoria Park
Canadian Falls
Tonawanda
384
Effingham
20
Thorold
Marineland
Chippawa
Ridgeville
Pelham Corners
Grand Island
58
White Pigeon
Cook Mills
Black Creek
290
Welland
Douglastown
Chippawa Canal
58
Netherby
425
58a
Snyder
QEW
140
190
384
58
Fort Erie
Gasline
Oak Hill
3
Ridgewood
3
Fort Erie Beach
Port Colborne
Lorraine
Elco Beach
Thunder Bay
Erie Beach
Crescent Park
33
Pine Crest Point
Cedar Bay
Bay Beach
1
Wavecrest
Waverly Beach
Buffalo
Sherkston Beaches
Crystal Beach
Point Abino

Lake Erie

CANADA
UNITED STATES

©ULYSSES

0   5   10km

5   90

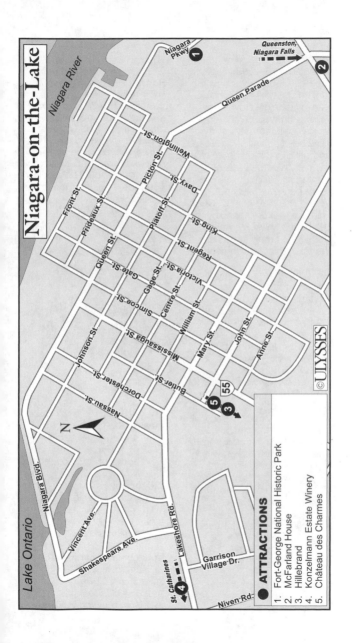

Niagara-on-the-Lake

Lake Ontario

Niagara River

Queenston,
Niagara Falls

Niagara Pkwy 1

2

Queen Parade

Wellington St.

Picton St.

Davy St.

Front St.

Prideaux St.

Platoff St.

King St.

Queen St.

Gate St.

Regent St.

Simcoe St.

Gage St.

Victoria St.

Centre St.

Johnson St.

Mississauga St.

William St.

Mary St.

John St.

Dorchester St.

Butler St.

Anne St.

Nassau St.

N

Niagara Blvd.

Vincent Ave.

Shakespeare Ave.

Lakeshore Rd.

St. Catharines 4

Garrison
Village Dr.

Niven Rd.

55

5
3

© ULYSSES

ATTRACTIONS

1. Fort-George National Historic Park
2. McFarland House
3. Hillebrand
4. Konzelmann Estate Winery
5. Château des Charmes

for the town was burned during the War of 1812, which pitted the British colonies against the United States. After the American invasion, the town was rebuilt and graced with elegant English-style homes, which have been beautifully preserved and still give this community at the mouth of the Niagara River a great deal of charm. Some of these houses have been converted into elegant inns, which welcome visitors attending the celebrated Shaw Festival (see p 247), or simply lured here by the town's English atmosphere.

After the American Revolution, the British abandoned Fort Niagara, which stands on the east side of the Niagara River. To protect their remaining colonies, however, they decided to build another fort. Between 1797 and 1799, Fort George was erected on the west side of the river. Within a few years, the two countries were fighting again. In 1812, war broke out, and the Niagara-on-the-Lake region, which shared a border with the United States, was in the eye of the storm. Fort George was captured, then destroyed in 1813, only to be reconstructed in 1815.

At the **Fort George National Historic Park** ★ *($6; Apr to Oct, every day 10am to 5pm; 26 Queen's Parade, ☎905-468-4257)*, you can tour the officer's quarters, the guard rooms, the barracks and other parts of the restored fort.

You can also visit the lovely, Georgian-style **McFarland House** *($2.50; mid-Apr to Jun, every day 10pm to 4pm; Jul and Aug, Sun-Thu 10am to 5pm, Fri and Sat 10am to 8pm; Sep every day 11am to 4pm; Oct, Fri-Sun 11am to 4pm, by appointment during the rest of the year; 15927 Niagara Pkwy. S., 2km south of town, ☎905-468-3322)*, built in 1800 for James McFarland and still decorated with furnishings dating from 1800 to 1840.

McFarland House

There are a number of **vineyards** in the Niagara-on-the-Lake region, large, striped fields all along the side of the highway. Some of these offer tours:

Hillebrand
1249 Niagara Stone Rd.
Niagara-on-the-Lake
☎*(905) 468-7123*
www.hillebrand.com

Konzelmann Estate Winery
1096 Lakeshore Rd.
Niagara-on-the-Lake
☎*(905) 935-2866*
www.konzelmannwines.com

Château des Charmes
1025 York Rd., St. Davids
☎*(905) 262-4219*
www.chateaudescharmes.com

Continue heading south on the Niagara Parkway, which runs alongside the Niagara River to Queenston.

Queenston

A pretty hamlet on the banks of the Niagara River, Queenston consists of a few little houses and verdant gardens. It is best known as the former home of Laura Secord.

Laura Secord Homestead
($3.50; Jun to Sep 11am to 5pm; Queenston St., ☎877-642-7275, www.niagaraparks. com). Laura Secord, born Ingersoll in Massachusetts in 1775, married James Secord in 1795, settling in Queenston a few years later. She became famous during the War of 1812 when, after learning of an imminent attack by the Americans, she ran some 25km to warn the British army, thus helping them succeed in pushing back the enemy troops. Today, her name is usually associated with a brand of chocolates, some of which you can taste in the shop located next to the homestead.

Farther south, you'll reach the foot of Queenston Height. If you're feeling energetic, you can climb the steps to the statue of Isaac Brock, a British general who died in this area

while leading his men to victory during the War of 1812. This spot also offers a splendid **view ★** of the region.

Keep heading south to Niagara Falls.

Niagara Falls

The striking spectacle of the Niagara Falls has been attracting crowds of visitors for many years, a trend supposedly started when Napoleon's brother came here with his young bride. Right beside the falls, the town of the same name is entirely devoted to tourism, and its downtown area is a series of nondescript motels, uninteresting museums and fast-food restaurants, accented by scores of colourful signs. These places have sprung up in a chaotic manner, and no one seems to have given a second thought to aesthetics. There's no denying that the Niagara Falls themselves are a natural trea-sure, but the town is best avoided.

The **Niagara Falls ★★★** were formed some 10,000 years ago, when the glaciers receded, clearing the Niagara Escarpment and diverting the aters of Lake Erie into Lake Ontario. This natural formation is remarkably beautiful, with two falls, one on either side of the border. The American Falls are 64m high and 305m wide, with a flow of 14 million litres

Exploring

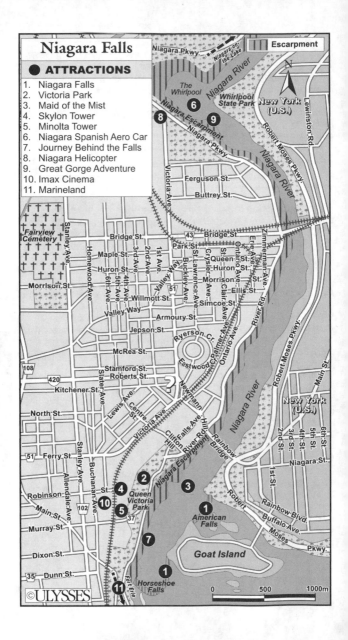

Niagara Falls

● ATTRACTIONS

1. Niagara Falls
2. Victoria Park
3. Maid of the Mist
4. Skylon Tower
5. Minolta Tower
6. Niagara Spanish Aero Car
7. Journey Behind the Falls
8. Niagara Helicopter
9. Great Gorge Adventure
10. Imax Cinema
11. Marineland

Escarpment

©ULYSSES

per minute, while Canada's Horseshoe Falls, named for their shape, are 54m high and 675m wide, with a flow of 155 million litres of water per minute. The rocky shelf of the falls is made of soft stone, and it was being worn away at a rate of 1m per year until some of the water was diverted to the nearby hydroelectric power stations. The rate of erosion is now about 0.3m per year.

It would be hard not to be impressed by the sight of all that raging water plunging into the gulf at your feet with a thundering roar. This seemingly un-tameable natural force has been a source of inspiration to many a visitor. In the early 20th century, a few daring souls tried to demonstrate their bravery by going over the falls in a barrel or walking over them on a tightrope, resulting in several deaths. In 1912, these types of stunts were outlawed.

During the summer, a huge number of visitors arrive every day to see the falls. Many come by car, so there tend to be traffic jams while everyone searches for a place to park. There is a huge parking lot at the entrance to the park–the **Fallsview Parking,** which charges a fee. To save a few dollars, you can brave the traffic downtown, where parking lots are cheaper.

You can also park your car at the **Rapids View Parking Lot**. Parking fees include an all-day People Mover Transportation Pass.

The **People Mover Buses** transportation service covers the entire falls area and allows visitors to travel effortlessly from one attraction to another.

Those only here for a short time can park at **Greenhouse Parking**.

Those wanting to visit several of the city's tourist attractions (Journey Behind the Falls, Butterfly Conservatory, Niagara Spanish Aero Car, Great Gorge Adventure, Fort Erie, Laura Secord Homestead and McFarland House) can buy the **Discovery Pass Plus**. This pass also includes all-day transportation aboard the People Mover Buses.

In 1885, **Victoria Park ★** was created in order to protect the natural setting around the falls from unbridled commercial development. This beautiful green space alongside the river is scored with hiking and cross-country ski trails.

There are **observation decks ★ ★ ★** in front of the falls, which can also be viewed from countless other angles; read on...

The **Maid of the Mist ★** *($12.25; early May to end Oct, departures every 15min, first and last departures vary throughout the season–call first, 9am to 7pm or later in high season; 5920 River Rd., ☎905-358-5781)* takes passengers to the foot of the falls, which make the boat seem very small indeed. Protected from getting drenched by a raincoat during the outing, you can view the American side of the falls and then the Canadian side, right in the middle of the horseshoe.

If you climb to the top of the **Skylon Tower** *($8.95; May to Oct, every day 8am to 10:30pm; Nov to Apr, every day 11am to 10:30pm; 5200 Robinson St., ☎905-356-2651 or 877-475-9566)*, you can **view the falls ★★** at your feet, a truly unique and memorable sight. You will enjoy a similar view from the **Minolta Tower** *($6.95; every day 7am to 11pm; 6732 Oakes Dr., ☎905-356-1501)*.

The **Spanish Aero Car** *($5; Mar to Nov, 10am to 4:40pm; Niagara Pkwy., ☎877-642-7275)* offers a bird's-eye view of the falls from a height of 76.2m.

To truly feel the power of the falls, head to the Table Rock Complex to participate in the **Journey Behind the Falls ★** *($10; Mon-Fri 10am to 6pm, Sat and Sun 9am to 6pm; ☎358-3268)*. An elevator takes visitors underground to one of three tunnels hollowed out of the rock that lead behind the falls, where the roaring torrents of water can be viewed up close.

How about soaring through the air over the falls? You can do just that, thanks to **Niagara Helicopters** *($90; every day from 9am on, weather permitting; 3731 Victoria Ave., ☎905-357-5672)*.

An elevator transports visitors all the way down to the rapids for the **Great Gorge Adventure** *($4.75; Apr to mid-Oct 9am to 5pm; 4330 River Rd., ☎905-374-1221)*.

Niagara has countless museums, some of little interest. A number of them are located in the downtown area known as Clifton Hill.

The **Imax Theatre** *($7.50; May to Oct every day; 6170 Buchanan Ave., ☎905-358-3611)* shows a film on the falls on a giant screen.

If you'd like to forget about the falls for a little while and watch some performing sea-lions, dolphins and whales instead, head to **Marineland** *(prices vary, $29.95 during summer; May to Oct 10am to 5pm, Jul and Aug 9am to 6pm; 7657 Portage Rd., ☎905-356-9565)*. The little zoo and carousels are sure to be a hit with the kids.

Maid of the Mist

Outdoors

M etropolitan Toronto
began as a collection of small, previously independent villages.

A s a result, it is graced with hundreds of lovely parks encompassing the city's largest natural areas, many of which include heritage buildings. Over 80km of maintained trails beckon to walkers, joggers, cyclists and in-line skaters. The outdoor possibilities are endless.

Parks

High Park (☎392-1111), located in the western part of the city and bounded by Bloor Street to the north, The Queensway to the south, Parkside Drive to the east and Ellis Avenue to the west, is Toronto's Central Park. It is accessible by both subway (Keele or High Park stations) and streetcar (College or Queen). Toronto's largest park, High Park features tennis courts, playgrounds, bike paths, nature trails, picnic areas and a swimming pool; skating and fishing on Grenadier Pond; rare flora; wildlife indigenous to the area plus animal paddocks where buffaloes, llamas and

sheep are kept; a beach on Lake Ontario and, finally, "Dream in High Park" (see p 239), a version of Shakespeare in the park.

Historic **Colborne Lodge** *($3.50; May to Sept, Tue-Sun noon to 5pm; Oct to Dec, Tue-Sun noon to 4pm; Jan to Apr, Sat and Sun noon to 4pm; year-round for booked groups, these* *hours change often so call ahead; High Park,* ☎392-6916) is also located in the park. Built in 1837, this Regency-style residence was built and inhabited by architect John Howard. Its lovely three-sided veranda once offered clear views of Lake Ontario and the Humber River. Howard deeded 67ha to the City of Toronto in 1873. The other 94ha that make up High Park were acquired separately. The house is now open to the public and run by guides in period dress. The nearby **Howard Tomb and Monument** is surrounded by an iron fence that was designed by Christopher Wren and once helped guard St. Paul's Cathedral in London, England.

The **Village of Yorkville Park** *(Cumberland St. between Avenue Rd. and Bellair St.)* is a fascinating example of urban ecology. Divided into 13 sectors, it represents local history and regional identity. A walk through the park from west to east begins in the Amelanchier Grove and leads through the Heritage Walk (Old York Lane), the Herbaceous Border Garden, the Canadian Shield Clearing & Fountain, the Alder Grove, the Ontario Marsh, the Festival Walk, the Cumberland Court Cross Walk, The Crabapple Orchard, The Fragrant Herb Rock Garden, The Birch Grove and the Prairie Wildflower Gardens, before ending up in the Pine Grove. The highlight of the walk is certainly the village rock in the Canadian Shield sector. The rock is approximately one billion years old and weighs 650 tonnes. It comes from the area northeast of Gravenhurst, in the Muskoka Lakes region of northern Ontario.

Allan Gardens *(between Dundas, Gerrard, Sherbourne and Jarvis Sts.)* is a pretty city park with a lovely old Victorian greenhouse overflowing with brightly coloured flowers year-round.

The Don River Valley wends its way through Toronto to Lake Ontario and harbours a net-. work of beautiful parks linked by bridges and trails. **Edwards Gardens** *(parking at Leslie St. and Lawrence Ave. E.,* ☎397-1340) is one of Toronto's first garden parks and features rock gardens, perennials, rose gardens, small waterfalls and dense forest. The river flows south past **Wilket Creek Park** and **Ernest Thompson Seton Park**.

Buffalo

The Ontario Science Centre overlooks the latter. Near Don Mills Road, **Taylor Creek Park** extends to the east all the way to Warden Woods. All of these parks are wonderful places for walking, bicycling, jogging, cross-country skiing and even bird-watching.

Scarborough Bluffs Park and **Cathedral Bluffs Park** command breathtaking views of Lake Ontario from atop the scenic bluffs, while **Bluffer's Park** and **Bluffer's West Park** offer beautiful, spacious beaches and picnic areas.

Toronto Islands Park is on a group of 17 islands collectively known as the Toronto Islands, an 8min ferry ride from Toronto Harbour. Three ferries, each departing from the Mainland Ferry Terminal at the foot of Bay Street, go to the islands. See p 92 for a walking tour of the islands.

Outdoor Activities

Bicycling

The **Martin Goodman Trail**, a 22km jogging and cycling path, follows the shore of Lake Ontario from the mouth of the Humber River west of the city centre, past Ontario Place and Queen's Quay to the Balmy Beach Club in The Beaches. Call ☎*392-8186* for a map of the trail.

Bicycle and jogging paths also weave their way through Metropolitan Toronto's parks, such as High Park. For maps and information on the trails call ☎*392-8186*.

Toronto Island Bicycle Rental
Centre Island
☎*203-0009*

Wheel Excitement
5 Rees St. (south of the SkyDome)
☎*260-9000*

Downtown Cycle
368 College St.
☎*923-8189*

High Park Cycle
High Park
☎*614-6689*

In-line Skating

Toronto's streets may be a bit hazardous for this sport, but the scenic paths on the Toronto Islands and near the water in The Beaches, or at the parks near the Bluffs, are ideal.

Wheel Excitement
5 Rees St. (south of the SkyDome)
☎*260-9000*
This shop rents skates and all the necessary equipment (pads)

Outdoors

and offers lessons. You will need at least 3hrs to tour the islands.

Ice Skating

There are several enchanting places to go ice-skating in the city. These include the rink in front of New City Hall, Grenadier Pond in High Park and York Quay at Harbourfront. For information on city rinks call ☎392-1111.

Golf

There are five municipal golf courses (two executive and three regulation), which operate on a first-come, first-served basis. The **Don Valley Golf Course** (☎392-2465) is a challenging regulation course with several water and bunker hazards.

For something more challenging, take a little jaunt out to Oakville, to the **Glen Abbey Golf Club** (green fees and cart $235, discount rates in off-season and on weekends after 2pm $135; ☎905-844-1800). This spectacular course was the first to be designed by Jack Nicklaus. The rates are high, but it's a real thrill to play where the

pros play. The Canadian Open Championship is held here.

Hiking and Cross-Country Skiing

Trails for both activities criss-cross the **Toronto Islands** (see p 175).

Toronto's many ravines are wonderful places to explore on foot or on skis. A lovely trail begins in **Edwards Gardens** and meanders along the **Don River** to **Taylor Creek**. Pedestrians can access the Don River Valley from Leslie Street between Lawrence and Eglinton, from Gateway Boulevard behind the Ontario Science Centre, from Moore Avenue near Mount Pleasant Cemetery and from the Gerrard Street overpass.

Much more pristine than the Don River Valley, **Highland Creek** to the east of Scarborough is also lined with scenic walking trails. This area is known for its spectacular fall colours. The woodsy trails of **Morningside Park** are perfect for cross-country skiing.

Accommodations

Travellers will discover a great variety of lodging options in all price categories in Toronto.

Rates vary greatly from one season to the next. They are much higher during the summer, but usually lower on the weekends than during the week. Remember that the weeks of the Caribana festival (end of July to early August) and the film festival (early September) are particularly busy. We recommend making reservations well in advance if you plan to be in Toronto during these events. In the off-season, it is often possible to obtain better rates than those quoted in this guide. Several establishments also offer discounts to automobile club members and corporate employees. Make sure to ask about these discounts, as they are easy to obtain. Please note that parking is available at most large hotels, usually at a cost of between $10 and $25 per day.

All Prices mentioned in this guide apply to a standard room for two people in peak

season and do not include taxes.

$	50$ or less
$$	50,01$ to 100$
$$$	100,01$ to 150$
$$$$	150,01$ to 200$
$$$$$	200,01$ and over

The Waterfront

Radisson Plaza Hotel Admiral
$$$$$
≡, ⊛, ≈
249 Queen's Quay W.
☎ *203-3333 or 800-333-3333*
⇄ *203-3100*
www.radisson.com
If you like the sea, you will feel at home at the Radisson Plaza Hotel Admiral. The decor of this charming hotel displays a seafaring motif, with the room decor reminiscent of a cruise ship. The view of the bay from the fifth-floor pool is quite magnificent. Regular shuttle service is offered between the hotel and the downtown area.

SkyDome Hotel
$$$$$
ℜ, ≈, ⊘, ⌂, ⊛, ≡
1 Blue Jays Way
☎ *341-7100 or 800-237-1512*
⇄ *341-5091*
www.renaissancehotels.com
The SkyDome Hotel has 348 rooms with panoramic views and also offers its customers 70 rooms facing the inside of the stadium. The latter cost more, but what a view! The hotel has a choice of restaurants, a business centre and a bar that also offers a view of the playing field. The modern rooms are adequate, but nothing special. Valet service and room service are available day and night.

Westin Harbour Castle
$$$$$
≡, ≈, ℜ, ⊘, ⌂, ⊛
1 Harbour Square
☎ *869-1600 or 800-228-3000*
⇄ *869-0573*
www.westin.com
The Westin Harbour Castle used to be part of the Hilton hotel chain. In 1987, Westin and Hilton decided to swap their respective Toronto hotels. Located in a calm and peaceful spot on the shore of Lake Ontario, the Westin Harbour Castle is just a few steps from the Harbourfront Centre and the ferry to the Toronto Islands. To help guests reach the downtown area, the hotel offers a free shuttle service. It also lies along a streetcar line.

The Theatre and Financial Districts

Global Village Backpackers
$$
sb/pb, ℝ, K
460 King St. W.
☎ 703-8540 or 888-844-7875
⇌ 703-3887
www.globalbackpackers.com
Global Village Backpackers is housed in what was once the infamous Spadina Hotel. Now totally refurbished as a youth hostel, it is just three blocks from the trendy, artsy area of Queen West. It is Toronto's largest international traveller's hostel (though not a member of the International Youth Hostel Federation), with 200 beds. Its dormitory-style accommodations lend it a great atmosphere for students. Internet facilities available.

Hotel Victoria
$$$ bkfst incl.
ℜ, ℝ
56 Yonge St.
☎ 363-1666 or 800-363-8228
⇌ 363-7327
www.toronto.com/hotelvictoria
The Hotel Victoria has a wonderful location, midway between the financial district and Union Station. The hotel offers simple rooms at very affordable prices. Although it does not have its own parking area, this should not be a problem, as there are a number of public parking lots nearby. The restaurant is open for breakfast only.

Strathcona Hotel
$$$
≡, ℜ
60 York St.
☎ 363-3321 or 800-268-8304
⇌ 363-4679
www.toronto.com/strathconahotel
Much smaller than its downtown counterparts, the Strathcona is a pleasant hotel, located just two steps from the Fairmont Royal York Hotel and a few minutes' walk from the Waterfront. Its attractive rooms offer a standard level of comfort.

Travelodge Toronto Downtown West
$$$
≡
621 King St. W.
☎ 504-7441 or 800-578-7878
⇌ 504-4722
www.travelodgetorontodowntown.com
Set back from the theatre and financial districts, the Travelodge Toronto Downtown West is one of the best low-budget options downtown. The 88 rooms of this small three-storey hotel are ideal for families, as are its room rates. Free parking.

Fairmont Royal York Hotel
$$$$$
≡, ≈, ☺, △, ℜ
100 Front St. W.
☎ 368-2511 or 800-441-1414
⇌ 368-2884
www.royalyorkhotel.com
The Fairmont Royal York lives up to its reputation: it's clear when you enter the luxurious

lobby that your stay will be an unforgettable and comfortable one. The rooms are pleasant and equipped with the latest in modern amenities, without sacrificing their old-world charm. Unlike most hotels, the Fairmont Royal York is a happening place, whether it's for watching the comings and goings in the lobby while having a cup of coffee in the restaurant, or for enjoying a beer in its famed Library Bar, you'll want to join in. Located right across the street from Union Station, this is one of the busiest hotels in Toronto.

🏨 Le Germain
$$$$$
30 Mercer St.
☎ *345-9500 or 866-345-9501*
www.germaintoronto.com
The Germain is the latest addition to the Financial and Theatre districts, and its appeal lies in its modest size and refined decor. The 120 rooms boast an elegant simplicity that marries comfort and pleasure with the more specific needs of business travellers. A gem…

Hilton Toronto
$$$$$
≡, ⊛, ≈, ℜ, ☺, △
145 Richmond St. W.
☎ *869-3456 or 800-445-8667*
⇄ *869-3187*
www.hilton.com
The Toronto Hilton International, with its pastel decor, resembles many other Hilton hotels. It offers comfortable, clean, well equipped rooms. Many visiting sports teams stay

at the Hilton, among them the Montreal Canadiens, the Los Angeles Kings and the Oakland A's.

Holiday Inn on King
$$$$$
≡, ≈, △, ☺
370 King St. W.
☎ *599-4000 or 800-263-6364*
⇄ *599-4785*
www.hiok.com
Located on busy King Street, the Holiday Inn on King is hard to miss thanks to its huge size, multi-tiered architecture and white exterior. The 425-odd rooms offer a pleasant, modern decor but no special charm. Some have balconies.

🏨 InterContinental Toronto Centre
$$$$$
225 Front St. W.
☎ *597-1400 or 800-422-7969*
⇄ *597-8128*
www.torontocentre
.intercontinental.com
A big favourite with business travellers, adjacent to the Metro Toronto Convention Centre, the InterContinental Toronto Centre has become one of the best hotels in Toronto, thanks in part to a recent 36-million-dollar renovation project. The avant-garde lobby and the huge stained-glass wall that overlooks Front Street from the restaurant are a foretaste of its tasteful rooms, which feature contemporary stylings and a modern uncluttered luxury. The Centre is also home to the Victoria Spa, one of the most popular day spas in Toronto.

Old Town of York

Hostelling International
$
K
76 Church St.
☎*971-4440 or 877-848-8737*
⇌*971-4088*
www.bostellingint-gl.on.ca
Hostelling International offers
180 beds in semi-private rooms
or dormitories at very affordable prices. Guests will find a
television lounge, a laundromat,
Internet facilities, a kitchen and
a pool table and dart board, as
well as an outdoor terrace.
Discount offered to members.

Cawthra Square Bed &
Breakfast
$$$-$$$$$ bkfst incl.
sb/pb, ≡, ✪
10 Cawthra Sq.
☎*966-3074 or 800-259-5474*
⇌*966-4494*
www.cawthrasquare.com
Cawthra Square Bed & Break-
fast comprises two elegant
Victorian and Edwardian homes
in the heart of Toronto's gay

village, near Church and
Wellesley. It has grand main
rooms, continental breakfast
rooms and a library on site.
Private bathrooms and terraces
are also available.

Ambassador Inn
Downtown Toronto
$$$-$$$$$ bkfst incl.
sb/pb, ≡
280 Jarvis St.
☎*260-2608*
⇌*260-1219*
www.ambassadorinntoronto.com
The Ambassador Inn Down-
town Toronto is an elegant,
upscale bed and breakfast in a
20-room Victorian mansion
with fireplaces, a cathedral
ceiling, gabled roof, stained-
glass windows and skylights.
The rooms are uniquely decorated, combining modern comfort with a classical style. Furthermore, the Ambassador Inn
provides all the usual services
for business travellers.

Novotel
$$$-$$$$$
≡, ⊛, ℜ, ⊘, ⌂, ≈
45 The Esplanade
☎*367-8900 or 800-668-6835*
⇌*360-8285*
www.novotel.com
French hotel chain Novotel
enjoys an ideal Toronto loca-
tion, just minutes from Har-
bourfront, the St. Lawrence
and Hummingbird centres, and
Union Station. Comfort is as-
sured at this hotel, except per-
haps for the rooms facing The
Esplanade whose peace and
quiet may be disturbed by
sounds from the outdoor bars.

Quality Hotel Downtown
$$$-$$$$

≡, ☉

111 Lombard St.

☎ *367-5555 or 800-228-5151*

⇝ *367-3470*

www.toronto.com/qualityhotel

The Quality Hotel by Journey's End caters to people who want simple but comfortable rooms at a reasonable price.

🖐 Royal Meridian King Edward Hotel
$$$$$

≡, ☉, ℜ

37 King St. E.

☎ *863-3131 or 800-543-4300*

⇝ *367-5515*

www.lemeridien-kingedward.com

Built in 1903, the Royal Meridian King Edward Hotel is the oldest hotel in Toronto and still one of the most attractive. Rooms at this very elegant spot each have their own character but do not, unfortunately, offer much in terms of views. However, the magnificent lobby and the two ballrooms make up for this. Airport buses stop here regularly.

Queen Street West

St. Lawrence Residences
$-$$ bkfst incl.

sb, ℜ, ≡

137 Jarvis St.

☎ *361-0053 or 800-567-9949*

⇝ *361-0837*

www.saintlawrenceresidences
.com

St. Lawrence Residences provides bed-and-breakfast, hotel- or dorm-style rooms. The rooms are bright and airy at this

downtown establishment that's close to the Eaton Centre, Yonge Street, the financial district and many restaurants.

Bond Place Hotel
$$$-$$$$

≡, ℜ

65 Dundas St. E.

☎ *360-6061 or 800-268-9390*

⇝ *360-6406*

The Bond Place Hotel is doubtless the best-located hotel for enjoying the rhythm of the city and mixing with the varied throng at the corner of Dundas and Yonge.

Cambridge Suites Hotel
$$$$-$$$$$ bkfst incl.

≡, ≈, ⊛, *K*, ℝ, ☉, ℜ

15 Richmond St. E.

☎ *368-1990 or 800-463-1990*

⇝ *601-3751/3753*

www.cambridgesuiteshotel.com

The Cambridge Suites Hotel offers large comfortable suites. They are equipped with a kitchenette and work space and are well suited for business travellers as well as families.

Sheraton Centre Toronto
$$$$$

≡, ≈, ℜ, ☉, △, ✿

123 Queen St. W.

☎ *361-1000 or 800-325-3535*

⇝ *947-4854*

www.sheratontoronto.com

The Sheraton Centre Toronto is an enormous complex including 40 shops, restaurants and bars as well as two movie theatres. This very comfortable hotel has many rooms, of which the most attractive are in the two towers, reached by private elevators. The lobby, with its magnificent 0.8ha (2 acre) in-door garden, is this hotel's most astonishing feature. Guests also have access to the network of indoor passageways linking many downtown points.

Toronto Marriott Eaton Centre
$$$$$
≡, ≈, ℜ, ⊛, △, ⊘
525 Bay St.
☎ *597-9200 or 800-905-0667*
⇌ *597-9211*
www.marriott.com
If you prefer to have everything under the same roof, the To-ronto Marriott Eaton Centre fits the bill. Linked to the famous Eaton Centre (a shoppers' mecca and one of the city's main attractions) the Marriott Hotel offers huge, well-equip-ped rooms (they even have irons and ironing boards). If you want to relax, there are two ground-floor lounges, one with pool tables and televisions.

Chinatown and Kensington

Alexandra Hotel
$$
≡, ℝ, *K*
77 Ryerson Ave.
☎ *504-2121 or 800-567-1893*
⇌ *504-9195*
www.alexandrahotel.com
Located in the heart of the trendy Queen West area and with the same owners as the

Grange Hotel, the Alexandra Hotel has comfortable studio suites equipped with kitchen-ettes, bathrooms, colour cable television, air conditioning, direct dial telephones and laun-dry facilities. Parking is available.

Grange Hotel
$$
≡, ℝ, *K*
165 Grange Ave.
☎ *603-7700 or 888-232-0002*
⇌ *603-9977*
www.grangehotel.com
Located downtown near Chi-natown, Kensington and Queen Street West, the affordable studio suites are comfortable and air conditioned with colour TV, telephone, laundry rooms and parking available.

Beaconsfield Bed & Breakfast
$$-$$$ bkfst incl.
≡, *pb/sb*
38 Beaconsfield Ave.
☎ *535-3338*
⇌ *535-3338*
www.bbcanada.com/771.html
The Beaconsfield is a superb Victorian house dating from 1882 in a quiet little neighbour-hood near Queen Street. It's a good place to turn if you are looking for something different from the big hotels. Rooms are charming and imaginatively decorated. Perhaps best of all, though, are the delightful and musical breakfasts.

Metropolitan Hotel
$$$$$
≡, ≈, ⊘, △, ℜ
108 Chestnut St.
☎*977-5000 or 800-668-6600*
⇄*977-9513*
www.metropolitan.com

The Metropolitan Hotel is one of the biggest additions to the Toronto hotel scene. Entering the lobby, you will discover an inviting atrium, giving you an idea of what to expect in the thoroughly pleasant rooms, which offer cable and Internet access.

Queen's Park and the University of Toronto

Les Amis
$$ bkfst incl.
≡, sb
31 Granby St.
☎*928-1348*
⇄*591-8546*
www.bbtoronto.com

Michelle and Paul-Antoine Buer, who moved here from France several years ago, have recently opened Les Amis, a small, unpretentious bed and breakfast where you'll feel right at home. Simply but carefully decorated, each of the house's three rooms features a comfortable bed with a German mattress, comforter and goosedown pillows. Though located on a small, quiet, residential street, it is only a few minutes from bustling downtown Toronto. The fresh, homemade vegetarian breakfast is made with organic products.

Neil Wycik College Hotel
$$ bkfst incl.
ℜ, △
96 Gerrard St. E.
☎*977-2320 or 800-268-4358*
⇄*977-2809*
www.neil-wycik.com/hotel

From mid-May to late August, the Neil Wycik College Hotel opens its student residences to travellers. Rooms are simple and offer only the basics, but there is a room-cleaning service, a television lounge and a laundromat at guests' disposal.

Victoria College University of Toronto
$$ bkfst incl.
140 Charles St. W.
☎*585-4524*
⇄*585-4530*

If you are visiting Toronto during the summer months and want a clean, economic place to sleep, you can take advantage of the 425 rooms at Victoria College. Guests also have a laundromat and cafeteria at their disposal.

St. George Campus
$$
K, ℝ, ℜ, ⊘
University of Toronto 214 College St.
☎*978-8045*

From May to August, at the St. George Campus, you will find an excellent, low-cost alternative to expensive hotels. The university has lodgings that can accommodate four to six persons, each with a fully equipped kitchenette. They are located near a cafeteria, a pub and a physical fitness centre.

 **Beverley Place Bed & Breakfast**
$$-$$$ bkfst incl.
sb/pb, ≈, ℝ
235 Beverley St.
☎*977-0077*
⇌*599-2242*
This 1887 Victorian house has been restored to its original beauty, complete with exquisite antique furnishings. Awarded the Government of Canada Tourism Ambassador Certificate, it is centrally located near the University of Toronto campus, Chinatown and the cafés and shops in the Annex.

 **The House on McGill**
$$-$$$ bkfst incl.
sb/pb, ≈
110 McGill St.
☎*351-1503 or 877-580-5015*
www.mcgillbb.ca
Canadian Dave Perks and Australian Adam Tanner-Hill welcome you to their delightful bed and breakfast, housed in a beautiful Victorian home erected in 1894. Located on a small residential street just steps away from Church Street and Toronto's Gay Village, the establishment offers six colourful, tastefully decorated rooms in a setting that combines the best of the Victorian era with modern comfort.

Guests appreciate the quiet and intimacy of the place, its polished decor, small garden and central location.

Victoria's Mansion
$$-$$$
ℝ, *K*, ≈
68 Gloucester St.
☎*921-4625*
⇌*944-1092*
www.victoriasmansion.com
Victoria's Mansion is a beautiful turn-of-the-20th century home located on a quiet street close to lively neighbourhoods, just a few streets south of Bloor. Its elaborate exterior gives a somewhat inaccurate idea of its modestly decorated interior and plainly furnished suites. Victoria's Mansion is particularly well suited for long-term stays since each room is equipped with a kitchenette and desk, offering a level of comfort similar to that of a small apartment.

Comfort Hotel Downtown
$$$
ℜ, ≈
15 Charles St. E.
☎*924-1222 or 800-228-5150*
⇌*927-1369*
The Comfort Hotel Downtown is near Bloor Street's upscale shopping district– a block from

the central intersection of Yonge and Bloor. This newly renovated hotel has elegantly decorated rooms.

Jarvis House
$$$
≡, ⊗, *K*
344 Jarvis St.
☎*975-3838*
⇌*975-9808*
www.jarvishouse.com
Jarvis House offers 11 spotless rooms, each with a private bathroom. This newly renovated Victorian house also offers laundry service and full or continental breakfasts.

Best Western Primrose Hotel
$$$$
≡, ≈, ℜ, △, ⊘
111 Carlton St.
☎*977-8000 or 800-268-8082*
⇌*977-6323*
www.bestwestern.com
Best Western Primrose Hotel is located in the heart of downtown Toronto, opposite Maple Leaf Gardens. It has spacious rooms with two double beds or a king- size bed and a sofa, meeting rooms, a lounge and an outdoor pool.

Delta Chelsea
$$$$$
≡, ⊛, ≈, ℜ, ⊘
33 Gerrard St. W.
☎*595-1975 or 800-243-5732*
⇌*585-4375*
www.deltahotels.com
The Delta Chelsea is very popular with visitors and justly so. The hotel offers more than 1500 rooms, each designed to

accommodate the specific needs of business travellers or to provide the comfort required by families travelling with children. Furthermore, guests under 18 can share their parents' room free of charge. The new tower draws business travellers thanks to its business centre equipped with ergonomically designed chairs, fax machines and telephones.

Ramada Hotel and Suites
$$$$$
≡, ≈, ℜ, ⊘, △
300 Jarvis St.
☎*977-4823 or 800-567-2233*
⇌*977-4830*
www.ramadahotelandsuites.com
Well situated, the Ramada Hotel and Suites offers over 100 comfortable rooms, decorated in the usual style associated with this type of establishment. The service is excellent.

Sutton Place Hotel
$$$$$
≈, ℜ, ⊘
955 Bay St.
☎*924-9221 or 800-268-3790*
⇌*924-1778*
www.suttonplace.com
The Sutton Place Hotel boasts a solid reputation for luxury and the highest standards of quality and service, and all this ideally located near Queen's Park, the Royal Ontario Museum and the shops of Bloor and Yorkville. Each of the rooms and suites is well equipped for business travellers. The suites also have a full kitchen and a stunning antique decor.

Bloor and Yorkville

Marlborough Place
$$ bkfst incl.
sb/pb, ≡
93 Marlborough Ave.
☎*922-2159*
www.bbcanada.com/591.html
Marlborough Place is a bed and breakfast in a charming 1880 Victorian townhouse located near the fashionable Yorkville shopping area. It offers a spacious loft and a private room.

Howard Johnson Inn Yorkville
$$$ bkfst incl.
≡, ℝ
89 Avenue Rd.
☎*964-1220 or 800-446-4656*
⇌*964-8692*
Howard Johnson Inn Yorkville is a quaint, 71-room hotel located in the trendy Yorkville area. It is a little less expensive than some of the five-star hotels in the area, but is still just a step from the shop-lined streets of Yorkville and Bloor and some of Toronto's finest galleries. Coffee and tea are always available in the lobby, and rooms offer high-speed Internet access.

Days Inn – Toronto Downtown
$$$-$$$$
≡, ≈, ℜ, ℝ, △
30 Carlton St.
☎*977-6655 or 800-329-7466*
⇌*977-2865*
Days Inn Toronto Downtown offers decent, affordable hotel accommodation. It is just half a block from the subway and within walking distance of Yonge Street and the Eaton Centre. Recently renovated,

the Days Inn has a laundry service, free parking, an indoor pool, and in-room movies at guests' disposal.

Quality Hotel Midtown
$$$$
≡, ℜ
280 Bloor St. W.
☎*968-0010 or 800-228-5151*
⇌*968-7765*
www.choicehotels.com
Quality Hotel Midtown is right on fashionable Bloor Street West amidst shops, museums and the beautiful, tree-lined grounds of the University of Toronto. The many restaurants found in the Annex area are an easy walk away, and the hotel is located near the city's transit system. The rooms are clean and spacious. Guests have access to a fitness centre just down the street.

Four Seasons Hotel Toronto
$$$$$
≡, ⊛, ≈, ℜ, ⊘
21 Avenue Rd.
☎*964-0411 or 800-268-6282*
⇌*964-2301*
www.fourseasons.com
If you are looking for top-of-the-line luxury accommodation, the Four Seasons Hotel Toronto is one of the most highly rated hotels in North America. This spot lives up to its reputation, with impeccable service and beautifully decorated rooms. It also has a sumptuous ballroom with Persian carpets and crystal chandeliers. The hotel's restaurant, Truffles (see p 220) is every bit as impressive as the hotel itself.

Hotel Inter-Continental Toronto
$$$$$
≡, ≈, ℜ, ☺, △
220 Bloor St. W.
☎*960-5200 or 800-267-0010*
⇄*960-8269 or 324-5920*
www.travelweb.com
Just a few steps from the Royal Ontario Museum and from Yorkville Street, the Hotel Inter-Continental Toronto is sure to seduce you with its vast, tastefully decorated rooms and its exemplary service.

Park Hyatt
$$$$$
≡, ℜ, ☺, ✪
4 Avenue Rd.
☎*925-1234 or 800-233-1234*
⇄*924-4933*
www.hyatt.com
The rooms at the Park Hyatt have been tastefully renovated–even the bathrooms are now covered in marble. It has a terrific location in the heart of Yorkville, just a few minutes' walk from the Royal Ontario Museum. Business centre available.

Cabbagetown

Homewood Inn
$$ bkfst incl.
ℜ
65 Homewood Ave.
☎*920-7944*
⇄*920-4091*
www.homewoodinn.com
Established in 1990, the Homewood Inn is an English-style bed and breakfast. Housed in a near-century-old home, it exudes a period ambiance, with its an-

tique furnishings, venerable decor and library, where guests enjoy five o'clock tea. The three rooms are in keeping with the rest of the house, comfortable and with the charm of yesteryear. A small garden is laid out behind the house.

1871 Historic House Bed & Breakfast
$$-$$$ bkfst incl.
sb/pb, ≡, ℜ, ⊛
65 Huntley St.
☎*923-6950*
⇄*923-1065*
www.bbcanada.com/3021.html
Built in 1871, the Historic House Bed & Breakfast is located between the Yonge and Bloor shopping area and Cabbagetown, and is an easy walk to either. This is a sunny, comfortable, antique-filled Victorian home with hardwood floors, a whirlpool bath, antique wicker furnishings and period paintings.

Aberdeen Guest House
$$-$$$ bkfst incl.
≡, *sb/pb*
52 Aberdeen Ave.
☎*922-8697*
⇄*922-5011*
www.bedandbreakfast.com/ontario/aberdeen-guest-house-bb.html
The Aberdeen Guest House is a charming bed and breakfast impeccably run by its owners, Gary and Richard, who put special care into the landscaping of the phenomenal garden. Their small brick house, typical of the neighbourhood, offers four rooms with antique decor. A place where guests feel right at home and enjoy attentive service.

Banting House
$$-$$$ bkfst incl.
≡, sb/pb
73 Homewood Ave.
☎*924-1458 or 800-823-8856*
⇌922-2718
www.bantinghouse.com

Built over a century ago in the Edwardian style, the extraordinary Banting House has hosted some famous guests throughout its history. Purchased by the University of Toronto in the 1920s, it served as the workplace of Dr. Frederick Banting, Dr. Charles Best and their colleagues while they conducted research that would lead to the discovery of insulin. Upon entering the venerable house, visitors are greeted by the impressive three-storey oak staircase. The current owners, who acquired the Banting House in 1997, have done a stellar job restoring the place, keeping the original stained-glass and lead-crystal windows intact and adorning it with magnificent antiques. The seven singularly charming rooms promote quiet and serenity. A wonderful place in which to relive history and enjoy remarkable comfort.

Mulberry Tree
$$$ bkfst incl.
≡
122 Isabella St.
☎*960-5249*
⇌960-3853

The Mulberry Tree is on shady, tree-lined Isabella Street near Cabbagetown, the gay village and the upscale shopping area at Yonge and Bloor. This downtown heritage home with a touch of European flair has a guest lounge, free parking and 24hr coffee and tea.

Selby Hotel
$$$ bkfst incl.
≡, ☺
592 Sherbourne St.
☎*921-3142 or 800-387-4788*
⇌923-3177
www.hotelselby.com

A charming, inexpensive option near Rosedale is the Selby Hotel. Built in 1880, this Victorian house has been lodging visitors since 1915, even hosting Ernest Hemingway and his wife for some time. Its 82 rooms offer modern comfort.

Toronto Downtown Bed and Breakfast
$$$$-$$$$$ bkfst incl.
572 Ontario St.
☎*941-1524 or 877-950-6200*
⇌941-1525
www.tdbab.com

Located on a small street in the heart of the very pleasant Cabbagetown district, the Downtown Toronto Bed and Breakfast offers three rooms and one suite in a relaxed family setting. Hosts Roger and Jim run a tight ship and offer their guests discreet but attentive service.

The Annex

Annex House Bed & Breakfast
$$ bkfst incl.
≡, ℝ, K
147 Madison Ave.
☎*/⇌920-3922*

Annex House Bed & Breakfast is located among beautiful Victorian and Georgian homes in the tree-lined streets of the Annex, and is within easy walking distance of Bloor Street's many restaurants as well as the subway line.

B & B in The Annex
$$ bkfst incl.
sb, ≡, ℝ, *K*
31 Dalton Rd.
☎*962-2786 or 888-272-2718*
⇌*964-8837*
B & B in The Annex is an elegant, affordable accommodation located in a historic building on the fringes of the Annex area (at the intersection of both the east-west and north-south subway lines). It has three rooms with oak woodwork, stained-glass windows and comfortable beds.

Global Guest House
$$
≡, *sb/pb*
9 Spadina Rd.
☎*923-4004*
⇌*923-1202*
The Global Guest House is a popular, inexpensive and ecologically sound alternative, ideally situated just north of Bloor Street. The nine rooms are all spotless and simply decorated.

Free coffee and tea, laundry service and kitchen privileges available.

The French Connection Bed & Breakfast
$$$-$$$$ bkfst incl.
sb/pb, ⊛, ≡
102 Burnside Dr.
☎*537-7741 or 800-313-3993*
⇌*537-0747*
www.thefrenchconnection.com
Located in a posh residential neighborhood accessible via Bathurst Street, the French Connection features six luxurious rooms and suites, including one with a private balcony. Housed in a large brick home built in 1925, the elegant establishment offers peace and quiet as well as cozy comfort, far from the hustle and bustle of downtown but only a subway ride away.

Lowther House
$$$-$$$$ bkfst incl.
≡, *pb/sb*, ⊛
72 Lowther Ave.
☎*323-1589 or 800-265-4158*
⇌*961-9322*
www.lowtherhouse.ca
Lowther House is a charming, beautifully restored Victorian mansion in the heart of the

Annex and just minutes from many of the city's best sights. A double whirlpool bath, sun room, fireplace, claw-footed tub and delicious Belgian waffles are just some of the treasures that await visitors at this home away from home.

Palmerston Inn
$$$-$$$$ bkfst incl.
pb/sb, ☜, ≡
322 Palmerston Blvd.
☎ *920-7842*
⇄ *960-9529*

A lovely Georgian house with two elegant white columns houses the Palmerston Inn Bed and Breakfast. Located on one of the city's few quiet streets, this establishment offers eight rooms for non-smokers only, five of them air-conditioned and all decorated with period furniture. Extra touches include bathrobes and fresh flowers in the rooms and complimentary afternoon sherry.

Madison Manor Boutique Hotel
$$$$ bkfst incl.
≡, ℜ
20 Madison Ave.
☎ *922-5579 or 877-561-7048*
⇄ *963-4325*
www.madisonavenuepub.com

The Madison Manor Boutique Hotel is part of a group of three old Victorian mansions that have served as a pub and hotel for nigh on 20 years. The Hotel, located at 20 Madison Avenue, houses 23 rooms distributed over four floors. Its period cachet has been preserved, thanks to original woodwork and antique furnishings. At nos. 14 and 18 is a typical English pub that serves light meals and a good selection of draught beer.

Terrace House B&B
$$$$ bkfst incl.
≡, *pb/sb*
52 Austin Terrace
☎ *535-1493*
⇄ *535-9616*
www.terracehouse.com

Antique furnishings and leaded-glass windows contribute to the beautiful surroundings at the Terrace House B&B, located close to Casa Loma and public transit. The friendly francophone hosts and two resident cats will make you feel right at home. The gourmet breakfasts are a sumptuous treat.

Rosedale, Forest Hill and North of Toronto

YWCA
$ bkfst incl.
80 Woodlawn Ave. E.
☎ *923-8454*

The YWCA is open only to women, who can choose between dormitories, semi-private or private rooms

Ainsley House Bed and Breakfast
$$ bkfst. incl.
≡, *pb/sb*
19 Elm Ave.
☎ *972-0533 or 888-423-3337*
⇄ *925-1853*

Conveniently located in the heart of Rosedale, Ainsley House is close to public transit, a museum, shopping, restaurants and galleries. Wake up to freshly baked bread, homemade muffins, fruit jam and freshly ground coffee before heading out to explore this historic area. Nonsmoking.

Vanderkooy Bed & Breakfast
$$ bkfst incl.
sb/pb, ≡
53 Walker Ave.
☎*925-8765*
⇌*925-8557*
www.bbcanada.com/1107.html
The Vanderkooy Bed & Breakfast is located in Toronto's upscale, residential, tree-lined Rosedale neighbourhood. It's just a 5min walk from the Summerhill subway station and a 15min walk from Yonge and Bloor. This bed and breakfast has a pond in the garden and a resident cat. The owners have a penchant for jazz music.

Eastern Toronto

Scarborough

Scarborough's Guild Inn
$$
≈, ℜ
201 Guildwood Pkwy.
☎*261-3331*
⇌*261-5675*
At Scarborough's Guild Inn, you can enjoy the pleasure of a traditional country inn just minutes from Toronto. The original 1930s building is set amidst a lush green forest, while the inn's 82 guestrooms occupy an adjoining modern

wing. The utmost in romance and charm, this inn is truly a must!

The Beaches

Beaches Bed & Breakfast
$$ bkfst incl.
sb/pb, ≡, ℝ, K
174 Waverley Rd
☎*699-0818*
⇌*699-2246*
www.members.tripod.com/beaches bb
Beaches Bed & Breakfast is a charming and unusual home right in the heart of the Beaches neighbourhood. It's close to the lake, parks, shops, cafés and the streetcar to downtown. Cats share the home with the hosts and the breakfast each morning is tasty and nutritious.

West of the City

Marigold Hostel
$ bkfst incl.
sb
2011 Dundas St. W.
☎*536-8824 after 7pm*
⇌*596-8188*
For an alternative to the big, expensive hotels, try the Marigold Hostel. This charming little hotel is often filled with young travellers and students who will forego a private bathroom to save a bit of cash. All of the rooms are dormitory style, except for one private room available for couples *($50)*. Open 24hrs.

Islington Bed & Breakfast House
$$ bkfst incl.
sb, ≡
1411 Islington Ave.
☎*236-2707*
⇌*233-3192*

Islington Bed & Breakfast House is located west of the city in one of Toronto's prestigious neighborhoods near the Humber Valley, just steps away from the subway line for downtown. Breakfast features home-baked treats, made from scratch, and lots of fresh fruit. No smoking.

Novotel Mississauga Hotel
$$$$
≡, ≈, ℜ, ⊘, △
3670 Hurontario St.
☎*(905) 896-1000 or 800-695-8284*
⇌*(905) 896-2521*

The Novotel Mississauga Hotel lies just west of the city in the centre of the suburb of Mississauga. Restaurants and shopping are close at hand and the airport is just a short drive away. In addition to its 325 rooms, a wealth of services and amenities is available here, including a racquetball court, indoor pool, whirlpool and free airport shuttle.

Near the Airport

Ramada Hotel Toronto Airport
$$$
≡, ≈, ℜ, ⊛, △, ⊘
2 Holiday Dr., Etobicoke
☎*621-2121 or 800-272-6232*
⇌*621-9840*
www.avari.com

The Ramada Hotel Toronto Airport is 5min from the airport and offers complementary shuttle service. Amenities include a whirlpool, indoor/outdoor pool and licensed dining room.

🌴 Quality Suites
$$$-$$$$ bkfst incl.
≡, ℜ
262 Carlingview Dr.
☎*674-8442 or 800-228-5151*

For middle-budget travellers, Quality Suites offers pleasant, unpretentious rooms. Although it is a little far from the airport, this place offers one of the best quality-to-price ratios in the area. A regular bus links the hotel and the airport every half-hour.

Holiday Inn Select Toronto Airport
$$$$
≡, ≈, ℜ, ⊛, △, ⊘
970 Dixon Rd.
☎*675-7611 or 800-695-8284*
⇌*675-9162*

The amenities at Holiday Inn Select Toronto Airport include heated indoor/outdoor pools, whirlpool, and a licensed dining room. There is a snooker lounge with light dining and a bar, and a business centre. Complimentary airport shuttle service available.

Regal Constellation Hotel
$$$$
≡, ≈, ℜ, ⊛, △, ⊘
900 Dixon Rd.
☎*675-1500 or 800-950-1363*
⇌*675-1737*
www.regal-hotels.com

Regal Constellation Hotel is a large hotel, convention and trade-show facility near Pearson International Airport. It has an

impressive array of amenities,
including a heated indoor/
outdoor pool, beauty salon,
travel agency, four restaurants
and a lounge.

**Best Western Carlton Place
Hotel**
$$$$$
≡, ⊛, ≈, ℜ, △, ℝ
33 Carlson Court
☎*675-1234 or 800-528-1234*
⇌*675-3436*
Close to the airport, the Best
Western Carlton Place Hotel
offers decent, comfortable
rooms at reasonable prices.
Laundry and babysitting services
available.

**Sheraton Gateway Hotel at
Terminal Three**
$$$$$
≡, ⊛, ℜ, ☉
Terminal 3, Toronto International
Airport
☎*(905) 672-7000* ✈
800-565-0010
⇌*(905) 672-7100*
www.sheraton.com
The Sheraton Gateway Hotel,
linked directly to Terminal 3 at
Toronto's Pearson International
Airport, has the best location
for in-transit passengers. It has
474 attractively decorated
rooms and is fully soundproof-
ed, with panoramic views of the
airport or the city.

Ulysses' Favourites

For the location:
    Toronto Marriott Eaton Centre, p 188
    Fairmont Royal York Hotel, p 179

For the view:
    SkyDome Hotel, p 178

For Victorian charm:
    Beaconsfield Bed & Breakfast, p 183
    Beverly Place Bed & Breakfast, p 185

For history buffs:
    Royal Meridian King Edward Hotel, p 182
    Fairmont Royal York Hotel, p 179

For the utmost in luxury:
    Sutton Place Hotel, p 186

Restaurants

Toronto abounds
in opportunities to sample international culinary delights.

As a cosmopolitan metropolis bustling with myriad cultures and varied neighbourhoods, its restaurants serve cuisines from all over the world that are as diverse as its population. Certainly Toronto offers plenty of fine-dining opportunities with prices to match, but even the penny-wise can find unique and interesting eateries within their budget.

The following descriptions are grouped according to location, in the same order as the tours in the "Exploring" chapter, to make it easier for visitors to find those hidden treasures while they are exploring a particular area. An index by type of cuisine can be found in this chapter; each restaurant is also in the main index at the end of the guide.

Prices and Symbols

Prices refer to a complete meal (usually dinner– including appetizer, main course and

dessert) for one person and are indicated as follow:

$	10$ or less
$$	10,01$ to 20$
$$$	20,01$ to 30$
$$$$	30,01$ and over

Restaurants by Type of Cuisine

Ulysses' Favourites

For the finest dining:
Truffles, p 220

For the innovative cuisine:
Fez Batik, p 208
North 44, p 223

For the interesting selection:
Marché Mövenpick, p 202

For the warm ambiance:
Select Bistro, p 214
The Paddock, p 213

For the view:
360 Restaurant, p 201

For the decor:
Addis Ababa, p 206
Bombay Palace, p 205
Fez Batik, p 208

For breakfast or brunch:
Café du Marché, p 204

For afternoon tea:
Queen Mother Cafe, p 207

For the price:
Epicure Cafe, p 211

For the terrasse:
By the Way Cafe, p 222
Pappas Grill, p 218

For people-watching:
Cafe Nervosa, p 218

For the desserts:
Bibiche Bistro, p 225

Restaurants

The Waterfront

Boathouse Bar & Grill
$$-$$$
207 Queen's Quay W.
☎ 203-6300
Situated inside the Queen's Quay Terminal, the Boathouse Bar & Grill has a nautical look with lots of brass accents. This busy family-style restaurant has an outdoor patio and serves roadhouse fare–steak, potatoes and pasta.

Hard Rock Cafe
$$-$$$
1 Blue Jays Way, in the SkyDome
☎ 341-2388
Toronto's Hard Rock Cafe, like other locations of this worldwide chain, is a tribute to the greats of rock and roll. The walls and ceiling are covered with paraphernalia that once belonged to the likes of Paul McCartney and Janis Joplin. With a view of the SkyDome's playing field, a meal here can be an experience to remember. The usual burgers and fries make up the menu.

Planet Hollywood
$$-$$$
277 Front St. W.
☎ 596-7827
Planet Hollywood, the giant American chain, goes for Hollywood glitz with movie memorabilia, flashing lights and big-screen televisions. Situated at the base of the CN Tower, it mainly attracts tourists. The food, however, isn't quite as glamourous as the restaurant tries to be. The typical American fare of burgers, pasta and sandwiches is over-priced and mediocre.

Wayne Gretzky's
$$-$$$
99 Blue Jays Way
☎ 979-7825
Wayne Gretzky's may be the last place to get close to the Great One, now that the stick-handling virtuoso has retired. Just around the corner from the CN Tower, this mega-sized sports bar seats hundreds and is a veritable shrine of Gretzky memorabilia with displays of sweaters, trophies and skates. The rooftop Oasis patio has a rock waterfall and fake palm trees, and serves up barbecue

food such as burgers and ribs, from an open grill. A good selection of pasta rounds out the regular pub fare on the rest of the menu.

Whistling Oyster Seafood Café
$$-$$$
11 Duncan St.
☎598-7707
The Whistling Oyster Seafood Café has a daily happy hour, but not for alcohol. Here, it's bargain-priced seafood and Thai-inspired items that bring people in. A few examples: a half-dozen fresh oysters cost just over $6, New England clam chowder is $2, and you pay only $4 for grilled chicken and shrimp satay. It has a casual, loungy atmosphere.

Captain John's Seafood
$$$
1 Queens Quay W.
☎363-6062
An imposing 1957 ocean liner permanently moored at the foot of Yonge Street is the setting for Captain John's Seafood. With such a name and locale, it's hardly surprising that seafood is front and centre on the menu! Shrimp, shark, salmon, scampi, coquilles Saint-Jacques and other bounties of the sea take pride of place on the menu of this establishment with a laid-back ambiance.

Pearl Harbourfront
$$$
207 Queen's Quay W.
☎203-1233
Pearl Harbourfront is a somewhat formal restaurant, also in the Queen's Quay Terminal. Its

many skylights make the room open and airy. The staff is very attentive. The Chinese specialties, including delicious chicken and prawn dishes, are cooked with market-fresh food.

360 Restaurant
$$$$
CN Tower, 301 Front St. W.
☎362-5411
Imagine savouring a meal and a bottle of wine, with a panoramic view of Toronto and Lake Ontario as the backdrop. The 360 Restaurant revolves atop the CN Tower, offering fine dining and undoubtedly the most spectacular views in town.

Susur
$$$$
601 King St. W
☎603-2205
For the ultimate taste sensation, Susur is a sure bet. Albeit pricey, the chef and owner Susur Lee continues to produce the finest of fusion cuisine. The five tasting menus are very popular with fans of this fine establishment, and the ambiance, service and decor is sure to please.

Toronto Islands

Island Paradise Restaurant
$$$
mid-May to mid-Oct
next to the Centre Island ferry
☎203-0245
The Island Paradise Restaurant is popular for its outdoor terrace and spectacular views of Lake Ontario and of Toronto, which can be enjoyed while

Restaurants

delighting in a choice of Caribbean dishes or a steak. Open until the departure of the last ferry.

The Theatre and Financial Districts

Shopsy's Deli & Restaurant
$-$$
33 Yonge St.
☎365-3333
Some establishments have continuously pleased their customers for decades. Such is the case of Shopsy's Deli & Restaurant, a delicatessen that opened in 1921 and has captured the hearts and stomachs of Torontonians with its traditional breakfasts and its hot dogs. The deli is located a few steps from the Hockey Hall of Fame, at the corner of Yonge and Front streets.

Hey Lucy
$$
295 King St. W.
☎408-3633
Hey Lucy puts a little panache into pizza-eating with exposed brick walls and a wood-fired pizza oven. Suits and theatre-goers congregate within or on the sidewalk patio out front for nachos or fresh mussel appetizers, a choice of gourmet salads, 16 different kinds of pizza, and pasta including seafood linguine. They even have a dessert pizza: a wood-fired crust baked with cinnamon and brown sugar, topped with raspberry sauce, fresh fruit and whipped cream. Martini Wednesdays.

Duke of Argyle
$$-$$$
86 John St.
☎340-9700
Located in the heart of Toronto, right near the SkyDome, Duke of Argyle is a traditional pub. Its draws include more than 60 single malts, many of them for less than $5, and over 50 sizzling hot sauces to put some fire into your burger or succulent ribs.

Golden Thai
$$-$$$
105 Church St.
☎868-6668
Golden Thai is a popular dinner spot specializing in pad Thai, but also offering the whole spectrum of Thai cuisine. Several combination dinners are available.

Marché Mövenpick
$$-$$$
inside BCE place at Front and Yonge Sts.
☎366-8986
At Marché Mövenpick, you can serve yourself from an array of gourmet food counters, offering everything from freshly made sushi to fresh pasta and salads. The only challenge is choosing between so many dishes, as each is as tempting as the next. This spot is very popular and often has line-ups, particularly during lunch hour.

N'Awlins Jazz Bar & Grill
$$-$$$
299 King St. W.
☎595-1958
You can't miss N'Awlins Jazz Bar & Grill—it's the one with

the piano hanging above the door outside! The place has a loungy atmosphere reserved for a hip, sophisticated crowd. There are excellent live jazz musicians every night except Monday, providing the musical soundscape while you sample the menu of tasty gourmet pasta and meat dishes.

Szechuan, Szechuan
$$-$$$
100 King St. W., First Canadian Place, mezzanine level
You'll escape Toronto's hectic downtown ambiance as soon as you set foot inside the warm atmosphere of Szechuan, Szechuan, an authentic Chinese restaurant. Dishes are perfectly prepared and include such traditional fare as garlic shrimp with vegetables, spicy shredded beef and chicken in peanut sauce. Service is attentive.

Acqua
$$$
BCE Place, 10 Front St. W.
☎368-7171
As the name suggests, Acqua takes water as its main theme. While observing the fine and rather unusual decor of this fashionable restaurant, you will enjoy succulent dishes drawn from the culinary traditions of the Mediterranean.

Friscos
$$$
133 John St.
☎595-8201
With its high ceilings, vibrant colours and red booths, Friscos is a great place to hang out with friends. The menu lists Parisian-inspired dishes like coq au vin and cassoulet, as well as pizzas and steaks and fries. Complete your meal with a bottle from Friscos' extensive wine list and let the spirits move you!

Kit Kat
$$$
297 King St. W.
☎977-4461
A popular, typical yet funky Italian restaurant run by longtime owner Al Carbone, Kit Kat serves authentic, fairly uncompromising cuisine well supported by a wine list featuring an ample choice of Italian, Californian and Australian selections. In a somewhat jumbled setting dotted with tables draped in red-checkered tablecloths, patrons enjoy a few top-notch specialities, notably the grilled polenta and osso bucco. Narrow and somewhat cramped, the place is lively, friendly and inviting, making it a favourite with business people, celebrities—including the likes of Keith Richards from the Rolling Stones—and more plebeian regulars alike.

Fenice
$$$-$$$$
319 King St. W.
☎585-2377
Fenice invites you to enjoy delicious Italian dishes prepared with fresh ingredients, and to delight in a warm atmosphere rocked by the sounds of classical music.

Restaurants

Fred's Not Here
$$$-$$$$
321 King St. W.
☎*971-9155*
The strip of King Street, between John and Peter streets, is popular with both the theatre and after-work crowds. Fred's Not Here has a crisp look, with white tablecloths and glass-sculpted decor. Menu offerings include steak, fish, seafood and game such as duck and pheasant. The atmosphere is civilized although noise from The Red Tomato, the bar below, can get quite loud.

Epic
$$$$
Fairmont Royal Hotel
100 Front St. W.
☎*860-6949*
The Epic is a perfect fit for the Fairmont Royal Hotel. Only the finest local and international ingredients are used in its fusion of classical European and North-American new cuisine. Every meal is a veritable feast, with exquisite desserts to top off a memorable dining experience.

Senses
$$$$
328 Wellington St. W.
☎*935-0400*
The recently re-opened Senses at the SoHo Metropolitan Hotel will have your taste buds in a frenzy. With Asian/Central American influences, dishes such as the roasted Arctic char and tea-smoked squab breasts are delicious. Desserts including banana cream pie are sheer heaven.

Old Town of York

Café du Marché
$$
45 Colborne St.
☎*368-0371*
Café du Marché serves only breakfast and lunch (it closes at 3pm), but is excellent value for your money. There is both a take-out counter and a dining room serving soups, salads, sandwiches, quiches, omelettes, entrees and a scrumptious selection of desserts.

C'est What
$$
67 Front St. E
☎*867-9499*
A wonderful medley of cuisines is served into the wee hours at this before- and after-theatre stop. The exciting menu features exotic salads and original sandwiches. The ambiance is almost pub-like, with cozy chairs, board games and mood music that runs the gamut from folk to jazz.

The Old Spaghetti Factory
$$
54 The Esplanade
☎*864-9761*
With seating for a few hundred, a lively ambiance and a charming decor of antiques and knick-knacks, there's nothing boring about the Old Spaghetti Factory. Young and old will enjoy a meal here, where pasta takes centre stage!

Le Papillon
$$
16 Church St.
☎363-0838

You are sure to be satisfied at Le Papillon, whose menu offers a tempting variety of dishes combining the delicacies of French and Québecois cuisines. The crepes are especially good. Two of the house specialties are steak and fries, and *tourtière* (meat pie).

Young Thailand
$$
81 Church St.
☎368-1368

The owner and chef Wandee Young was one of the first to introduce Canadians to Thai food back in 1980, when the first Thai restaurant in Canada was opened at the Yonge St. location. With three locations in Toronto, classic favourites including green mango salad, satays with fiery peanut sauce and, of course, phad thai are sure to please.

Bombay Palace
$$-$$$
71 Jarvis
☎368-8048

Bombay Palace has a dimly lit, ornate interior decorated with typical Indian art. It manages to transcend the bright lights and tacky dinette sets which typify so many of Toronto's Indian restaurants. White tablecloths and uniformed waiters give it a reserved air, but the food is excellent and well-priced. There is an extensive menu as well as a steaming buffet table.

Hiro Sushi
$$$
171 King St. E.
☎304-0550

Hailed as the best sushi chef in town, Hiro Yoshida makes sushi-lovers very happy at his popular namesake restaurant. Though he relies on the most classic recipes of the Land of the Rising Sun, where he sometimes returns to get back to his roots, Yoshida also turns out a few in-house specialties, to the great pleasure of patrons. The intimate establishment features a sparse decor that gives centre stage to the sushi-master's creations.

Biagio Ristorante
$$$-$$$$
155 King St. E.
☎366-4040

A few steps from St. Lawrence Hall, you can enjoy Italian food worthy of the finest palates at Biagio Ristorante. This elegant restaurant serves some of the best fresh pastas in town. After struggling to settle on one of the very tempting dishes, you can choose from among an excellent selection of wines. Not sure which one to choose? Not to worry, your server can help.

Restaurants

Queen Street West

Addis Ababa
$
1184 Queen St. W.
☎*538-0059*
Looking for something different? Well, Addis Ababa is an intoxicatingly heady den that serves up traditional Ethiopian cuisine. Dinner is a communal rite, as the spicy dishes come on a platter shared by everyone at the table. Diners eat with their hands, scooping up the food with *injera*–the flat, crepe-like Ethiopian bread. Clouded by the smoke of burning frankincense and animated by African music, its tables are covered with colourful woven tablecloths, the walls with wooden carvings and paintings from Ethiopia. Patrons can enjoy live jazz on Friday and Saturday evenings.

Salad King
$
335 Yonge St.
☎*971-7041*
The Salad King, tucked on the corner of Yonge and Gould streets, is a place so unassuming that you would walk right by it if you weren't looking for it. But the food, which is ordered cafeteria-style from an open kitchen, is worth stopping for. The ambiance scores low (most of the tables are in a dim, windowless room), but the authentic Thai fare is excellent and one of the best deals in town. Open for lunch and dinner.

Babur
$$
273 Queen St. W.
☎*599-7720*
Babur is a typical Indian restaurant with specialties from different parts of India–from chicken tandoori to *paneer korma*. The vegetable *pakoras* (deep-fried Indian fritters) make a savoury appetizer. Like many of the restaurants on Queen West, Babur gets very busy, especially on the weekends, so it's a good idea to reserve ahead of time.

Everest Cafe & Bar
$$
232 Queen St. W.
☎*977-6969*
Though both Tibetan and Indian, the Everest Cafe & Bar features a resolutely Western, polished and Spartan decor. Although some may find this setting ill-suited to the fare on offer, they will no less appreciate the top-notch Himalayan specialties, notably the Tibetan *momos* and the Indian curries with chick peas and potatoes.

Korean Grill House
$$
214 Queen St. W.
☎*263-9850*
The Korean Grill House promises an original and unforgettable culinary experience. The all-you-can-eat set-up lets you cook your own meat or fish on small round barbecues built into each table, and dress them up with Korean condiments. The decor is a refined and modern combination of red and steel tones. Be sure to reserve a table as this is a very popular

spot, particularly among local Koreans. There is also an à la carte menu with Korean specialties.

Little India
$$
255 Queen St. W.
☎205-9836
For authentic Indian food head to Little India. With a great selection of both vegetarian and meat choices, favourites include tandoori dishes, butter chicken, *aloo gobi* and *palak paneer*. There is also a daily lunch buffet.

Sushi Bistro on Queen
$$
204 Queen St. W.
☎971-5315
A popular little eatery enlivened by a loyal clientele, Sushi Bistro on Queen predictably serves typically Japanese seaweed-wrapped raw-fish rolls. Daily consignments of fish round out a menu selection that may appear somewhat limited. The very sparse decor and bright lighting, coupled with friendly service and reasonable prices, give the place a much appreciated, simple and decent character.

Sushiman Japanese Restaurant
$$
20 Richmond St. E.
☎362-8793
Sushiman Japanese Restaurant serves excellent sushi and tempura at reasonable prices along with a traditional sushi bar and Japanese decor. Lunchtime specials draw a crowd that usually packs the place at midday.

Tiger Lily's Noodle House
$$
257 Queen St. W.
☎977-5499
The interior of Tiger Lily's Noodle House is simple, almost pristine, and the service is lightning-fast. Ambrosial Thai and Chinese soups are served, arriving in something more akin to a serving dish than a soup bowl, and are large enough for a meal. Soup may be the specialty here, but the menu is rounded out with a tasty array of noodle dishes.

Hard Rock Cafe
$$-$$$
279 Yonge St.
☎362-3636
Hard Rock Cafe is in the heart of Toronto's downtown core. Directly opposite the Eaton Centre, this tourist hot-spot lives up to its reputation with memorabilia and paraphernalia honouring decades of rock and roll history. The fare is all-American burgers and fries.

Queen Mother Cafe
$$-$$$
208 Queen St. W.
☎598-4719
Queen Mother Cafe is owned by the same people who run the popular Rivoli restaurant and bar down the road. Hardly a place for afternoon tea, the Queen Mum serves up an eclectic range of dishes from Laos and Thailand. Cozy booths and tables fill three rooms and there is a small patio out back. Their pad Thai has been a favourite since long before every other place on the

Restaurants

street was serving it. The sticky rice with peanut sauce is a pure delight. There is an extensive menu of specials every day, and the desserts are divine.

Fez Batik
$$$
129 Peter St.
☎**204-9660**
Fez Batik is the result of the efforts of a pair of successful local restaurateurs who transformed a club into what is now a Moroccan-themed dinner lounge. It's a large, three-level space with a massive sculpted Buddha head dominating the entrance and a lounge area where couches are piled high with Moroccan cushions. The food is an outstanding fusion of culinary styles, from Moroccan to Japanese, as artfully displayed as they are carefully prepared. The friendly, hipster-type servers will bring you fresh bread with a delicious tapenade of roasted tomatoes, olives and garlic as you pore over the enticing menu. In addition to a fine wine list, there are more than 40 types of tea to choose from. There are also numerous beers on tap, which can be enjoyed in front of cozy fireplaces. DJs play live music every night.

Peter Pan
$$$
373 Queen St. W.
☎**593-0917**
Peter Pan has a beautiful 1930s decor and serves delicious and imaginative dishes. Pasta, pizza and fish take on an original look here. Service is distinguished.

Rivoli
$$$
332 Queen St. W.
☎**597-0794**
With a fusion menu that changes with the seasons and dishes that are inspired by Italian, French and Thai influences, there is something for everyone at the Riv. The back room plays host to live music, comedy acts and spoken word readings. There is also a cocktail bar, pool hall and a great sidewalk patio to observe the happenings on Queen St. W.

Mildred Pierce
$$$-$$$$
99 Sudbury St.
☎**588-5695**
Named after a classic Joan Crawford film, this restaurant with its high ceilings and Romanesque murals sets the mood for an enchanting evening. Featuring an eclectic menu with influences from all over the world including Mediterranean, Italian and Thai, the dishes are of the highest calibre. The in-house desserts are simply delicious.

Avalon
$$$$
270 Adelaide St. W.
☎**979-9918**
For an intimate evening, head to one of Toronto's best. With a Mediterranean-French inspired menu that changes almost every day, the freshest ingredients are featured. The raw milk cheese and "to-die-for" desserts are a sure pleaser. Impeccable service and attention to detail are guaranteed.

Barberian's Steak House
$$$$
7 Elm St., toward Bay and Dundas
☎597-0335
There is nothing quite like a tender grilled sirloin steak the way it is done at Barberian's Steak House. Steak dominates the menu at this restaurant but you can also select from among items like fresh fish, Bay of Fundy salmon, ribs or chicken. The not-to-be-outdone wine list features over 1,500 labels, and the well-stocked cellar holds an impressive 15,000 bottles! The decor is distinctly Canadiana, with Inuit carvings and some original artwork from the Group of Seven. It is preferable to reserve in advance.

The Fifth
$$$$
225 Richmond St. W.
☎979-3005
To reach this 5th level, chic romantic loft, you first pass bouncers in the alley of the upscale nightclub Easy, then into an old freight elevator up to this superbly designed restaurant. Fine French food is served and during the summer months you can enjoy one of Toronto's most stylish patios. The crème brûlée is fabulous.

Monsoon
$$$$
100 Simcoe St.
☎979-7172
Monsoon's stunning and altogether unique decor tends to banish the delicious, subtle character of the food from diners' minds. While it's true that the upscale restaurant's outstanding, polished, two-toned decor can't help but hold patrons' attention, gourmets are sure to appreciate the inventiveness and daring of the chef, who turns thoroughly North American vegetables, fish and meats into veritable Asian-flavoured culinary delights.

Chinatown and Kensington

Amato Ristorante & Bar
$
534 Queen St. W.
☎703-8989
Pizza aficionados can find their heaven at Amato, a part of a chain of restaurants where a $3 or $4 slice constitutes a quarter of a large pizza. Every day, there are at least 30 gourmet pizzas to choose from, ranging from your standard pepperoni pie to vegan pizzas, white pizzas (no tomato sauce), and pizzas with snazzy toppings like artichoke hearts, feta cheese and spinach. Amato also has a cozy sit-down section at the back with large comfortable booths where you can order gorgeous pastas, salads, focaccia sandwiches and custom pizzas.

Canteena Azul
$
open for dinner only, except for Sunday brunch
181 Bathurst St.
☎703-9360
Canteena Azul, tucked around the corner from Queen on Bathurst Street, exudes a casual, laid-back air with a coffee

table scattered with magazines in one corner. The owner/chef has managed to combine a casual atmosphere with an impressive menu specializing in fusion foods that feature Asian and Latin influences. No matter which meal you try, the emphasis is on health-conscious food, with lots of veggie options and a selection of virtuously wholesome vegetable and fruit juices and smoothies. Enticing drinks, such as Mind Fuzz Be Gone (carrot, apple, ginger, beet and a shot of gingko), live up to their names.

Dufflet Pastries
$
787 Queen St. W.
☎ 504-2870
Dufflet Pastries makes some of the most divine cakes, tarts and pies in the city. Its goods fill the dessert cases of a number of restaurants, but there's nothing like getting it from the source. You can buy an entire cake for a special occasion, or sit in the bright little shop sipping a cappuccino or café latte while you indulge in sinfully sweet delights.

Lotus Garden Vietnamese Vegetarian Restaurant
$
393 Dundas St. W., Unit G
☎ 598-1883
Lotus Garden Vietnamese Vegetarian Restaurant is a unique Vietnamese eatery that attracts younger types who come for its soya and tofu dishes, salads and soups. There is no MSG used in the cooking and very little salt. Some dishes are made with organic vegetables.

Pho Hung Vietnamese Restaurant
$
350 Spadina Ave.
☎ 593-4274
Pho Hung Vietnamese Restaurant on Spadina at Baldwin is affectionately known as the "laughing cow" due to its chuckling bovine logo. It serves up good, bargain Vietnamese food, complemented by cheap beer. It is also fully licensed.

Tequila Bookworm
$
490 Queen St. W.
☎ 504-7335
Drawing a young, hip, alternative crowd, Tequila Bookworm offers light meals to "bookish types" and provides them with books and magazines to buy or leaf through. An unpretentious and pleasantly bohemian place.

Vienna Home Bakery
$
626 Queen St. W.
☎ 703-7278
The Vienna Home Bakery looks like it should be in a small town in northern Ontario rather than a stone's throw from Queen and Bathurst. This simple, cozy lunch counter is characterized by its pale-pink walls and the smell of bread baking. Homemade vegan soups are prepared fresh every day and the bread is always straight from the oven. They also make sandwiches and some of the best pies in town. Everything here is made fresh and entirely from scratch. Watch for the daily specials, such as their popular quiche or chili.

Happy Seven
$-$$
358 Spadina Ave.
☎ 971-9820
Happy Seven is another China-town institution and like so many others, it has glaring lighting but pristine cleanliness. There are a dizzying 298 items to choose from on the menu, including dozens of soups and many seafood selections, as well as pork, chicken, duck, bean curd, noodle and vegetable dishes. All are served in generous portions. Although mainly Cantonese, the menu also offers several Szechuan items.

Citron
$$
813 Queen St. W.
☎ 504-2647
Across the road from Terroni (see p 212), the candle-lit Citron has more of an air of casual sophistication than some of its neighbours. The staff is friendly and relaxed and an open kitchen ensures that the small dining room is always filled with delicious aromas. The tone for the main dishes is set by the near-perfect salad with organic greens, grilled pears, walnuts and feta and starters such as vegetable Thai bundles in rice paper with lemon grass-mint sauce. Entrees are very reasonably priced and include a lot of vegan and vegetarian dishes, as well as duck (no red meat is served here). A variety of fine wines are available by the glass. Open nightly for dinner, and for brunch on Friday to Sunday.

Epicure Cafe
$$
512 Queen St. W.
☎ 504-8942
The Epicure Cafe has a warm, bistro-like atmosphere with two levels and two patios—one right on Queen and a quieter outdoor retreat on the rooftop. In addition to a standard menu of hamburgers, pasta and sandwiches, Fried Cajun calamari and mussels provençale add a French-Louisiana element to the fare. A variety of beers are on tap and there is a cappuccino bar.

Margarita's Fiesta Room
$$
14 Baldwin St.
☎ 977-5525
Margarita's provides quite an escape, with its infectious Latin music and its tasty dishes, including Toronto's best nachos and delicious guacamole. This piece of Mexico will transport you far from the rush of urban Toronto.

Squirly's
$$
807 Queen St. W.
☎ 703-0574
Squirly's has a casual atmosphere and a menu of pizzas, pastas, stir-fries, quesadillas, hamburgers and salads that you can enjoy without emptying your pockets. It's just dingy and sufficiently artsy in decor to double as a cool late-night drinking spot. Don't expect to find any fine wines here, and the music can get loud after

Restaurants

11pm. The back room, with its red-velvet sofas and candlelight, is a casual, intimate den that turns into a patio when the roof comes off in the summertime.

Terroni
$$
720 Queen St. W
☎ 504-0320

This outlet of Terroni, a chain of restaurants, is a long, narrow, gourmet pizzeria with wooden booths surrounded by shelves crammed with Italian groceries. There is also a tiny patio at the back. Italian salads, sandwiches and pizzas are made fresh with top-quality ingredients (interestingly, they don't serve pasta). Frequented by those in the local arts scene, this is the place to linger over an espresso, surrounded by the area's actors, photographers and artists.

Tortilla Flats
$$
429 Queen St. W.
☎ 593-9870

Tortilla Flats is a Tex-Mex emporium, near the corner of Queen and Spadina, decorated with bright colours and typical Mexican trinkets. There is a bar, booths, tables and a patio at the back. The food is passable Tex-Mex–lots of cheesy burritos, nachos, enchiladas and fajitas. Try their head-clearing, fiery-hot Jalapeno poppers – whole jalapeno peppers stuffed with cream cheese, breaded and deep fried. Two-for-one-fajitas available on Tuesdays.

Gypsy Co-Op
$$-$$$
815 Queen St. W.
☎ 703-5069

Gypsy Co-Op is a hipster mainstay in this part of town. The restaurant serves a fancy fusion menu, with entrees that include several pasta and vegetarian dishes, as well as pork, chicken and salmon. The rear half is a loungy bar with couches, comfy chairs and some of the city's best DJs. The noise and smoke from the bar can cloud the dining experience, so if you're looking for dinner and conversation, go early.

Lee Garden
$$-$$$
331 Spadina Ave.
☎ 593-9524

On certain days, the little Lee Garden restaurant is so crowded you may believe all of China has squeezed in here. People come for the delectable Chinese cuisine, (mainly Cantonese, with some Szechuan), especially the seafood and duck, and the mango chicken.

Cafe La Gaffe
$$$
24 Baldwin St.
☎ 596-2397

Cafe La Gaffe is housed in a converted store on Baldwin. Known as "the Gaffe," it attracts both the Queen West and student crowds to its front and rear patios. Most of the decorative items from the shaky chairs to the art on the walls are mismatched. Patrons are greeted with a basket of Portuguese corn bread to start before digging into seafood appetizers, homemade soups, and entrees like hearty pastas, steak, fish, seafood and organic chicken. All this is rounded out by a good wine list, with several whites and reds available by the glass. Also a popular spot for weekend brunch, when eggs Benedict has pride of place.

Cities
$$$
859 Queen St. W.
☎ 504-3762

Cities exemplifies the joy of cooking and eating. Both the decor and the menu are exceptionally imaginative, with "fresh market cuisine" figuring prominently. The menu changes daily and highlights pork, beef, lamb, fish and seafood dishes, which can be topped off with a homemade dessert. Very good value considering the variety and freshness of ingredients. Good wine list.

Lai Wah Heen
$$$
108 Chestnut St., Metropolitan Hotel, second floor
☎ 977-9899

Toronto is home to many excellent Chinese restaurants, but few can compare to Lai Wah Heen. Its menu features mostly Cantonese *haute cuisine*. Signature items include Peking duck, fresh lobster and seafood and the "lustrous peacock salad," a colourful creation comprised of barbequed duck,

chicken, melon and mango. Remarkable attention to detail is shown in both preparation and presentation. A place of great refinement for its food, decor, and service. Dim Sum is also served in the afternoons.

Left Bank
$$$
567 Queen St. W.
☎ 504-1626

Cavernous and austere decor, exquisite presentation, attitude, and mood lighting all set the stage for this restaurant's North American–style bistro menu. Salmon, steaks and braised lamb shanks are among the enticing entrees. Vegetarian options are also available, as are a variety of fresh pasta, made every day from scratch. Save some room for the homemade desserts, and enjoy the sounds of a live band or DJ in the nightclub.

The Paddock
$$$
178 Bathurst St.
☎ 504-9997

Not long ago, The Paddock was a notorious saloon-style drinking hole—one of those places your mother warns you about. Now totally refurbished, it's a warm, jazzy den where the neighbourhood's thirty-somethings go for fine dining. The portions are small but beautifully presented. They include treats such as sweet potato and Gorgonzola crumpet with baby greens and mesquite-smoked steak with potato gaufrette and grilled peppers. The place becomes a cocktail lounge in the evenings.

Select Bistro
$$$
328 Queen St. W.
☎ 596-6405

Upon entering Select Bistro, the smooth jazz in the background will tempt you to stay for hours. But this Parisian-style bistro offers more than a warm, relaxing atmosphere. It also has a mouth-watering menu that draws a clientele of connoisseurs who come back time and again for such savoury specialities as bouillabaisse, *cassoulet*, *bavette*, lamb and duck *confit*. Winner of the *Wine Spectator* award of excellence for the year 2000, this establishment has an exhaustive wine list of over 1,000 vintages. A very inviting outdoor terrace is open in summer.

Swan Restaurant
$$$
892 Queen St. W.
☎ 532-0452

Just west of Trinity Bellwoods Park, Swan Restaurant attracts local film and theatre people with a taste for fine food. The long, narrow space is filled with retro-style booths and cool, jazzy music. The brunches are a step above most in the city, and include fresh shellfish (it's an oyster bar, and you can watch the chef shucking them fresh). The menu is an exquisite roster of delicacies, including home-made soups served with Portuguese bread.

Bodega
$$$$
30 Baldwin St.
☎ 977-1287

Bodega serves resolutely gastronomic French dishes made with the freshest of ingredients. The wall coverings, the lace and the music that wafts across the dining room help create an authentic French atmosphere. The mere mention of their specialties, such as *crème brûlée*, house escargot with port, rack of lamb with Dijon, duckling breast with orange, goat cheese and apple chutney, may well set your mouth to watering.

Taro Grill
$$$$
492 Queen St. W.
☎ 504-1320

Taro Grill is one of those places you go to not only to eat, but also to be seen. The spectacle is complete with the chef visible through the open kitchen.

Queen's Park and the University of Toronto

 Kalendar's Coffee House
$
546 College St.
☎923-4138
The relaxed setting at Kalendar's Coffee House is ideal for an intimate tête-à-tête over coffee and cake, or a light lunch. The menu lists an array of interesting sandwiches, their signature scrolls and simple yet tasty dishes.

Lucky Dragon
$
418 Spadina Ave.
☎598-7823
The Lucky Dragon is typical of Spadina's Chinese restaurants with bright lights, plain decor and a massive fish tank. The menu is extensive, with hundreds of selections drawing on culinary traditions from all over China: spicy specialty rices with such toppings as squid in chilli and garlic sauce, and whole braised fish in a soy-ginger sauce.

Maggie's
$
400 College St.
☎323-3248
The few tables at pint-sized Maggie's are usually taken up by young people chatting over coffee or eating a light meal. With its spare decor it's clear why the place, which specializes in breakfast meals served all

day, draws a few regulars for whom the simplicity of the setting and food matter little.

Not Just Noodles
$
570 Yonge St.
☎960-8898
A tiny Sino-Vietnamese eatery with a handful of tables, Not Just Noodles offers a good choice of Asian specialties in an atmosphere typical of this type of establishment: patrons are urged to leave their North American habits at the door and give in to Asian informality and conviviality.

Irie Caribbean Restaurant
$-$$
808 College St.
☎531-4743
The Irie Caribbean Restaurant happens to make some of the best *rotis* in the city. Frequented mainly by a West Indian crowd, you know you're getting the real thing here. A jerk chicken salad is accented with heaps of tropical fruits. In addition to the delicious *rotis*, there are spicy main dishes cooked island-style, such as steamed red snapper and jerk specialties.

Peter's Chung King
$-$$
281 College St.
☎928-2936
Peter's Chung King serves up the almost-forgotten Chinatown culinary tradition of sizzling Szechuan. Long an institution in this part of town, Peter's has a nondescript ambiance and

Restaurants

indifferent staff. Although the food still rates well, you've got to put in a special request to get your Szechuan-spiced flamered chilli as hot as it should be.

Swatow
$-$$
309 Spadina
☎ 977-0601
Swatow is a no-fuss eatery with an extensive menu that is guaranteed to satisfy your palate. There is nothing fancy about this place, but you can't beat it for its genuine Cantonese cooking served up fast and good, just like in China.

Bar Italia
$$
582 College St.
☎ 535-3621
Bar Italia is a sleek, swanky pasta spot attracting beautiful people until the wee hours. Mirrors at eye level running all the way around the restaurant's simple wood booths make it easy to check out and be checked out. Panini are gourmet affairs, and the pastas are quite rich in cream and Gorgonzola cheese sauces. Tenderloin, roast chicken and seafood are also very popular. Homemade Italian ice cream is a sweet ending to the meal.

El Bodegon
$$
537 College St.
☎ 944-8297
El Bodegon is awash in typical South American decor: village scenes are painted in primary colours on orange stucco, sombreros and pan flutes hang from the walls and fake parrots hover on perches beneath a ceiling of plastic vines. Peruvian music compounds the thematic effect. An impressive list of seafoodrich broths is upstaged only by the calamari, grilled to tender perfection. A host of hearty, simple Peruvian dishes, such as *ceviche*, hearty meat stews and frittatas (thick omelettes) round out the menu that also includes inexplicably disparate items such as pasta, BLT sandwiches and won ton soup.

The Living Well
$$
692 Yonge St.
☎ 922-6770
A small "bar-restaurant" with a stylish but funky decor of brick walls, modern paintings, flowery banquettes and a wooden bar, the Living Well offers varied and resolutely international fare. The chef, originally from South Asia, adds a touch of exoticism to the menu and transforms what could be unoriginal dishes into pleasant culinary surprises. Among the standouts are the Moroccan vegetarian stew, the pumpkin soup and the stir-fries.

Oasis
$$
294 College St.
☎ 975-0845
Despite its proximity to Chinatown, Oasis leaves the Asian cuisine behind, and instead offers *tapas* with a twist. You can order from among 80 items on the menu, including many vegan and vegetarian dishes. There are various dips, all made

in-house, and the chefs add their own creations to the Spanish fare, like Thai coconut rice balls and Malaysian vegetable curry. For dessert, try the brie and pear turnover with raspberry sauce. The ambiance here is casual and laid back, the food is good and the price is right.

Pony
$$
488 College St.
☎*923-7665*
Soft lighting, crisp white tiles, freshly cut flowers and simple chairs with gold-stencilled and white slipcovers come together to create a romantic ambiance in which to enjoy the Italian specialties at Pony. The veal and calamari are particularly noteworthy.

Utopia Cafe & Grill
$$
586 College St.
☎*534-7751*
Neither the menu nor the interior of Utopia Cafe & Grill is remarkable at first glance, but the dark wood, low lighting and candles on each of the tables give this small place a warm ambiance. Quiet strains of North African and New-Age music waft around the eight to 10 tables. Monthly art exhibits are held here, and there's a backyard patio for fine summer days. Both the beef burger and the all-natural veggie burgers are savoury delights, and the fries are a perfect crispy brown. Utopia's fare of homemade charbroiled hamburgers, grilled chicken breast, smoked salmon

sandwiches, burritos, quesadillas and New York strip sirloin may not be unique, but quality makes up for originality, and the meals are excellent value. Inquire about their daily specials.

College Street Bar
$$$
574 College St.
☎*533-2417*
Boasting a tasty Mediterranean menu and lively atmosphere, the College Street Bar is a hot spot, frequented by a young crowd; many people just stop in to have drinks and soak up the atmosphere.

Kensington Kitchen
$$$
124 Harbord St.
☎*961-3404*
This kitchen specializes in Mediterranean dishes like Moroccan couscous, Istanbul lamb and homemade appetizers such as hummus, tabouli and baba ghanouj. The warm, comfortable dining room is adorned with tapestries, and an interesting collection of antique model airplanes is suspended from the ceiling. This is a good spot to go on fine summer days when you can enjoy the same specialties on the rooftop terrace.

Bloor and Yorkville

Flo's
$-$$
70 Yorkville St.
☎*961-4333*
Among the chic stores in the Yorkville district, you might be

surprised to discover a traditional diner. Like most establishments of this type, Flo's Diner is a good spot for hamburgers. In the summer, there is a patio.

Swiss Chalet
$$
345 Bloor St. E
☎944-2472

The Swiss Chalet has been slow-roasting chicken to perfection since 1954. This popular family restaurant serves a variety of chicken dishes, ribs, fries, salads and stir-fries. Kids will love the special children's menu which comes with a drink, dessert and small gift.

Allen's
$$-$$$
143 Danforth Ave.
☎463-3086

Located in Greektown, Allen's offers a pub-style menu enhanced by the creativity of its clever chef who marries Irish and Asian flavourings: grilled calamari with Mongolian fire sauce, Kilkenny steamed mussels, Guinness-flavoured lamb on baguette with wasabi mayonnaise… The subtle and polished decor, with its wood accents and Guinness carpets, combined with a jolly clientele make it a favourite in Greektown.

Cafe Nervosa
$$-$$$
75 Yorkville Ave.
☎961-4642

The patio at Cafe Nervosa is a prime spot from which to watch the Yorkville socialites pass by. The interior has that trendy modern jungle look with lots of leopard prints and wrought iron. Upper-crust guests from the nearby Four Seasons Hotel vie with American tourists for table space from which they can see and be seen while enjoying average fare of fancy salads, pastas and pizzas. There are live jazz performances on Thursday and Friday nights.

Pappas Grill
$$-$$$
440 Danforth Ave.
☎469-9595

One of the most popular spots in Greektown-on-the-Danforth, Pappas Grill is a cosy place with its Mediterranean blue decor, big windows and Greek music. The menu is just as easygoing as the staff: try one of the local specialties like the pizzas fresh from the big oven near the entrance or the hamburgers and sandwiches, unless you'd prefer a classic kebab…

Serra
$$-$$$
378 Bloor St. W.
☎944-9211

This casually chic Italian restaurant serves a fabulous selection of delicious fresh pasta, grilled focaccia sandwiches and thin-crust pizzas straight from the wood-burning oven. Main dishes include beef tenderloin, herb-rubbed free range chicken breast and Atlantic salmon.

Opus Restaurant on Prince Arthur

$$$

37 Prince Arthur Ave.

☎921-3105

Recently renovated, with a contemporary decor, Opus serves refined and modern cuisine described as "contemporary Canadian," mixing traditional recipes with other culinary traditions. A new private room with seating for 22 people has recently been added, and the back garden features an outdoor patio. Exceptional wine list.

Yamato

$$$

18 Bellair St.

☎927-0077

Yamato features Japanese cuisine with a twist–the chef prepares your meal right before your eyes! The menu includes classics, such as teriyaki steak, seafood, chicken, sushi and vegetable tempura, which are always fresh and tasty.

Bistro 990

$$$$

990 Bay St.

☎921-9990

Bistro 990 is quite simply one of the best dining spots in Toronto. Delicious country French and continental cuisine are offered in a Mediterranean setting–escargot with mushrooms in a wine and garlic sauce, rack of lamb stuffed with garlic and Camembert, and sea bass with braised vegetables are but a few of the house recommendations.

Boba

$$$$

90 Avenue Rd.

☎961-2622

Boba is an inviting and charming little restaurant which has acquired a solid reputation thanks to its fine cuisine and courteous service. In-house specialties include beef, duck, fish and lamb, and the desserts are particularly delicious.

Jacques Bistro du Parc

$$$$

126-A Cumberland St.

☎961-1893

It is really worth taking the trouble to find Jacques Bistro du Parc. This charming little spot is located upstairs in a fine Yorkville house. The very friendly French owner offers simple but high-quality food, such as fresh Ontario rabbit and rack of lamb with Dijon mustard. The fresh Atlantic salmon and the spinach salad are among the pleasant surprises on the menu.

Sassafraz

$$$$

100 Cumberland St.

☎964-2222

Sassafraz is a big bar and bistro with bay windows looking out onto the street for a view of the passing scene. The decor is done in pastel shades with wooden floors and furniture. On the left, a pleasant dining room with modern furnishings and lighting greets guests who prefer a quieter atmosphere. The menu is a fusion of French and California cuisine, with a

Restaurants

definite Italian flair. Among its noteworthy items are the purple-rice-crusted salmon, lamb, seafood, sea bass and tenderloin of veal.

🍵 Truffles
$$$$
Four Seasons Hotel Toronto
21 Avenue Rd.
☎ **928-7331**
This restaurant is not within the reach of every budget, but if you have the resources, you will be absolutely delighted. Truffles has truly earned its reputation as one of the most esteemed dining establishments in town.

Cabbagetown

Mocha Mocha
$
489 Danforth Ave.
☎ **778-7896**
A small, family-run neighbourhood bistro, Mocha Mocha serves breakfast, brunch, sandwiches and salads, as well as wine by the glass. Patrons, who are invited to peruse the chalkboard menu and order at the counter, enjoy a warm, friendly setting.

Peartree
$$
507 Parliament St.
☎ **962-8190**
From the outside, you'll never imagine what this pleasant little establishment harbours. The secret lies at the back, where patrons discover an appealing veranda adjoining a charming garden courtyard, both enhanced with warm, cheerful colours–a little haven of peace in the heart of the city. The simple menu offers salads, burgers, sandwiches on wholewheat bread, pasta and fish, as well as a few Sunday-brunch specials. Friendly, attentive service.

Rashnaa
$$
307 Wellesley St. E.
☎ **929-2099**
Rashnaa, a modest Tamil/Sri Lankan joint in Cabbagetown, is a great place to linger over a meal with friends, especially if your budget is tight. Rashnaa's interior, with its dinette sets and paintings of Hindu gods, is a warm place that's always filled with the scent of floral incense and the sound of sitar music. Most of Rashnaa's dishes are fairly mild, but the chutneys are deliciously piquant. They also do an excellent rendition of Sri Lankan specialties, including *masala dosa*, *kottu roti* and string hoppers. It's simple Sri Lankan fare but the prices and the chutneys make it worth going back for.

Timothy's Tikka House
$$
556 Parliament St. (at Wellesley)
☎ **964-7583**
Timothy's Tikka House prepares tandoori, vindaloo and jalfrezi-style chicken and chicken tikka rolls. The flavours of India are at their best in the melt-in-your-mouth nan bread and savoury mulligatawny soup.

Keg Mansion
$$$
515 Jarvis St.
☎964-6609
The Keg Mansion has a wonderful location in an old mansion on Jarvis Street. Traditional North American–style cuisine, with an emphasis on steak and roast beef, is served in a charming atmosphere.

Myth
$$$
417 Danforth Ave.
☎461-8383
This beautiful bar-cum-restaurant is sure to please with its stylish decor. The mostly Grecian menu consists of Mediterranean delights with a twist, such as Moroccan chicken with braised eggplant, dried fruit and nut ragout and herbed couscous. A Greek band and DJs start to play after 10pm on Fridays and Saturdays, and the front patio is very popular during the warmer months.

Pan on the Danforth
$$$
516 Danforth Ave.
☎466-8158
The Pan on the Danforth serves a classic yet inventive take on Greek cuisine, with sunny original versions of modern and traditional recipes. Though the hip crowd is a testament to the chef's inventive side, it nevertheless appreciates finding good, standard Greek fare here.

🌴 Provence
$$$$
12 Amelia St.
☎924-9901
In a fabulous, bright and cheerfully coloured dining room with typical black-and-white tiled floors, Provence brings the flavours of France to Toronto with a most refined seasonal menu. As an appetizer, the chef offers, among other things, an innovative cold apple-mint soup, while main courses such as lobster *pastilla* and *confit* of calf's liver are definite standouts. The servers, dressed to the nines, provide professional service worthy of a high-class establishment.

The Annex

Future Bakery and Cafe
$
483 Bloor St. W.
☎922-5875
A café, bakery and cafeteria serving hot meals all rolled into one, this place is patronized by a fairly young and trendy

Restaurants

crowd. The large space has been successfully exploited, with a designated place for each of the establishment's functions. Customers can thus simply buy their bread or have a coffee here without having to wait in line behind those ordering a hot meal. Moreover, the setting is pleasant and open, with high ceilings, wooden furnishings and murals.

Country Style
$$
450 Bloor St. W.
☎536-5966
This unpretentious neighbour-hood restaurant is the Annex's last bastion of Eastern-Euro-pean cooking. The gingham tablecloths, home style Hungar-ian cooking (ragouts, goulash, cabbage rolls) and the good-natured staff are what attract the neighbourhood regulars.

Nataraj Indian Restaurant
$$
394 Bloor St. W.
☎928-2925
The Nataraj is a typical Indian restaurant with sparse, clean decor and too-bright lighting. While the northern Indian cui-sine is very good, the service is a bit slow. Breads from the tandoori oven are almost flaw-less.

Sushi on Bloor
$$
515 Bloor St. W.
☎516-3456
Sushi on Bloor is all the rage. Seated in a long and narrow dining room, boisterous patrons enjoy the low prices and no-

nonsense ambiance. That being said, the top-rate sushi and other Japanese specialties are anything but ordinary! Popular with neighbourhood regulars, passers-by and Japanese locals and visitors.

By the Way Cafe
$$$
400 Bloor St. W.
☎967-4295
This small, cosy and intimate restaurant in the heart of the Annex, with its huge painted mural, offers French-style daily specials with a Mediterranean accent. The large patio is popu-lar, especially for brunch and lunch.

Dooney's
$$$
511 Bloor St. W.
☎536-3293
Dooney's is a good place to stop for tea or coffee, or even for a meal. The menu is remi-niscent of a French bistro and also includes pizzas and pasta dishes. During the warmer months, patrons enjoy the outdoor patio and its view of life in the Annex.

Korea House
$$$
666 Bloor St. W.
☎536-8666
There are a number of Korean restaurants and supermarkets clustered along Bloor west of Bathurst. Among them is Korea House, which has a pleasant wood-and-stucco decor. Com-plete dinners include rice or noodles with mixed meat or seafood and an array of vegeta-

ble and pickle dishes. Not to be confused with the Korean Grill House (see p 206).

Le Paradis
$$$
166 Bedford Rd.
☎*921-0995*

Le Paradis serves authentic French bistro cuisine at authentic bistro prices. They specialize in casseroles (lamb, duck and rabbit) as well as fish dishes. The decor is simple and the service reserved, but a devoted following and the delicious cooking make it a must.

Rosedale, Forest Hill and North of Toronto

Five Doors North
$$$
2088 Yonge St.
☎*480-6234*

Five Doors North, on Yonge south of Eglinton, is a challenge to find but worth the effort. It doesn't have a sign, but lies beneath a banner for "Future Furniture" (the shop above it). Inside, a narrow hallway opens into a large, lively backroom. There are no windows and the restaurant is heady with smells from the open kitchen. The menu is based on a four-course meal (sort of like tapas), with a selection of antipasto, pasta, meat or fish, and vegetables. You need quite an appetite, however, to finish off all four courses. Both the food and the service are excellent.

Millie's Bistro
$$$
1980 Avenue Rd
☎*481-1247*

With an extensive menu consisting of Spanish, Italian, Moroccan and Southern French fare, this Mediterranean restaurant has something for everyone. A wide range of tapas, vegetarian and organic dishes including rib eye or tuna steak are featured, as well as a kid's menu.

North 44
$$$-$$$$
2537 Yonge St.
☎*487-4897*

North 44 is one of the *in* restaurants with the hip Toronto crowd. This is not just a place to see and be seen, however, since its food is also exquisite. The chef culls from several culinary traditions to create a decidedly innovative menu.

Auberge du Pommier
$$$$
4150 Yonge St.
☎*222-2220*

For a memorable evening, Auberge du Pommier is the place to go. With its quiet, elegant atmosphere and refined French cuisine, its specialties include caviar and *foie gras*. Meals here can be accompanied by fine wines from a very elaborate list.

Filippo's
$$$$
744 St. Clair Ave. W.
☎*658-0568*

Filippo's serves savoury gourmet pizzas and pastas with a

Mediterranean accent. A cozy and chic atmosphere for the trend-setter in everyone.

Eastern Toronto

The Beaches

Sunset Grill
$
2006 Queen St. E.
☎*690-9985*
Hankering for a big traditional breakfast just like on the farm? Eggs, bacon, sausages and home fries are cooked up all day long at the Sunset Grill. The French toast and omelettes are also done to perfection. Burgers and sandwiches complete the menu. Expect a line-up for the famous Sunday brunch. Open 7am to 4pm weekdays, and 7am to 5pm on weekends.

Whitlock's
$$
1961 Queen St. E.
☎*691-8784*
Whitlock's is a longstanding tradition in the Beach. Located in a lovely old building, the atmosphere is simple, casual and unpretentious. The menu is varied and down-to-earth, offering such standard fare as pasta, steaks, sandwiches and oriental stir-fries. This place is said to typify the real "Beach," as opposed to the glitz and trendiness of what some like to call the "Beaches."

Yumei Sushi
$$
2116-F Queen St. E.
☎*698-7705*
With its excellent sushi and sashimi, its choice of tempuras and teriyaki dishes, Yumei Sushi satisfies lovers of Japanese cuisine. The small eatery's setting is very appealing and its Japanese-style partitioned cubicles give it a noteworthy cachet.

Dwarfed by modern Toronto's skyscrapers, the Gooderham Building stands out with its castle-like architecture. - *Patrick Escudero*

A modern glass and steel structure towers over a "loose moose" standing guard in front of Toronto's Old City Hall. - *Patrick Escudero*

Horse-drawn buggies are a great way to tour
Niagara-on-the-Lake in the summertime. - *Patrick Escudero*

A mirrored skyscraper towers over Toronto's old city hall,
which dates from 1889. - *Patrick Escudero*

Quigley's
$$$
2232 Queen St. E.
☎**699-9998**
From the outside, Quigley's looks like it could just be a pub, but beyond the bar and the beer on tap there is a comfortable dining area at the back. Serving pub food with an exotic touch, from pasta to pad Thai, this is a casual place to eat, just east of the hustle and bustle of the Beach's main drag. Patrons can enjoy Celtic music on Saturday afternoon, and jazz on Sunday afternoon.

Spiaggia Trattoria
$$$
2318 Queen St. E.
☎**699-4656**
The Beach is a wonderful place to watch the world go by from a sidewalk café, and Spiaggia Trattoria is just the place. A wonderful mix of people frequent this spot, all the better to people-watch. All the exotic ingredients that we've come to expect from a trendy trattoria figure on the menu here, from fresh herbs to Asiago and sun-dried tomatoes.

The Danforth

Bibiche Bistro
$$
1352 Danforth Ave.
☎**463-9494**
The owner of the Bibiche Bistro is so friendly that you will overlook the very ordinary decor. In fact, you'll soon forget all about the surroundings as you enjoy your meal, especially the fabulous desserts.

Christina's Ristorante
$$-$$$
492 Danforth Ave.
☎**463-4418**
Christina's Ristorante is probably the most famous of the trendy Danforth Greek eateries. The restaurant is known for its Wall of Fame that features dozens of framed pictures of famous customers, from Tom Hanks to Alanis Morissette. They serve a full Greek menu until 4am on the weekends and present live Greek music and belly-dancing shows.

La Carreta Cuban Tapas Bar
$$$
469 Danforth Ave.
☎**461-7718**
A bright-yellow sign framed with flashing lights hangs above the door of La Carreta, making it look more like a karaoke joint than a Cuban tapas bar. Inside, it's polished and modern, with mint-green textured walls, a long bar of glass and mahogany, blue glass lamps and hand-painted tables. A unique selection of meat, vegetarian and seafood tapas offers abundant choice for the undecided. Smoking section available.

Silk Road Cafe
$$$
341 Danforth Ave.
☎463-8660

Stop in at Silk Road and you'll think you've really embarked on this historic route. This is, in fact, a culinary journey through the cuisines of Tibet, India, Thailand and China, in an exotic ambiance.

Ouzeri
$$$-$$$$
500-A Danforth Ave.
☎778-0500

One of the Danforth's typical eateries, Ouzeri is often noisy and crowded, but what a great menu! The freshest ingredients come together in a fine selection of Greek dishes, including several vegetarian meals.

Entertainment

W**hether it be** cultural activities, major festivals, professional hockey, baseball or basketball games or automobile racing, Toronto has something for everyone, any time of the year.

R**ave** culture and after-hours, all-night dance clubs (mainly catering to a very young crowd) ensure that parts of the town, at least, are going all night. Toronto also has a vibrant underground live-music scene that has only become stronger in recent years. On any night of the week there are numerous bands, from big names to local acts, playing live at one or another of the city's many watering holes. Along lively strips such as Queen Street West, College Street in Little Italy and the Annex's Bloor Street, there is always something going on, and even just strolling along the sidewalks to soak up the atmosphere can be entertaining.

T**he** flourishing of the city's theatre industry has also had an enormous impact on

Toronto's entertainment scene. Toronto is now the third-largest theatre city in the English-speaking world, surpassed only by New York and London. Summertime brings festivals celebrating everything from jazz to the music of the Caribbean.

Bars and Nightclubs

The Waterfront

The Docks
11 Polson St.
☎461-3625
The Docks is a renovated entertainment complex located east of downtown near Cherry Beach. The patio, which is over 3,700m^2 and extends out over the waters of Lake Ontario, has outdoor pool tables and boat docking facilities. Live DJs play on weekends and for special events in three different nightclubs.

The Guvernment
132 Queen's Quay E.
☎869-0045
This massive warehouse that was retrofitted in the '80s (it was formerly called RPM) has been one of the city's coolest clubs ever since. From Thursday to Saturday, hot live DJs spin house and dance music. The Guvernment is actually one of seven rooms in a trendy complex that includes two outdoor terraces. Each room has its own DJ and offers its own unique ambiance: you'll find Toronto's who's who in The Drink room, a Moroccan-style decor in the Tanja room and raves and popular live acts within the Kool Haus (previously known as the Warehouse).

Loose Moose
146 Front St. W.
☎977-8840
The Loose Moose serves typical pub-grub, burgers and wings, but is more recommended as a popular pick-up joint! The dance floor and the latest top-40 hits and retro tunes set the pace.

The Theatre and Financial Districts

Though a few of the bars listed in this section are found just slightly west of the official boundaries of the Financial and Theatre Districts, they still make this downtown area one of the most vibrant in the city. Very hip, sometimes even bordering on showy and pretentious, with its happening and jam-packed nightclubs, the area also has its fair share of small cosy pubs and unassuming bohemian dives.

The 606
606 King St. W.
☎504-8740
A hip crowd of journalists, actors and film people gathers at this combined restaurant, bar and lounge to sip martinis while DJs spin acid jazz, R&B and funk.

Afterlife
250 Adelaide St. W.
☎593-6126
Not only are there two bars here, but two hot tubs as well! With different DJs on different floors on different nights, their repertoire is incredibly diverse, spanning dance and progressive underground house, retro, electronica and classic alternative sounds.

C'est what?
67 Front St. E.
☎867-9499
C'est what?, located in the basement of an older building, is a charming pub with regular live blues, jazz, funk and rock performances. Great selection of beer and scotch.

Crocodile Rock
240 Adelaide St. W.
☎599-9751
This casual, laid-back club is a great place to dance to Top 40, disco, 80s and rock music. There are also pool tables and a new rooftop patio.

The Devil's Martini
473 Adelaide St. W.
☎603-9300
It's not hard to surmise what the drink of choice is at this establishment, which has a patio and three pool tables.

Easy
225 Richmond St. W.
☎979-3000
Catering to a sophisticated crowd with various bars serving a wide range of wine, champagne, scotch and cognac, there is also a cigar bar and guests can enjoy live jazz here.

Elephant & Castle Pub
212 King St. W.
☎598-4455
In front of Roy Thompson Hall, Elephant & Castle Pub offers all the warm charm typical of an authentic English pub.

Fairmont Royal York
100 Front St. W.
☎368-2511
If you aren't lucky enough to be staying at the Fairmont Royal York, but want to admire its timeless elegance, you can enjoy a drink in one of its bars. Both the **Lobby Bar** and the **Library Bar** give a taste of the classic charm of this turn-of-the-century hotel. This is an excellent place to sit and relax before catching a train at Union Station located directly in front of the hotel.

Fez Batik
129 Peter St.
☎204-9660
Fez Batik is a Moroccan-themed restaurant and lounge, with a fabulous outdoor patio. The upper level is a lounge where couches are littered with colourful Moroccan cushions, and later at night DJs spin soul, deep sounds and drum 'n' bass.

Fluid Lounge
217 Richmond St. W.
☎593-6116
Fluid Lounge is a swanky basement nightclub with chill-out

Entertainment

areas filled with animal-print '70s couches and DJs spinning eclectic grooves from disco to R&B to old school. Their hip hop nights are always very packed, and very steamy.

Helium
473 Adelaide St. W.
☎ *603-9300*
Helium is one of Toronto's newest slick nightclubs, with a 929m² warehouse/dance floor setting. DJs spin a commercial dance mix.

Horizons Bar
301 Front St. W., CN Tower
☎ *601-4719*
Perched at the top of the CN Tower, Horizons justly prides itself on being the world's loftiest bar. Light meals are served in the evening.

Joe
250 Richmond St. W.
☎ *971-6563*
Caters to a young crowd with four floors of fun. DJs spin house, retro, Top 40 and alternative music. Drinks are reasonably priced and the dress code is casual.

Joker
318 Richmond St. W.
☎ *598-1313*
This is one of the Theatre and Financial district's most popular four-floor emporiums, with pool tables in the basement, prominent local DJs rotating on the next two levels, spinning everything from R&B to old school to progressive house, and a rooftop patio that seats 200 and provides an aerial view through the skylight to the third-floor dance floor.

My Apartment
81 Peter St.
☎ *348-9884*
My Apartment is a stylish and happening nightclub centred around a rectangular bar. The music is loud right from the get-go, but this doesn't seem to bother the well-dressed young urban professionals who pack the place. There is a patio in the back.

N'Awlins
299 King St. W.
☎ *595-1958*
Here you'll find an elegant jazz restaurant with a bar at the back and excellent live jazz and R&B nightly.

Peel Pub
276 King St. W.
☎ *977-0003*
Toronto's incarnation of the infamous university hangout on Montreal's Peel Street is no less popular than the original. Basically a pub-like watering hole, it attracts big crowds on the weekends.

Reservoir Lounge
52 Wellington St. E.
☎ *955-0887*
This 1950s-style jazz and piano bar attracts a local and international clientele. Drinks after work are popular with local business people, who also appreciate the swing, jazz and blues shows.

Room 471
471 Richmond St. W.
☎703-6239
This chic yet comfortable martini bar lounge plays acid jazz and house mixes. Great place to chill and enjoy yourself.

Shmooze
15 Mercer St.
☎341-8777
Located in an old brick building, the prestigious Shmooze is all the rage. Some 900 lucky patrons make it inside to party the night away beneath high ceilings and flashy candelabras. The oh-so-chic clientele comes first for a meal, and finishes the night off on the dance floor. On weekends, line-ups to join the fun start at 6:30pm.

Smokeless Joe
125 John St.
☎591-2221
Smokeless Joe is a tiny place, but imported beer connoisseurs will love it. They'll find an impressive selection of brews from Belgium, England, Germany and Eastern Europe. There's even a beer from Trinidad-Tobago and another from Kenya!

This is London
364 Richmond St. W.
☎351-1100
A stylish bar and dance club catering to well-off yuppies, This is London features a stylized, inspired decor, with sleek leather couches and wooden floors. The DJ spins a good variety of music, ranging from the latest hits to disco, soul and R&B.

Tonic
117 Peter St., entrance on Richmond
☎204-9200
A popular nightclub on the strip, where DJs spin Top 40, R&B, dance and house music.

Top O' the Senator
249 Victoria St.
☎364-7517
Top O' the Senator, a jazz bar which first opened its doors in the 1920s, is a real Toronto institution. International jazz stars perform regularly here. Inside the same building is the Victory Lounge, a cigar lounge with a quieter ambiance.

Old Town of York

Montreal Bistro-Jazz Club
65 Sherbourne St.
☎363-0179
Local and international celebrities give shows at the Montreal

Bistro-Jazz Club, considered one of the city's finest jazz clubs.

Queen Street West

Queen Street West offers a succession of happening alternative bars and hip clubs, notably the recently opened Drake Hotel. The street is particularly lively on weekends; revellers start here with a meal out and stay until the wee hours for drinks, a show or a twirl on the dance floor!

The 360
326 Queen St. W.
☎ *593-0840*
Just a few doors down from the Rivoli, The 360 is an old legion hall, with beer on tap and live music in the back-room. Its bare-bones patio lacks glamour but has a prime Queen West people-watching location.

The Bishop and the Belcher
361 Queen St. W.
☎ *591-2352*
This traditional English-style pub offers 16 beers on tap.

The Black Bull Tavern
298 Queen St. W.
☎ *593-2766*
Here is where you'll find the best patio on Queen Street, a huge patio that sprawls along the side of the building near Soho Street. Once frequented mainly by bikers who lined their Harleys up on the sidewalk, the "Bull" is now a meeting place for all sorts of people looking for a summertime beer in the sun.

The Bovine Sex Club
542 Queen St. W.
☎ *504-4239*
The name alone might be enough to keep some people away and to attract others. There is no sign on the door, but it's hard to miss the tangle of recycled bicycle wheels and twisted steel adorning its facade. The crowd is alternative and there is live music the last week of every month.

The Cameron
408 Queen St. W.
☎ *703-0811*
Take a look at the psychedelic mural on the exterior of this building: you're about to enter the Cameron, one of the last bastions of classic Queen Street West. Newcomers and old regulars converge here to listen to acid jazz, house music and eclectic live shows or just to sit and stare at the local music celebrities who gather here.

The Drake Hotel
1150 Queen St. W.
☎ *531-5042*
Patrons of The Drake Hotel come in all sizes, shapes and ages, and they all seem to love it! It is noisy and eclectic, and the DJ plays everything from rock to jazz and blues. If you had to pin it down though, the place does tend toward the hip bohemian side of Queen Street West. Obviously, the Drake must offer something more, how else do you explain the

masses of people who crowd its sidewalks on weekends, waiting to get inside?

Gypsy Co-Op
815 Queen St. W.
☎ *703-5069*
Gypsy Co-Op features funky DJs and live bands every night in its lounge/bar at the back. Its "General Store" is stocked full of nostalgic candy.

The Horseshoe Tavern
370 Queen St. W.
☎ *598-4753*
The Horseshoe Tavern is a long-standing Queen West tradition, with a tavern and live rock in the front room, and indie bands in the back.

Left Bank
567 Queen St. W.
☎ *504-1626*
This Parisian Renaissance style bar caters to an over-25 crowd. The DJ creates an upbeat and relaxed environment and there is also a billiard room with fireplaces and couches.

Raq n Waq
739 Queen St. W.
☎ *504-9120*
Top-40, Latin and R&B music predominate here. This establish-ment is mainly an upscale pool hall, with 13 Brunswick tables.

Reverb/Big Bop/Holy Joe's
651 Queen St. W.
☎ *504-6699*
A live music venue with different acts playing on all three floors most nights of the week.

Rex Hotel Jazz Bar & Grill
194 Queen St. W.
☎ *598-2475*
The Rex has a casual pub-like atmosphere with live jazz and blues acts nightly.

The Rivoli
332 Queen St. W.
☎ *596-1908*
The Rivoli is one of the trendiest spots on the strip, with a cozy bar, a small, crowded outdoor patio in the heart of Queen West's alternative scene, an Asian-fusion restaurant and a back-room showcasing live alternative music or comedy.

Savage Garden
550 Queen St. W.
☎ *504-2178*
Savage Garden is all Goth, every night, with industrial, retro, Goth and electronic music.

Velvet Underground
508 Queen St. W.
☎ *504-6688*
Here's where Canadian singer Alanis Morrissette got her start. A mixed crowd gathers here to dance to alternative music or simply to sit and talk. A good choice for those who'd prefer to avoid noisy nightclubs.

College Street/ Queen's Park and the University of Toronto

The stretch of College Street west of Bathurst still has all the

Entertainment

Mediterranean flavour of Little Italy, with sidewalk cafés galore serving *gelato* and cappuccino, and *trattorias* open well into the night. But the area has also been adopted by a young, trendy crowd of students and musicians, who while away the evenings in the area's many bars.

Bar Italia
582 College St.
☎ *535-3621*
This Italian eatery doubles as a chic night spot, with DJs throughout the week and live bands on Saturdays.

The Chelsea Room
923 Dundas St. W.
☎ *364-0553*
Located in a residential neigh-bourhood where the sidewalks aren't overrun every weekend, the Chelsea Room is a nice change from the chic and the hip of the usual underground scenes. This subdued moody place, with its uncluttered but gutsy decor, is one of those new bars on Dundas Street West that likes to celebrate its difference. As does its clientele, a funky mix of young profes-sionals, artists and students who come to chat and discuss, or to dance to the soul, funk and house DJ offerings. A real find!

College Street Bar
574 College St.
☎ *533-2417*
The College Street Bar is a U of T student hangout.

The Comfort Zone
480 Spadina Ave.
☎ *763-9139*
The aura surrounding "The Zone" verges on religious cult territory. And for good reason: during its Devine Sunday events, the party starts at 6am and lasts for the next 24 hours, with different DJs entertaining a mostly young crowd. Other mornings and afternoons have DJs and local bands playing. An ideal spot for your after... after hours, to kick off or continue a night of revelry at any and all hours.

El Covento Rico
750 College St.
☎ *588-7800*
This sizzling Latin dance bar plays dance, disco and Latin music, and gives free Latin dance lessons.

El Mocambo
462 Spadina Ave.
☎ *777-1777*
Since the Rolling Stones played here in the 1960s, the El Mocambo has been one of Toronto's most legendary live music venues.

Free Times Cafe
320 College St.
☎ *967-1078*
A cozy spot with live acoustic and folk music nightly in the backroom.

Fuse Room
418 College St. W.
☎ *920-5937*
The Fuse Room is a surprising and truly cosy spot, a real ha-

ven on hip College Street. This bar feels like a café, with its vibrant blue walls and exhibits of works by local artists. The calendar of events here is varied, including everything from DJ nights to poetry readings and musical shows. Simple, but you'll love it. A clientele of regulars and neighbourhood residents.

Lava Lounge & Restaurant
507 College St.
☎*966-LAVA*
With a suave '70s look, this club attracts a trendy set who combine lounging and dancing to a mixture of live music and DJs.

The Midtown
552 College St.
☎*920-4533*
The Midtown is a College Street student hot spot for sharing a drink with friends, with draft beer, single malts and three pool tables.

Oasis
294 College St.
☎*975-0845*
This earthy, no-frills tapas bar presents live bands, DJs and stand-up comedy.

Orbit Room
580-A College St.
☎*535-0613*
The Orbit Room is a popular spot featuring some of the city's best R&B bands.

The Silver Dollar Room
486 Spadina Ave.
☎*975-0909*
The Silver Dollar Room, a club very much in the Chicago tradi-

tion, showcases local and international blues acts.

Sneaky Dee's
431 College St.
☎*603-3090*
This smoky Tex-Mex joint is where the local grungy student crowd hangs out to drink beer on tap and play pinball and pool to a background of alternative music. Live bands provide the entertainment.

Souz Dal
636 College St.
☎*537-1883*
Souz Dal is all acid jazz and worldbeat, with candles and martinis.

Sutra
612 College St.
☎*537-8755*
Like the name suggests, Sutra is hot and exotic! Officially, this is a Tiki Bar: with lots of bamboo and the requisite Tiki statues, a big selection of cocktails, from *pina coladas* to *mojitos*, not to mention the homegrown *martikis*! As with most of the bars on College Street, Sutra is somewhere to go to see and be seen… though here things are just a bit more relaxed.

The Annex

Brunswick House
481 Bloor St. W.
☎*964-2242*
Toronto's most popular student hangout is the Brunswick House. Large-screen televisions, shuffle board, billiard

Entertainment

tables, cheap beer and a local character named Rockin' Irene are the mainstays here.

Dooney's
511 Bloor St. W.
☎536-3293

Dooney's quiet charm, world music and patio attract a hushed crowd of students come evening. They come to discuss and debate the state of world affairs, or maybe just to chat with friends over drinks. Unpretentious and just right...

Insomnia
563 Bloor St. W.
☎588-3907

A trendy bar-restaurant, Insomnia welcomes a young crowd in a polished, Spartan setting. A DJ spins every night.

James Joyce Irish Pub
386 Bloor St. W.
☎324-9400

The name is fairly self-explanatory: imported beer on tap, traditional live Irish music in a lively atmosphere, and pool tables.

Lee's Palace
529 Bloor St. W.
☎532-1598

Lee's Palace stands out, with its colourful facade, adorned with cartoon characters. This is where Nirvana and Oasis played before they became famous and it remains a popular spot to see good rock and alternative shows or to discover new talent. DJs spin in the upstairs Dance Cave.

Madison Avenue Pub
14 Madison Ave.
☎927-1722

With four floors and four patios, this British style pub is one of the city's most popular gathering places—especially for current or former U of T students. There is also a piano bar and a new billiard room with 10 tables.

Panorama
55 Bloor St. W., 51st floor
☎967-5225

Just east of the Annex's main drag, Panorama sits atop the ManuLife Centre. The drinks and cocktails are pricey, but then again the view is spectacular. Proper dress is required. The patio is open all summer long.

Pauper's Pub
539 Bloor St. W.
☎530-1331

Housed in what used to be a bank, the Pauper's Pub attracts a mixed crowd to its cozy easy-going environment. The rooftop patio offers a nice panoramic view.

Niagara-on-the-Lake

The Oban
160 Front St.
☎468-2165

The Oban is *the* place in town for a drink with friends, or even alone, ensconced in a comfortable armchair by the fireplace.

Gay Bars

5ive
cover charge
5 St. Joseph St.
☎*964-8685*
A trendy bar and dance club,
5ive hosts theme nights and a
revolving cast of DJs.

The Black Eagle
457 Church St.
☎*413-1219*
The Black Eagle is a men's leather cruising bar, with a pool
table, videos playing and dun-
geon equipment.

Byzantium
499 Church St.
☎*922-3859*
Byzantium is a swanky martini
bar and neighbourhood lounge
with one of the city's most extensive martini lists.

Ciao Edie
489 College St.
☎*927-7774*
A '70s cocktail lounge in the
trendy College Street area,
Ciao Edie has a lesbian night on
Sundays with excellent DJs
spinning soul and drum 'n' bass.
Men and straight clientele are
welcome. Different from the
Church Street scene, Ciao
Edie's Sunday nights draw the
city's funky, artsy, tattooed
lebians out of the woodwork.
The martinis are fabulous but
the music is deafening after
11pm.

Crews/Tango
508-510 Church St.
☎*972-1662*
A grand old Victorian house has
been converted into these two
bars, with everything from karaoke to pool to live comedy
shows and drag performances.
Tango, a cozy bar with bay-
window seating, is primarily a
lesbian bar but men are welcome.

Pegasus Billiard Lounge
489 Church St., 2nd floor
☎*927-8832*
An alternative to the dance
clubs, with professional-sized
pool tables and dart boards,
Pegasus is a good place to sit
and relax. The clientele is both
gay and straight, men and
women.

Remington's
cover charge
379 Yonge St.
☎*977-2160*
Remington's offers two levels of
dance floors, graced with video
screens, where a strictly male
crowd gets down and dirty.

Slack Alice Bar & Grill
562 Church St.
☎*969-8742*
Slack Alice is artfully decorated
with wrought iron and a modern, industrial-style decor.
There is a decent restaurant in
the back, but the front half,
which spills ever-so-slightly
onto the Church Street sidewalk, is a funky, lively cocktail
bar and meeting place for both
men and women.

Entertainment

The Stables / The Barn
418 Church St.
☎977-4702
At this three-storey dance club, men are more into jeans than leather. There is, however, a leather shop inside that sells pants, vests and fetish items.

Tallulah's Cabaret
cover charge
12 Alexander St.
☎975-8555
Tallulah's Cabaret is located within the Buddies in Bad Times Theatre. The cabaret welcomes a gay and lesbian crowd for dancing after the end of the often controversial shows presented by the theatre company.

Woody's
465-467 Church St.
☎972-0887
Set in the heart of the gay village, Woody's is a popular meeting place for gay men, with a casual and friendly pub-like atmosphere.

Zelda's
542 Church St.
☎922-2526
If you're into 1970s music, head to Zelda's, a lively, "zesty" bar-restaurant that also hosts theme nights on Saturdays and Sundays.

Zipperz
cover charge
72 Carlton St.
☎921-0066
A piano bar, pool tables and a dance floor await party hounds at Zipperz.

Cultural Activities

Theatre, Dance and Opera

Toronto is the third-largest theatre centre in the English-speaking world, after New York and London. More than 200 professional theatre and dance companies perform the season's lineup. The offerings are astounding, and a night at the theatre, the opera or the symphony is fast becoming a must for any visit to Toronto.

Buddies in Bad Times Theatre
12 Alexander St.
☎975-8555
One of the biggest gay and lesbian theatre companies in the world, Buddies in Bad Times produces radical, controversial and influential Canadian stage works. **Tallulah's Cabaret** is Buddies' cabaret bar for smaller performances, art shows, book launches and screenings.

Canon Theatre
263 Yonge St.
☎872-1212
This refurbished vaudeville theatre, formerly known as the Pantages, was renamed the Canon Theatre in September 2001.

Dream in High Park
High Park at Bloor and Keele Sts.
☎367-1652 ext. 2
Summertime productions of Shakespeare in a magical setting, a tree-lined hollow in High Park.

Elgin and Winter Garden Theatres
189 Yonge St.
☎872-5555
The Elgin and Winter Garden are spectacular stacked theatres that play host to classic theatre, musicals, opera, jazz, etc. Guided tours offered (see p 116).

Factory Theatre
125 Bathurst St.
☎504-9971
The Factory Theatre stages the latest in Canadian theatre.

Harbourfront Centre Theatre
231 Queens Quay W.
☎973-4000
Located within what used to be a cold storage warehouse, the Harbourfront Centre Theatre presents renowned theatre works.

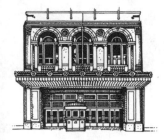

Elgin and Winter Garden Theatres

Hummingbird Centre
O'Keefe Centre, 1 Front St. E.
☎872-2262
The Hummingbird centre stages **Canadian Opera Company** and the **National Ballet of Canada** productions, as well as hit Broadway shows and big-name concerts.

Lorraine Kimsa Theatre for Young People
165 Front St. E.
☎862-2222
A terrific option for younger visitors. All of the productions are entirely devoted to children.

Massey Hall
178 Victoria St.
☎872-4255
Massey Hall's excellent acoustics enhance all types of spectacles, from rock and roll to theatre.

Premiere Dance Theatre
207 Queens Quay W., Queen's Quay Terminal
☎973-4000
Located on the third floor of the Queen's Quay Terminal, a building with stunning architecture, the Premiere Dance Theatre hosts local and international modern dance companies.

Princess of Wales Theatre
300 King St. W.
☎872-1212
This relatively new theatre (1994) was built for the production of the musical *Miss Saigon*.

Entertainment

Royal Alexandra Theatre
260 King St. W.
☎872-1212
Opened in 1907, this venerable Beaux-Arts theatre is a joy to behold. Broadway-style musicals and the like are showcased here.

Roy Thompson Hall
60 Simcoe St.
☎593-4828
The **Toronto Symphony Orchestra** and **Toronto Mendelssohn Choir** both make their home in this hall, which boasts outstanding acoustics.

St. Lawrence Centre for the Performing Arts
27 Front St. E.
☎366-7723
The **Canadian Stage Company** performs here, and classical music concerts round out the bill.

Tafelmusik Baroque Orchestra
St. Paul Centre at Trinity Church
427 Bloor St. W.
☎964-6337
An intimate opportunity to enjoy "table music" played on period instruments.

Théâtre français de Toronto
26 Berkeley St.
☎534-6604
Established in 1967 as the *Théâtre du P'tit Bonheur*, this is the only French-language theatre in Toronto. Its repertoire covers everything from French classics to new French-Canadian works.

Theatre Passe Muraille
16 Ryerson Ave.
☎504-7529
Innovative productions of independent Canadian theatre.

Toronto Centre for the Arts
5040 Yonge St.
☎872-1111
This new complex hosts the best Broadway shows.

Cabaret/Dinner Theatre

Famous People Players Dinner Theatre
110 Sudbury St.
☎532-1137 or 888-453-3385
This Canadian performing troupe showcases a uniquely dazzling performance with exciting music.

Medieval Times Dinner and Tournament
Exhibition Place
☎260-1234 or 800-563-1190
Guests will be regaled with an evening of sorcery, pageantry, horsemanship and excitement in this medieval theatre show. Knights on horseback re-enact an authentic 11th-century Spanish tournament while dinner guests feast on a four-course banquet.

Mysteriously Yours.Mystery Dinner Theatre
Various locations
☎486-7469 or 800-NOT-DEAD
Participate in solving an interactive "whodunit" with dinner and a show, or come just for the show.

Yuk Yuk's Comedy Cabaret

1280 Bay St.
☎967-6425
Toronto's hottest showcase stand-up comedy club, with alumni including Jim Carrey, Norm McDonald and Howie Mandel.

Ticket Agencies

Tickets for these and other shows are available through:

Ticketmaster
☎870-8000

Ticket King
☎872-1212

T.O. Tix
corner of Yonge and Dundas Sts., in the Eaton Centre
☎536-6468, ext. 1
Reduced-price tickets for same-day musical and theatrical events. In-person sales only, *(Tue-Sat noon to 7:30pm, Sun 11am to 3pm).*

Cinemas

Toronto has many movie houses. Check local listings in newspapers for schedules and times of first-run movies in the city. Special rates are offered on Tuesdays and for matinees.

Carlton Cinemas

20 Carlton St.
☎598-2309
Plays a lot of art-house and independent festival-type films.

National Film Board

150 John St.
☎973-3012

IMAX Theatres

There is an Imax theatre located in the Paramount complex *(☎925-4629)* and another at Ontario Place *(☎314-9900).*

Repertory Theatres

Cinematheque Ontario

317 Dundas St. W., Art Gallery of Ontario's Jackman Hall
☎968-3456
A repertory cinema, the Cinematheque screens foreign films in their original language and art house films, mostly in English or with English subtitles.

Toronto has six repertory cinemas, called **Festival Cinemas:**

The Fox

2236 Queen St. E.
☎691-7330

Kingsway Theatre

3030 Bloor St. W.
☎236-1411

The Music Hall

147 Danforth Ave.
☎778-8272

Paradise Cinema

1006 Bloor St. W.
☎537-7040

Revue Cinema

400 Roncesvalles Ave.
☎531-9959

Entertainment

The Royal Cinema
608 College St.
☎ *516-4845*

Many of the Festival cinemas are in beautiful, ornate old theatres. For schedules and prices, you can call the Festival Hotline at ☎ *690-2600*.

Sporting Events

The Air Canada Centre
40 Bay St.
☎ *815-5500*
In 1999, the Air Canada Centre replaced Maple Leaf Gardens as the arena where The National Hockey League's Toronto Maple Leafs play from November to April. The play-offs follow the regular season and can last right into June. It is also home to Toronto's National Basketball Association (NBA) team, the Raptors.

The **Canadian International Marathon** (☎ *972-1062*) takes place along Toronto's avenues and streets at end of October.

The **Molson Indy** (☎ *872-4639*) races through the streets of Toronto in mid-July.

The **Royal Agricultural Winter Fair** (☎ *872-7777*) is held every year in November on the grounds of the Canadian National Exhibition. This premier

event includes the Royal Horse Show.

SkyDome
1 Blue Jay Way
☎ *341-3663*
The Toronto Blue Jays of the American Baseball League and the Toronto Argonauts of the Canadian Football League (CFL) play their matches at the SkyDome.

The biggest names in tennis are matched in the **Tennis Masters Canada** international tennis competition (☎ *665-9777*) which is held at the National Tennis Centre, north of downtown at the Rexall Centre on the campus of York University. The men's and women's competitions alternate every other year.

Lake Ontario hosts the historic **Toronto International Dragon Boat Race Festival** (☎ *364-0046*) in early June.

The Woodbine Race Track
north of Hwy. 401, on Hwy. 27 at Rexdale
☎ *675-RACE (7223)*
This track is the largest racing property in North America and home of the Queen's Plate thoroughbred races in August, the longest-running uninterrupted event in North America. Thoroughbred racing post times: *Mar to Dec, Wed 6pm, Thu-Sun 1pm.* Harness Racing post times: *Jan to Mar and Jun to Sep, Mon, Tue, Thu-Sat 7:30pm.*

Festivals and Special Events

Harbourfront Centre
231-235 Queen's Quay W.
☎ *Information: 973-3000*
☎ *Tickets: 973-4000*
In a breezy, picturesque waterfront setting, the Harbourfront Centre offers arts, culture and recreation all year round. Annual events include free and ticketed concerts and musical performances (showcasing folk, jazz, worldbeat and pop artists), dance, theatre, art exhibitions, craft activities and festive celebrations.

Wintercity
start of February
☎ *395-0490*
Toronto hosts a party to celebrate the season of snow. Three family-friendly sites feature everything from skating shows and midway rides to pancake breakfasts.

Canada Blooms, The Flower and Garden Show
mid-Mar
☎ *800-730-1020*
Canada's largest annual indoor flower and garden show, with six acres of gardens,

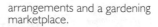

arrangements and a gardening marketplace.

North by Northeast
mid-Jun
☎ *863-6963*
More than 300 folk, rock, blues and funk groups gather in the bars and venues of Toronto for this music festival.

Toronto International Festival Caravan
☎ *856-6582*
This festival celebrates the city's many ethnic communities as well as cultures from around the world with dancing, international cuisine, films, theatre and music.

International Fireworks Festival, the Symphony of Fire
mid-Jun through Jul
Ontario Place, by the lake
☎ *870-8000 or 314-9900*

Toronto Downtown Jazz
end of Jun
www.tojazz.com
Jazz, gospel and blues performers are booked into venues big and small all over the city. The festival includes a parade and free shows.

Lesbian and Gay Pride Week
last week in Jun
☎ *927-7433*
One of the summer's most colourful events is the parade that caps off a week of festivities and one of the largest gay and lesbian pride celebrations in North America.

Entertainment

Gay Pride

The largest gay-pride festival in Canada, indeed in all of North America, **Pride Toronto** is a celebration of the gay, lesbian, bisexual and transgender (GLBT) communities. A week-long festival held every June and centred on Church Street, **Pride Toronto** culminates in two days of amazing marches and oh-so-hot and fabulous parades, as well as a cornucopia of shows and events of all kinds. More than a simple festive celebration that draws hundreds of thousands of onlookers, **Pride Toronto** is a highly political statement of great importance to Toronto's and Canada's GLBT community, with more than 750,000 people coming together every year to celebrate diversity and sexual freedom as well as human respect.

The history of **Pride Toronto** goes back more than 35 years. In 1969, then–Justice Minister Pierre Elliott Trudeau decriminalized homosexuality. Two years later, on August 1, 1971, the first **Gay Day Picnic** was held at Hanlan's Point in Toronto, an event that raised funds to send a few activists to Ottawa to take part in a march commemorating the second anniversary of the decriminalization of homosexuality. The following year, the second annual **Gay Day Picnic** was held, but this time as part of the first **Gay Pride Week**. Activists took advantage of this to present a brief to the Ontario government. After a few years without celebrations— punctuated by police harassment, demonstrations that sometimes turned sour and unjustified mass arrests—the **Lesbian and Gay Pride Day Toronto** pressure group was officially formed, and over 1,500 people gathered at Grange Park on June 28, 1981. It was the beginning of a great adventure. Since then, thousands, then hundreds of thousands of people from the gay community from all over the country and beyond have flooded Toronto and celebrated under a different theme every year for an entire week in June.

The Fringe–Toronto's Theatre Festival
early Jul
☎*966-1062*
More than 90 theatre companies participate, staging shows that can only be described as unique, diverse and unexpected.

Toronto Outdoor Art Exhibition
mid-Jul
☎*408-2754*
Canadian and international artists display their work in Nathan Phillips Square.

Caribana
mid-Jul to early Aug
☎*465-4884*
The premier festival of Caribbean music and culture, culminating in the famous parade, which is the largest in Canada and lasts 12 hours!

Beaches International Jazz Festival
third week of Jul
☎*698-2152*
More than 100 bands perform free on indoor and outdoor stages at this five-day festival, held in Toronto's most summery spot. Thousands of people picnic in the Beaches' main park, where beer gardens and vendors add to the atmosphere.

Fringe Festival of Independent Dance Artists
Aug
☎*410-4291*
More than 90 dance artists stage performances at various venues around the city.

Canadian National Exhibition
mid-Aug to early Sep
☎*393-6000*
Midway rides and games in a carnival atmosphere, plus pavilions with various exhibits, music and a wide variety of entertainment.

Krinos Taste of the Danforth
first week of Aug
☎*469-5634*
Greektown is transformed into a massive street festival during this weekend event, with outdoor stalls featuring food from the area's many restaurants. There is also live entertainment on special stages.

International Film Festival
early Sep
☎*968-FILM*
Toronto's own film festival is fast becoming a truly star-studded event. *Variety* magazine calls it the best film festival in North America.

International Festival of Authors
third week of Oct
☎*973-4000*
Marking its 23rd season in 2002, this event continues to dazzle literary buffs by bringing in the most popular writers of the moment to read from their latest works.

Kensington Festival of Lights
third week of Dec
☎*598-3729*
This festival celebrates the winter solstice, Hanukkah and Christmas with a costumed, lantern-lit procession through the Kensington Market neighbourhood.

Entertainment

The Caribana Festival

A colourful, music-filled festival, Caribana is one of the largest ethnic cultural events in North America. Every summer, over a million people gather on the shores of Lake Ontario for 18 days of sunny festivities.

Founded in 1967 by a group of academics and professionals anxious to spotlight the role of Afro-Canadians within Canada's cultural mosaic, the **Caribana Festival** now generates more than $200 million in annual revenue for the city of Toronto. Although the event has grown much larger than its founders ever imagined, the festival's mission remains the same, namely to promote, showcase and celebrate the culture and development of Canada's Caribbean and African communities.

The highlight of Caribana is definitely the spectacular parade that is held on the last Saturday of the festival, livened up by dazzling, brilliantly coloured costumes and pulsating African and Caribbean rhythms. In full swing on Lake Shore Boulevard, it brings together thousands of revellers and hundreds of participants from all backgrounds. The Caribana Festival is a vibrant event that helps forge bonds between the diverse communities of the very multicultural city of Toronto.

The festival is held every year from mid-July to the first Monday of August, which is a public holiday in Ontario.

Toronto International Pow Wow
late Nov to early Dec
at the SkyDome
☎ *(519) 751-0040*
This festival celebrates native dancing and culture.

The "One of a Kind" Canadian Craft Show & Sale
Dec and late Mar
at Exhibition Place
☎ *960-3680*

Canadian Aboriginal Festival

The **Canadian Aboriginal Festival** is one of Toronto's biggest cultural events. A unique opportunity to discover, share and learn about Canada's First Nations peoples, the festival has something for everyone. The crowning event of the festival, the two-day **Pow Wow** brings hundreds of Aboriginal dancers, singers and percussionists from across the country to Toronto's SkyDome stadium. The Pow Wow's opening ceremony, the "Great Entry," definitely constitutes one of the most fascinating Aboriginal ceremonies, with hundreds of dancers entering the huge dance circle.

The term "Pow Wow" dates back to the beginning of colonization. During Aboriginal gatherings, early settlers often heard an expression that actually referred to the medicine man. The central figure of a community, the medicine man always attended gatherings, and his title, which sounded like "Pow Wow," was often heard. The term was misinterpreted by white colonists to mean a gathering, a garbled definition that has survived to this day.

A Pow Wow is many things to many people and can be the opportunity to thank the Creator, pay homage to warriors, see old friends and meet new ones as well as exhibit and buy crafts. In short, to celebrate every aspect of the rich Aboriginal culture and heritage.

The tradition lives on every year in November.

Niagara-on-the-Lake

Shaw Festival
$42 to $77
☎(905) 468-2172 or 800-511-7429
⇒(905) 468-3804
www.shawfest.com
The internationally renowned Shaw Festival has been held every year since 1962. From April to October, visitors can take in various plays by George Bernard Shaw at one of the three theatres in town; the **Festival Theatre**, the **Court House Theatre** and the **Royal George Theatre**.

Shopping

Toronto is perfect
for window-shopping along busy streets lined with elegant boutiques and little shops that sell interesting merchandise.

You can find just about anything in the city's myriad stores and shopping centres. However, to find exactly what you're looking for, you have to know where to go. This chapter provides you with brief descriptions of some of the stores found in the various neighbourhoods. While the list is, of course, far from complete, it will point you in the right direction to help you find that perfect buy.

The Waterfront

Antiques

Harbourfront Antique Market
390 Queen's Quay W.
☎ *260-2626*
If you have the time and enjoy rummaging through old-fashioned items, antiques and other treasures from another era, head to the Harbourfront Antique Market which has about 100 antique sellers, some with very handsome wares.

Beer, Wine and Liquor

Here are two useful addresses to remember:

Beer Store
Mon-Wed 10am to 8pm, Thu-Fri 10am-9pm, Sat 9:30am to 9pm, Sun 11am to 6pm
350 Queen's Quay W.
☎ *581-1677*

**Liquor Control Board
of Ontario**
*Mon-Sat 9am to 10pm, Sun
noon to 6pm*
2 Cooper St., corner of Yonge St. and
Queen's Quay
☎*864-6777*

The former sells beer only,
while the latter sells wine and
liqueurs.

Clothing

Tilley Endurables
207 Queen's Quay W.
☎*203-0463*
Travellers have been coming to
Tilley Endurables for a long
time. The brand has a reputation for designing clothes that
are perfectly suited to travellers'
needs, made with waterproof
materials that don't wrinkle.
Tilley's heavy-duty hats are
perhaps the most popular.

Crafts

Arctic Canada
207 Queen's Quay W.
☎*260-7889*
For Aboriginal handicrafts, try
Arctic Canada, a shop that sells
attractive pieces, especially
prints and sculptures, as well as
leather and fur apparel.

The Bounty Shop
235 Queens Quay W.
☎*973-4993*
The Bounty Shop carries
Canadian-made crafts, perfect
to indulge yourself or offer as a
gift, such as handmade blown-

glass pieces, pottery and jewellery. Several of the items for
sale are created by artists from
the Harbourfront Centre's
Craft Studio.

Shopping Centres

Queen's Quay Terminal
207 Queens Quay W.
☎*203-0510*
A great shopping centre on the
shores of Lake Ontario,
Queen's Quay Terminal en-
compasses more than 50 shops
(most of which offer Canadian
goods) and restaurants. The
mall is housed in one of the
city's former warehouses.

The Theatre and Financial Districts

Books

Open Air Books and Maps
25 Toronto St.
☎*363-0719*
Travellers, adventurers and
nature lovers alike will be
amazed at the vast variety of
travel related guides, books and
maps available in this unique
shop.

Crafts

Native Stone Art
4 McCaul St.
☎*593-0924*
Native Stone Art features a
beautiful collection of First

Nations and Native American crafts acquired right from the source. Wares include Inuit, Iroquois and Mohawk carvings, Cree and Ojibway moccasins, Cowichan clothing as well as Navajo, Zuni and Hopi jewellery.

Gifts

Spirit of Hockey
181 Bay St., BCE Place, bottom floor
☎*360-7765*
The famous Hockey Hall of Fame's shop, Spirit of Hockey, sells an incomparable selection of hockey sweaters, sweatshirts, T-shirts, caps, books and other merchandise related to the world of professional hockey.

Rainwear and Umbrellas

Rainmakers Queens Shop
100 Front St. W., inside the Fairmont Royal York Hotel
☎*203-7246*
If a chorus of "Rain, rain, go away..." doesn't clear up those rain clouds, drop by Rainma-

kers, where you'll find a wide selection of umbrellas (including wind-resistant models) and raincoats, some of which are very well designed.

Queen West and St. Lawrence

Books

Pages Books and Magazines
256 Queen St. E.
☎*598-1447*
This alternative bookshop, appreciated by Toronto's intellectual elite, offers a good many specialty magazines and books on such subjects as gender politics, art, design and architecture, travel, social sciences and philosophy.

World's Biggest Bookstore
20 Edward St.
☎*977-7009*
We can't say if this is *really* the biggest bookstore on earth, but there's no doubt this Toronto institution offers a vast and impressive collection of reading material.

Clothing

The Bay
176 Yonge St.
Near the Eaton Centre is another Toronto institution, The Bay department store, with nine storeys bursting with all kinds of items.

Shopping

Eaton Centre
220 Yonge St., corner of Queen St. W.
☎ *598-8700*
Eaton Centre is so well-known in Toronto that it has almost become an attraction in itself. With some 320 stores, it is a must for shopping of any kind. Among the more mainstay boutiques are Harry Rosen, Mexx, Banana Republic and Gap for clothes, Bowrings for home furnishings, Disney Store for children and the Liquor Control Board of Ontario for wine and liqueurs.

Marilyn's
200 Spadina Ave.
☎ *504-6777*
Marilyn's sells discount clothing for women in sizes 2 through 24. Weekly consignments run from loungewear to very chic attire.

Out on the Street
551 Church St.
☎ *967-2759*
Located in the heart of the Gay Village, Out on the Street advertizes itself as "your friendly neighbourhood queer store." It's an apt description, as the service is indeed friendly and the clientele gay and lesbian. The place mainly sells clothing, but also offers jewellery, accessories, postcards and other small items.

Queen Street
Boutiques catering to a young and well-off clientele can be found along Queen Street. Among them, **La Cache** is especially well-known for its hats and scarves, and cotton and linen clothing for women, while

Gap clothes and **Roots** leather jackets and wool sweaters are also popular.

Crafts

Timbuktu
39 Front St. E.
☎ *366-3169*
This shop, located in the heart of the bustling St. Lawrence Market District, offers clothing, home furnishings, blankets, china, embroidered items imported from India and a host of other creations from more than 50 countries.

Gifts

Art Gallery of Ontario
317 Dundas St. W.
☎ *979-6610*
Selling books, decorative items and jewellery, the gift shop at the Art Gallery of Ontario is worth checking out. High quality items can be found in the several rooms, including unique gift ideas for adults and children of all ages.

The Condom Shack
231 Queen St. W.
☎ *596-7515*
Small ones, long ones, pink ones, blue ones, funny, practical and original ones, the Condom Shack has them all—and in all shapes and sizes, too! Besides imported Japanese, European and American latex goods, the shop offers everyday clothes, body lotions, books, games, gifts and novelties.

Down East
508 Bathurst St.
☎961-7400
Customers know exactly what they're in for upon walking into Down East, where they're greeted by the following sign: "Some awful and some good stuff from Atlantic Canada." Ain't that the truth! Indeed, virtually everything can be found here, from horrible, tacky thingamajigs to beautiful handicrafts. The only thing these goods have in common is that they all come from Canada's Atlantic provinces.

The Japanese Paper Place
887 Queen St. W.
☎703-0089
The Japanese Paper Place features a great selection of top-quality Japanese paper, both modern and traditional, as well as photo albums, books on the time-honoured Japanese art of paper-folding (*origami*), paper jewellery and handmade cards.

Groceries

St Lawrence Market
91 Front St. E.
One of the best places in town to shop for food is St. Lawrence Market, where you'll find an abundant selection of fresh fruits and vegetables, as well as a variety of meats. Saturday mornings are particularly enjoyable here, when local farmers sell fresh produce at the farmer's market.

Music

The Music Store
60 Simcoe St., Roy Thomson Hall
☎593-4822
This lovely looking shop sells several Toronto Symphony Orchestra's CDs of choral and classical music.

Outdoor Gear and Apparel

Europe Bound – Travel Outfitters
47 Front St. E.
☎601-1990
Here you'll find clothing, specialty products and books related to outdoor activities such as rock climbing and mountaineering, hiking, kayaking and cycling. You can also rent camping gear here.

Mountain Equipment Co-op
400 King St. W.
☎340-2667
Mountain Equipment Co-op is frequented by outdoor buffs who know where to find quality merchandise (backpacks, clothing, sports equipment) at good prices.

Photography

Henry's
119 Church St.
☎868-0872
Specializing in photo equipment, both new and second-

Shopping

hand, Henry's displays its merchandise over several floors. A good choice of cameras, camcorders, darkroom equipment, camera bags, tripods, digital cameras and, of course, film is available here. What's more, Henry's offers photo-development and equipment-repair services.

Shoes

The Australian Boot Company
791 Queen St. W.
☎504-2411
The above address specializes in comfortable, sturdy Australian-made footwear, with brands such as R.M. Williams and Blundstone.

John Fluevog
242 Queen St. W.
☎581-1420
If you're looking for high-fashion, if sometimes uncomfortable, shoes with which to put your best foot forward, John Fluevog is a good bet.

Bloor Street

Beer, Wine and Liquor

Liquor Control Board of Ontario
55 Bloor St. W., ManuLife Centre
☎925-5266
This is the place to stock up on beer, wine and liqueurs.

Books

Toronto has its share of megabookstores where you can spend hours browsing and still not have had enough time to check out everything. Two such establishments are located in this area: Chapters and Indigo, and both have beautifully designed stores.

Chapters
110 Bloor St. W.
☎920-9299

Indigo Books, Music and Café
55 Bloor St. W.
☎925-3536

Mable's Fables
2939 Bloor St. W.
☎233-8830
This bookshop caters exclusively to young readers, offering a wide selection of titles dividedby age group, from toddlers to teenagers.

Clothing

The Bay
2 Bloor St. W.
☎972-3333
The oldest retailer in Canada, the Hudson's Bay Company was founded in 1670. The retail giant's The Bay stores have it all, from clothing and household goods to cosmetics and gifts or souvenirs. There are 14 branches in Greater Toronto alone.

Maxmara
131 Bloor St. W.
☎928-1884
Bloor Street is a succession of clothing stores, including some of the world's biggest names in fashion. Your eye will inevitably be attracted by the alluring window displays at Maxmara, a huge Italian design house which creates more than 20 high quality clothing lines, including Weekend by Maxmara and Sportmax.

Other stores also have stylish collections, many with a more relaxed look. Among them are:

Banana Republic
80 Bloor St. W.
☎515-0018

Club Monaco
157 Bloor St. W.
☎591-8837

Gap
60 Bloor St. W.
☎323-3391

Roots
95-A Bloor St. W.
☎323-3289
Roots is sure to have something that appeals to you, and shopping here won't break the bank.

Discount Stores

Honest Ed's
581 Bloor St. W.
☎537-1574
Known for more than half a century as the place to find bargain deals on merchandise of all sorts, Honest Ed's is an absolute must for anyone looking to save. Here you'll find a huge inventory of a wide assortment of items, including everything from food to clothing.

Fashion

Chanel Boutique
131 Bloor St. W.
☎925-2577
The renowned Chanel Boutique offers classic, elegant top-quality clothing, leather handbags, jewellery, shoes, perfume and cosmetics. A place that needs no further introduction.

Hermès
131 Bloor St. W.
☎968-8626
Founded in 1837, Hermès is world famous for its elegant scarves, leather goods, neckties, chic ready-to-wear clothes, perfume and jewellery.

Shopping

Holt Renfrew
50 Bloor St. W.
☎922-2333
Holt Renfrew has carved out a choice place for itself among the city's major stores, thanks to its selection of clothing for men, women and children, accessories, cosmetics and perfume. A one-stop couture destination with such prestigious labels as Giorgio Armani, Calvin Klein, Donna Karan and Birger Christensen Furs.

Games

Science City
Holt Renfrew Centre, 50 Bloor St. W.
☎968-2627
Science City specializes in clever, educational games for all ages.

Gifts

The ROM Shops
100 Queen's Park Cr.
☎586-5551
You can live your zaniest dreams at The ROM Shops, which sells some of the museum's collection. Of course, the items for sale are reproductions of the "real thing," but they are painstakingly crafted and make fabulous gifts. Books, jewellery and decorative objects are also for sale.

Gardiner Museum
111 Queen's Park Cr.
☎586-8080
The Gardiner Museum is known for its magnificent collection of porcelain and pottery, and draws collectors and afficionados. The gift shop caters to this clientele with a lovely selection of porcelain and ceramic pieces by contemporary artists.

Home Decoration

Boutique Sérénité
87 Yorkville Ave.
☎924-6398
Be swept away to Provence and Tuscany with this unique concept-shop. Here you will find the finest of modern and traditional furniture, decorative home accessories and bath product lines.

Urban Mode
389 Queen St. W.
☎591-8834
This boutique specializes in home decor, with a good selection of household articles at affordable prices.

Jewellery

Birks
55 Bloor St. W.
☎922-2266
Founded in 1879, Birks needs little introduction. The prestigious shop sells jewellery, watches, silver and crystalware made by the biggest names in the business.

Tiffany & Co.
85 Bloor St. W.
☎921-3900
This world-renowned jeweller's boasts a fabulous collection of

the most beautiful diamonds, pearls, and gold and silver jewellery by the biggest jewellers, including Elsa Peretti, Paloma Picasso and Jean Schlumberger. Moreover, the elegant boutique offers crystalware, scarves, watches and scores of other gift ideas.

Leather Goods

Louis Vuitton
100 Bloor St. W.
☎*968-3993*
Over the years, the name Louis Vuitton has become synonymous with quality luggage and leather goods. It goes without saying that the prices are upscale.

Taschen!
162 Cumberland St., Renaissance Court
☎*961-3185*
This renowned leather goods store sells fabulous handbags, luggage, briefcases and other high-quality articles. The shop carries the biggest designer-name brands, such as the German Bree and Italian Mandarina Duck labels.

Music

HMV
50 Bloor St. W.
☎*324-9979*
Looking for a new CD? You are almost guaranteed to find it at HMV, which has a boggling selection of albums representing just about every musical genre.

Shopping Centres

Holt Renfrew Centre
50 Bloor St. W.
☎*923-2255*
Over 25 shops are housed here, including HMV, Eddie Bauer, Emporio Armani, Mephisto and Femme de Carrière, which offer everything from haute couture and sportswear to shoes and lingerie.

ManuLife Centre
55 Bloor St. W.
☎*923-9525*
The ManuLife Centre is home to 50 specialty shops in the heart of the swank Bloor-Yorkville shopping district. Linked to its neighbour the Holt Renfrew Centre, it comprises such big-name retail outlets as William Ashley, the Julian Edwards Boutique and Indigo Books.

Shopping

Yorkville Avenue

Yorkville is the best area in Toronto for walking around and stopping in at charming boutiques.

Aboriginal Crafts

Yorkville has several shops worth checking out if you like Aboriginal art. Among them are:

The Arctic Bear
125 Yorkville Ave.
☎*967-7885*
Whether you are looking for moccasins, leather or fur apparel, prints or sculptures by Aboriginal artists, you are sure to find it at The Arctic Bear.

The Guild Shop
118 Cumberland St.
☎*921-1721*

Feheley Fine Arts
14 Hazelton Ave.
☎*323-1373*

Antiques

Hazelton Avenue is one of Toronto's prettiest streets, largely because of the charming boutiques that are found here. Among them there are several antique dealers whose wares are worth browsing through if you are interested in period furniture.

Antique Prints

Elisabeth Legge Antique Prints
37 Hazelton Ave.
☎*972-1378*
There is nothing ordinary about this shop which has a collection of vintage prints, some of which are over 100 years old. You are sure to find something you like among the beautiful pieces that add a wonderful classic touch to any home.

Books

David Mirvish Books on Art
596 Markham St.
☎*531-9975*
This store is hidden among a row of craft and antique shops. Specializing in fine-art books, the shops also offers books on photography, interior design, architecture and fashion.

The Cookbook Store
850 Yonge St.
☎*920-2665*
The Cookbook Store predictably specializes in cookbooks: Canadian cuisine, desserts, vegetarian and healthy cooking.

Children's Clothing

You can find some designers who cater specifically to children—and their parents, who are sure to swoon over the creations. **Jacadi** *(87 Avenue Rd., ☎923-1717)* has a good selection of apparel for the little princes and princesses. Careful, though: the prices are sky-high.

Clothing

Over the Rainbow
101 Yorkville Ave.
☎967-7448
Sells a variety of the latest styles of funky jeans, casual wear and accessories. Caters to both men and women.

Handbags

Jeanne Lottie
106 Yorkville Ave.
☎975-5115
For the past 15 years Jeanne Lottie has been creating original handbags, in colourful and imaginative designs, at relatively reasonable prices.

Housewares

The Compleat Kitchen
18 Hazelton Ave.
☎920-6333
All great chefs need well-equipped kitchens, and this is just the place to pick up all sorts of indispensable kitchen items.

Multi Ceramica Italiana
88 Yorkville Ave.
☎969-0253
This is another address to keep in mind, where you will find a vast array of utensils, casseroles and tableware.

Souleiado en Provence
20 Hazelton Ave.
☎975-9400
The fabrics and tablecloths at Souleiado en Provence evoke the warm, rich colours of this lovely region of France.

Shopping Centres

Hazelton Lanes
55-57 Avenue Rd.
☎968-8602
The fancy Hazelton Lanes shopping centre encompasses more than 70 middle- and top-of-the-range clothing and jewellery stores. Big-name retail outlets such as Monaco Boys and Girls, Jacadi and Browns are featured here.

Toys

The Toy Shop
62 Cumberland St.
☎961-4870
The Toy Shop is crammed with educational toys, dolls, teddy bears and doll houses with miniature furniture—in short, with everything to delight the little ones.

Index

Index